E. P. Crowell

The Andria and Adelphoe of Terence

E. P. Crowell

The Andria and Adelphoe of Terence

ISBN/EAN: 9783337008604

Printed in Europe, USA, Canada, Australia, Japan

Cover: Foto ©ninafisch / pixelio.de

More available books at **www.hansebooks.com**

CHASE AND STUART'S CLASSICAL SERIES.

THE
ANDRIA AND ADELPHOE

OF

TERENCE.

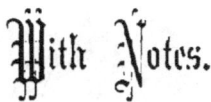

BY

E. P. CROWELL,

MOORE PROFESSOR OF LATIN IN AMHERST COLLEGE.

PHILADELPHIA:
ELDREDGE & BROTHER,
No. 17 North Seventh Street.
1880.

Entered, according to Act of Congress, in the year 1874, by
ELDREDGE & BROTHER,
in the Office of the Librarian of Congress, at Washington.

J. FAGAN & SON,
ELECTROTYPERS, PHILAD'A.

CAXTON PRESS OF SHERMAN & CO.

Preface.

ACCORDING to the eminent critic, Fr. Ritschl, all the more ancient MSS. of Terence, except one, bear the subscription of Calliopius, and are none of them earlier than the ninth century. That one, now in the Vatican Library, by far the oldest and best, though the first 785 lines of the Andria are lost, belongs to the fifth century, was once in the possession of the Cardinal Pietro Bembo of Venice, and is called the Bembine. Of a collation of this MS. by Petrus Victorius, now in the Royal Library at Munich, Fleckeisen availed himself in the preparation of his text published in the Teubner series of classics in 1857; and this text is adopted in the present edition of the *Andria* and *Adelphoe*. With it, however, has been carefully compared the edition of Francis Umpfenbach, Berlin, 1870, which contains exact collations of all the important MSS., and furnishes the most complete critical apparatus which has yet appeared. The more important various readings are mentioned in the Notes, and in a very few instances only a different reading has been preferred to that of Fleckeisen.

The comedies of Terence, in comparison with those of Plautus, stand in very little need of expurgation; and the omission of the few lines in these plays, indicated by the numbering, will not, it is believed, detract at all from their value or interest to the student.

The principal object in the Notes has been to aid the pupil in understanding the forms, meanings, and constructions of words peculiar to Terence or to his age, and the numerous elliptical colloquial expressions that occur, as well as to explain the plot of each play. In their preparation, use has been made chiefly of the commentaries of Wilhelm Wagner, Cambridge, Eng., 1869, E. St. J. Parry in the *Bibliotheca Classica*, London, 1857, Reinhold Klotz (The *Andria*), Leipsic, 1865, J. A. Phillips, Dublin, 1846, and occasionally of the older works of Klotz (1838), Stallbaum, and Westerhovius, which also contain the commentaries of the ancient grammarians Donatus and Eugraphius.

A brief account of Terence and his writings has been prefixed to the Notes, and an Appendix added upon the prosody and metres, with the metrical key to the *Andria* and *Adelphoe*.

No American edition of Terence has been published since that of Dillaway in 1839. It is therefore hoped, with the more confidence, that this edition may be of service to the pupil in his study of the language in the earlier period of its history, and may contribute to the better appreciation of an author who, in purity of idiom and elegance of style, was not surpassed by Cicero or Caesar, and whose plays are among the finest specimens of Roman comedy extant.

AMHERST COLLEGE, August 18th, 1874.

ANDRIA
P. TERENTI.

GRAECA · MENANDRV · ACTA · LVDIS · MEGA-
LENSIBVS · MARCO · FVLVIO · MANIO · GLA-
BRIONE · AEDILIB · CVRVLIB · EGERE · L ·
AMBIVIVS · TVRPIO · L · ATILIVS · PRAEN-
ESTINVS · MODOS · FECIT · FLACCVS ·
CLAVDI · TIBIIS · PARIBVS · TOTA · FACTA ·
PRIMA · M · MARCELLO · C · SVLPICIO · COS

PERSONAE.

SIMO .... *senex.*
SOSIA .... *libertvs.*
DAVOS .... *servos.*
PAMPHILVS .... *advlescens.*
GLYCERIVM .... *mvlier.*
MYSIS .... *ancilla.*

CHREMES .... *senex.*
CHARINVS .... *advlescens.*
BYRRIA .... *servos.*

CRITO .... *hospes.*
LESBIA .... *obstetrix.*
DROMO .... *lorarivs.*

PROLOGVS.

Poëta quom primum ánimum ad scribendum ádpulit,
Id sibi negoti credidit solum dari,
Populo ut placerent quas fecisset fabulas.
Verum áliter evenire multo intéllegit:
Nam in prólogis scribúndis óperam abútitur,　　　5
Non qui árgumentum nárret, sed qui máliuoli
Veterís poëtae máledictis respóndeat.
Nunc, quám rem uitio dént, quaeso animum atténdite.
Menander fecit Ándriam et Perínthiam.
Qui utrámuis recte nórit, ambas nóuerit:　　　10
Non íta sunt dissimili árgumento, séd tamen
Dissímili oratióne sunt factae ác stilo.
Quae cónuenere in Ándriam ex Perínthia
Fatétur transtulísse atque usum pró suis.
Id istí uituperant fáctum atque in eo dísputant　　　15
Contáminari nón decere fábulas.
Faciúntne intellegéndo, ut nil intéllegant?
Qui quom húnc accusant, Naéuium Plautum Énnium
Accúsant, quos hic nóster auctorés habet,
Quorum aémulari exóptat neglegéntiam　　　20
Potiús quam istorum obscúram diligéntiam.
Dehinc út quiescant pórro moneo et désinant
Male dícere, malefácta ne noscánt sua.
Fauéte, adeste aequo ánimo et rem cognóscite,
Vt pérnoscatis, écquid spei sit rélicuom:　　　25
Posthác quas faciet de íntegro comoédias,
Spectándae an exigéndae sint uobís prius.

7

ACTVS I.

SIMO. SOSIA.

Si. Vos ístaec intro auférte : abite. Sósia,
Adés dum : paucis té uolo. *So.* Dictúm puta :
Nempe út curentur récte haec. *Si.* Immo aliúd.
    So. Quid est,   30
Quod tíbi mea ars efficere hoc possit ámplius?
Si. Nil ístac opus est árte ad hanc rem, quám paro,
Sed eís, quas semper ín te intellexí sitas,
Fide ét taciturnitáte. *So.* Expecto quíd uelis.
Si. Ego póstquam te emi, a páruolo ut sempér tibi 35
Apúd me iusta et clémens fuerit séruitus,
Scis. Féci ex seruo ut ésses libertús mihi,
Proptérea quod scruíbas liberáliter.
Quod hábui summum prétium persoluí tibi.
So. In mémoria habeo. *Si.* Haud múto factum.
    So. Gaúdeo,   40
Si tíbi quid feci aut fácio quod placeát, Simo,
Et id grátum fuisse aduórsum te habeo grátiam.
Sed hoc míhi molestumst : nam ístacc commemo-
    rátio

	Quasi éxprobratióst inmemori bénefici.	
	Quin tu úno uerbo díc, quid est quod mé uelis.	45
Si.	Ita fáciam. Hoc primum in hác re praedicó tibi:	
	Quas crédis esse has, nón sunt uerae núptiae.	
So.	Quor símulas igitur? *Si.* Rem ómnem a principio aúdies:	
	Eo pácto et gnati uítam et consiliúm meum	
	Cognósces, et quid fácere in hac re té uelim.	50
	Nam is póstquam excessit éx ephebis, Sosia,	
	Liberius uiuendi fuit potestas — nam ántea	
	Qui scíre posses aút ingenium nóscere,	
	Dum aetás metus magíster prohibebánt? *So.* Itast.	
Si.	Quod plérique omnes fáciunt adulescéntuli,	55
	Vt ánimum ad aliquod stúdium adiungant, aút equos	
	Alere aút canes ad uénandum, aut ad philosophos:	
	Horum ílle nil egrégie practer cétera	
	Studébat, et tamen ómnia haec medíocriter.	
	Gaudébam. *So.* Non iniúria: nam id árbitror	60
	Adpríme in uita esse útile, ut ne quíd nimis.	
Si.	Sic uíta erat: facile ómnes perferre ac pati:	
	Cum quíbus erat quomque úna, eis sese dédere:	
	Eórum óbsequi studiis, aduorsus nemini,	
	Numquam praeponens se illis: ita facíllume	65
	Sine inuídia laudem inuénias et amicós pares.	
So.	Sapiénter uitam instítuit: namque hoc témpore	
	Obséquium amicos, uéritas odiúm parit.	

Si. Intérea mulier quaédam abhinc triénnium
Ex Ándro commigráuit huc uicíniae, 70
Inópia et cognatórum neglegéntia
Coácta, egregia fórma atque aetate íntegra.
So. Ei, uéreor nequid Ándria adportét mali.
Si. Primo haéc pudice uítam parce ac dúriter
Agébat, lana ac téla uictum quaéritans: 75
Sed póstquam amans accéssit pretium póllicens,
Vnús et item alter: íta ut ingeniumst ómnium
Hominum áb labore prócliue ad lubídinem,
Accépit condiciónem, dein quaestum óccipit.
Qui tum íllam amabant, fórte, ita ut fit, fílium 80
Perdúxere illuc, sécum ut una essét, meum.
Egomét continuo mécum ' certe cáptus est:
Habet.' Óbseruabam máne illorum séruolos
Veniéntis aut abeúntis: rogitabam 'heús puer,
Dic sódes, quis heri Chrýsidem habuit?' nam
Ándriae 85
Illi íd erat nomen.' *So.* Téneo. *Si.* Phaedrum
aut Clíniam
Dicébant aut Nicáretum: nam hi tres túm simul
Amábant. 'Eho, quid Pámphilus?' "Quid?
súmbolam
Dedít, cenauit." Gaúdebam. Item alió die
Quaerébam: comperiébam nil ad Pámphilum 90
Quicquam áttinere. Enim uéro spectatúm satis
Putábam et magnum exémplum continéntiae:
Nam quí cum ingeniis cónflictatur eíus modi

Neque cómmouetur ánimus in ea ré tamen,
Scias pósse habere iam ípsum suae uitaé modum. 95
Quom id míhi placebat, tum úno ore omnes
    ómnia
Bona dícere et laudáre fortunás meas,
Qui gnátum haberem táli ingenio praéditum.
Quid uérbis opus est? hác fama inpulsús Chremes
Vltro ád me uenit, únicam gnatám suam   100
Cum dóte summa fílio uxorem út daret.
Placuít : despondi : hic núptiis dictúst dies.

So. Quid ígitur obstat, quór non fiant? *Si.* Aúdies.
Ferme ín diebus paúcis, quibus haec ácta sunt,
Chrysís uicina haec móritur. *So.* O factúm bene : 105
Beásti : ei metui a Chrýside. *Si.* Ibi tum fílius
Cum illís, qui amarant Chrýsidem, una aderát
    frequens :
Curábat una fúnus : tristis ínterim,
Non númquam conlacrumábat. Placuit tum íd
    mihi.
Sic cógitabam 'hic páruae consuetúdinis   110
Causa húius mortem tám fert familiáriter :
Quid si ípse amasset? quid hic mihi faciét
    patri?'
Haec égo putabam esse ómnia humani íngeni
Mansuétique animi offícia. Quid multís moror?
Egomét quoque eius caúsa in funús pródeo,   115
Nil suspicáns étiam mali. *So.* Hem quid ést?
    Si. Scies.

Ecfértur. imus. ínterea inter mulieres,
Quae ibi áderant, forte unam áspicio adulescén-
    tulam,
Formá. *So.* Bona fortásse. *Si.* Et uoltu, Sósia,
Adeó modesto, adeó uenusto, ut níl supra.   120
Quae quóm mihi lamentári praeter céteras
Visást, et quia erat fórma praeter céteras
Honésta ac liberáli, accedo ad pédisequas,
Quae sít rogo. Sorórem esse aiunt Chrýsidis.
Percússit ilico ánimum. Attat hoc íllud est, 125
Hinc íllae lacrumae, haec íllast misericórdia.
So. Quam tímeo, quorsum euádas! *Si.* Funus ín-
    terim
Procédit. Sequimur: ád sepulcrum uénimus:
In ígnem impositast: flétur. Interea haéc soror,
Quam díxi, ad flammam accéssit inprudéntius, 130
Satis cúm periclo. Ibi tum éxanimatus Pám-
    philus
Bene díssimulatum amórem et celatum índicat:
Adcúrrit: mediam múlierem compléctitur:
'Mea Glýcerium' inquit 'quíd agis? quor te is
    pérditum?'
Tum illa, út consuetum fácile amorem cérneres, 135
Reiécit se in eum fléns quam familiáriter.
So. Quid aïs? *Si.* Redeo inde irátus atque aegré
    ferens:
Nec sátis ad obiurgándum causae. Díceret
'Quid féci? quid commérui aut peccauí, pater?

Quae sése in ignem iní̆cere uoluit, próhibui: 140
Seruáui.' Honesta orátiost. *So.* Recté putas:
Nam si íllum obiurges, uítae qui auxiliúm tulit,
Quid fácias illi, quí dederit damnum aút ma-
 lum?
Si. Venít Chremes postrídie ad me clámitans:
Indígnum facinus: cómperisse, Pámphilum 145
Pro uxóre habere hanc péregrinam.   Ego illud
 sédulo
Negáre factum.   Ille ínstat factum.   Dénique
Ita túm discedo ab íllo, ut qui se fíliam
Negét daturum.   *So.* Nón tu ibi gnatum?   *Si.*
 Ne haéc quidem
Satis uémens causa ad óbiurgandum.   *So.* Quí
 cedo? 150
Si. 'Tute ípse his rebus fínem praescripstí, pater:
Prope adést, quom alieno móre uiuendúmst mihi
Sine núnc meo me uíuere intereá modo.'
So. Quí igitúr relictus ést obiurgandí locús?
Si. Si própter amorem uxórem nolet dúcere, 155
Ea prímum ab illo animáduortenda iniúriast.
Et núnc id operam do, út per falsas núptias
Vera óbiurgandi caúsa sit, si déneget:
Simúl sceleratus Dáuos siquid cónsili
Habet, út consumat núnc, quom nil obsínt doli: 160
Quem ego crédo manibus pédibusque obnixe
 ómnia
Factúrum: magis id ádeo, mihi ut incómmodet,

Quam ut óbsequatur gnáto. *So.* Quaproptér?
Si. Rogas?
Mala méns, malus animus. Quém quidem ego
si sénsero . .
Sed quíd opust uerbis? sín eueniat, quód uolo, 165
In Pámphilo ut nil sít morae: restát Chremes,
Qui mi éxorandus ést: et spero cónfore.
Nunc tuómst officium, has béne ut adsimules
núptias:
Pertérrefacias Dáuom: obserues fílium,
Quid agát, quid cum illo cónsili captét. *So.*
Sat est: 170
Curábo. *Si.* Eamus núnciam intro. *So.* I praé,
sequor.

ACTVS II.

SIMO. DAVOS.

Si. Non dúbiumst, quin uxórem nolit fílius:
Ita Dáuom modo timére sensi, ubi núptias
Futúras esse audíuit. Sed ipse exít foras.
Da. Mirábar, hoc si síc abiret: ét eri semper lénitas
Verébar quorsum euáderet: 176
    Qui póstquam audierat nón datum iri fílio
        uxorém suo,
    Númquam quoiquam nóstrum uerbum fécit
        neque id aegré tulit.
Si. Át nunc faciet, néque, ut opinor, síne tuo magnó
        malo.
Da. Id uóluit, nos sic néc opinantis dúci falso
        gaúdio,
    Sperántis iam amotó metu, interea óscitantis
        ópprimi, 181
    Vt ne ésset spatium cógitandi ad dísturbandas
        núptias:
    Astúte. *Si.* Carnuféx quae loquitur? *Da.*
    Érus est, neque prouíderam.

Si. Daue. *Da.* Hém, quid est? *Si.* Eho dum ád
me. *Da.* Quid hic uolt? *Si.* Quíd
aïs? *Da.* Qua de ré? *Si.* Rogas?
Meum gnátum rumor ést amare. *Da.* Id pópu-
lus curat scílicet. 185
Si. Hocíne agis an non? *Da.* Égo uero istuc. *Si.*
Séd nunc ea me exquírere,
Iníqui patris est: nám quod antehac fécit, nil
ad me áttinet.
Dum témpus ad eam rém tulit, siui ánimum ut
explerét suom:
Nunc híc dies aliam uítam adfert, álios mores
póstulat.
Dehinc póstulo siue aéquomst te oro, Dáue, ut
redeat iam ín uiam. 190
Da. Hoc quíd sit? *Si.* Omnes, quí amant, grauiter
síbi dari uxorém ferunt.
Da. Ita áiunt. *Si.* Tum siquís magistrum cépit ad
eam rem ínprobum,
Ipsum ánimum aegrotum ad déteriorem pártem
plerumque ádplicat.
Da. Non hércle intellegó. *Si.* Non? hem. *Da.*
Non: Dáuos sum, non Oédipus.
Si. Nempe érgo aperte uís quae restant mé loqui?
Da. Sané quidem. 195
Si. Si sénsero hodie quícquam in his te núptiis
Fallaciae conári, quo fiánt minus,
Aut uélle in ea re osténdi, quam sis cállidus:

Verbéribus caesum te ín pistrinum, Dáue,
  dedam usque ád necem,
Ea lége atque omine, út, si te inde exémerim,
  ego pro té molam. 200
Quid, hoc íntellextin? án non dum etiam ne
  hóc quidem? *Da.* Immo cállide:
Ita apérte ipsam rem módo locutus, níl circum
  itione úsus es.
Si. Vbiuís facilius pássus sim quam in hác re me
  delúdier.
Da. Bona uérba, quaeso. *Si.* Inrídes? nil me fállis.
  Edicó tibi,
Ne témere facias: néque tu haud dices tíbi non
  praedictúm. Caue. 205
Da. Enim uéro, Daue, níl locist segnítiae neque
  socórdiae,
  Quantum íntellexi módo senis senténtiam de
    núptiis:
  Quae sí non astu próuidentur, me aút erum
    pessúm dabunt.
  Nec quíd agam certumst: Pámphilumne adiú-
    tem an auscultém seni.
  Si illúm relinquo, eius uítae timeo: sín opitulor,
    huíus minas, 210
  Quoi uérba dare difficilest: primum iám de
    amore hoc cómperit:
  Me inférsus seruat, néquam faciam in núptiis
    falláciam.

Si sénserit perii aut sí lubitum fúerit causam
  céperit,
Quo iúre quaque iniúria praecípitem in pistri-
  núm dabit!   214
Ad haéc mala hoc mi accédit etiam: haec
  Ándria,
Si ista úxor siue amícast, grauida e Pámphilost.
Audíreque eorumst óperae pretium audáciam:
Nam incéptiost améntium, haud amántium:
Quidquíd peperisset, décreuerunt tóllere:
Et fíngunt quandam intér se nunc falláciam,   220
  Ciuem Átticam esse hanc. 'Fúit olim *hinc*
  quidám senex
Mercátor: nauem is frégit apud Andrum ín-
  sulam:
Is óbiit mortem. Ibi tum hánc eiectam Chrý-
  sidis
Patrém recepisse órbam, paruam.' Fábulae.
[Mihi quidem hercle non fit ueri simile; atqui
  ipsis commentum placet.]   225
Sed Mýsis ab ea egréditur. At ego hinc me ád
  forum, ut
Conueniam Pámphilum, ne [de hac re] páter
  inprudentem ópprimat.

MYSIS. PAMPHILVS.

My. Sed quíd nam Pamphilum éxanimatum uídeo?
  uereor quíd siet.

| | Oppériar, ut sciám numquid nam haec túrba |
| | tristitiae ádferat. 235

Pa. Hocinést humanum fáctu aut inceptu? hócinest
officiúm patris?
My. Quid íllud est? *Pa.* Pro deúm fidem, quid est,
si hóc non contuméliast?
Vxórem decrerát dare sese mi hódie: nonne
opórtuit
Praescísse me ante? nónne prius commúnicatum
opórtuit?
My. Miserám me, quod uerbum aúdio? 240
Pa. Quíd? Chremes, qui dénegarat sé commissu-
rúm mihi
Gnátam suam uxorem, íd mutauit, quía me
inmutatúm uidet?
Itane óbstinate dát operam, ut me a Glýcerio
miserum ábstrahat?
Quod sí fit, perco fúnditus.
Adeon hominem esse ínuenustum aut ínfelicem
quémquam, ut ego sum! 245
Pró deum atque hominúm fidem!
Núllon ego Chremétis pacto adfínitatem ecfú-
gere potero?
Quót modis contémptus, spretus! fácta, trans-
acta ómnia. Hem,
Répudiatus répetor: quam obrem? nísi si id
est, quod súspicor:
Áliquid monstri alúnt: ea quoniam némini ob-
trudí potest, 250

Ítur ad me. *My.* Orátio haec me míseram ex-
    animauít metu.
Pa. Nam quíd ego dicam dé patre? ah
    Tantámne rem tam néglegenter ágere! prac-
        teriéns modo
    Mi apúd forum ' uxor tíbi ducendast, Pámphile,
        hodie' inquít, ' para :
    Abí domum.' Id mihi uísust dicere ' úbi cito
        ac suspénde te.' 255
    Óbstipui: censén me uerbum pótuisse ullum
        próloqui aut
    Ullam causam, inéptam saltem fálsam iniquam?
        obmútui.
    Quód si ego resciuíssem id prius, quid fácerem,
        siquis mé roget :
    Áliquid facerem, ut hóc ne facerem. Séd nunc
        quid primum éxequar?
    Tót me inpediunt cúrae, quae meum ánimum
        diuorsaé trahunt : 260
    Amor, misericordia húius, nuptiárum sollicitátio,
    Tum pátris pudor, qui mé tam leni pássus ani-
        most úsque adhuc
    Quae meó quomque animo lúbitumst facere.
        eine égo ut aduorser? eí mihi.
    Incértumst quid agam. *My.* Mísera timeo
        ' íncertum' hoc quorsum áccidat.
    Sed núnc peropus est, aút hunc cum ipsa aut de
        ílla me aduorsum húnc loqui. 265

Dum in dúbiost animus, paúlo momento húc
  uel illuc inpéllitur.
Pa. Quis hic lóquitur? Mysis, sálue. *My.* O salue,
  Pámphile. *Pa.* Quid agít? *My.*
  Rogas?
Labórat e dolóre, atque ex hoc mísera sollici-
  tást, diem
Quia ólim in hunc sunt cónstitutae núptiae.
  tum autem hóc timet,
Ne déseras se. *Pa.* Hem, egone ístuc conarí
  queam? 270
Egon própter me illam décipi miserám sinam,
Quae míhi suom animum atque ómnem uitam
  crédidit,
Quam ego ánimo egregie cáram pro uxore há-
  buerim?
Bene ét pudice eius dóctum atque eductúm
  sinam
Coáctum egestate íngenium inmutárier? 275
Non fáciam. *My.* Haud uerear, si ín te sit soló
  situm:
Sed ut uím queas ferre. *Pa.* Adeon me ignauóm
  putas,
Adeón porro ingratum aút inhumanum aút
  ferum,
Vt néque me consuetúdo neque amor néque
  pudor
Commóueat neque commóneat, ut seruém fidem? 280

My. Vnum hóc scio, esse méritam, ut memor essés
sui.

Pa. Memor éssem? O Mysis Mýsis, etiam núnc
mihi
Scripta ílla dicta súnt in animo Chrýsidis
De Glýcerio. iam férme moriens mé uocat:
Accéssi: uos semótae. Nos soli: íncipit 285
'Mi Pámphile, huius fórmam atque aetatém
uides:
Nec clám te est, quam illi núnc utraeque in-
útiles
Et ád pudicitiam ét ad rem tutandám sient.
Quod égo per hanc te déxtram oro et geniúm
tuom,
Per tuám fidem perque húius solitúdinem 290
Te obtéstor, ne abs te hanc ségreges neu déseras.
Si te ín germani frátris dilexí loco
Siue haéc te solum sémper fecit máxumi
Seu tíbi morigera fúit in rebus ómnibus,
Te istí uirum do, amícum tutorém patrem: 295
Bona nóstra haec tibi permítto et tuae mandó
fide.'
Hanc mi ín manum dat: mórs continuo ipsam
óccupat.
Accépi: acceptam séruabo. *My.* Ita speró
quidem.

Pa. Propera. atque aúdin?
Verbum únum caue de núptiis, ne ad mórbum
hoc etiam. *My.* Ténco. 300

ACTVS III.

CHARINVS. BYRRIA. PAMPHILVS.

Ch. Quíd aïs, Byrriá? daturne illa Pámphilo hodie
    núptum? *By.* Sic est.
Ch. Quí scis? *By.* Apud forúm modo e Dauo
    aúdiui. *Ch.* Vae miseró mihi.
    Vt ánimus in spe atque ín timore usque ántehac
        attentús fuit,
    Íta, póstquam adempta spés est, lassus cúra
        confectús stupet.
By. Quaéso edepol, Charíne, quoniam nón potest id
    fíeri quod uis,   305
    Íd uelis quod póssit. *Ch.* Nil uolo áliud nisi
        Philúmenam. *By.* Ah,
    Quánto satiust te íd dare operam, qui ístum
        amorem ex ánimo amoueas,
    Quam íd loqui, quo mágis lubido frústra incenda-
        túr tua.
Ch. Facile ómnes, quom ualémus, recta cónsilia
    aegrotís damus.

Tu si híc sis, aliter séntias. *By.* Age age, út
    lubet. *Ch.* Sed Pámphilum   310
Video. ómnia experíri certumst príus quam
    pereo. *By.* Quíd hic agit?
Ch. Ipsum húnc orabo, huic súpplicabo, amórem
    huic narrabó meum:
Credo ínpetrabo, ut áliquot saltem núptiis
    prodát dies:
Intérea fiet áliquid, spero. *By.* Id 'áliquid'
    nil est. *Ch.* Býrria,
Quid tíbi uidetur? ádeon ad eum? *By.* Quíd
    ni? si nil ínpetres,   315
Vt te árbitretur síbi paratum moéchum, si illam
    dúxerit.
Ch. Ábin hinc in malám rem cum suspítione istác,
    scelus?
Pa. Charínum uideo. sálue. *Ch.* O salue, Pám-
    phile:
Ád te aduenio spém salutem cónsilium auxilium
    éxpetens.
Pa. Néque pol consilí locum habeo néque ad
    auxilium cópiam.   320
Séd istuc quid namst? *Ch.* Hódie uxorem
    dúcis? *Pa.* Aiunt. *Ch.* Pámphile,
Si íd facis, hodié postremum mé uides. *Pa.*
    Quid ita? *Ch.* Eí mihi,
Véreor dicere: huíc dic quaeso, Býrria. *By.*
    Ego dicám. *Pa.* Quid est?

By. Spónsam hic tuam amat. *Pa.* Né iste haud
        mecum séntit. Eho dum díc mihi:
Númquid nam ampliús tibi cum illa fuít, Cha-
        rine? *Ch.* Ah, Pámphile,   325
Níl. *Pa.* Quam uellem! *Ch.* Núnc te per
        amicítiam et per amorem óbsecro,
Príncipio ut ne dúcas. *Pa.* Dabo equidem
        óperam. *Ch.* Sed si id nón potest
Aút tibi nuptiae haéc sunt cordi, *Pa.* Córdi?
    Ch. saltem aliquót dies
Prófer, dum profícíscor aliquo, né uideam. *Pa.*
        Audi núnciam.
Égo, Charine, ne útiquam officium líberi esse
        hominís puto,   330
Quom ís nil mereat, póstulare id grátiae adponí
        sibi.
Núptias ecfúgere ego istas málo quam tu
        apíscier.
Ch. Réddidisti animúm. *Pa.* Nunc siquid pótes aut
        tu aut hic Býrria,
Fácite fingite ínuenite efficite qui detúr tibi:
Égo id agam, mihi quí ne detur. *Ch.* Sát
        habeo. *Pa.* Dauom óptume   335
Vídeo, quoius consílio fretus sum. *Ch.* Át tu
        hercle haud quicquám mihi,
Nísi ea quae nil ópus sunt sciri. Fúgin hinc?
    By. Ego uero ác lubens.

DAVOS. CHARINVS. PAMPHILVS.

Da. Dí boni, boní quid porto? séd ubi inueniam Pámphilum,
Vt metum in quo nunc est adimam atque éxpleam animum gaúdio?
Ch. Laétus est nescio quid. *Pa.* Nil est: nón dum haec resciuít mala.   340
Da. Quem égo nunc credo, sí iam audierit síbi paratas núptias,
Ch. Aúdin tu illum? *Da.* tóto me oppido éxanimatum quaérere.
Séd ubi quaeram aut quó nunc primum inténdam? *Ch.* Cessas ádloqui?
Da. Hábeo. *Pa.* Daue, adés, resiste. *Da.* Quís homost, qui me . . ? O Pámphile,
Te ípsum quaero. eugaé Charine: ambo ópportune: uós uolo.   345
Pa. Dáue, perii. *Da.* Quín tu hoc audi. *Pa.* Intérii. *Da.* Quid timeás scio.
Ch. Méa quidem hercle cérte in dubio uítast. *Da.* Et quid tú, scio.
Pa. Núptiae mi. *Da.* Etsí scio? *Pa.* hodie. *Da.* Obtúndis, tam etsi intéllego?
Íd paues, ne dúcas tu illam: tu aútem, ut ducas. *Ch.* Rém tenes.
Pa. Istuc ipsum. *Da.* Atqui ístuc ipsum níl periclist: mé uide.   350

Pa. Óbsecro te, quám primum hoc me líbera miserúm metu. *Da.* Hem,
Líbero; uxorém tibi non dat iám Chremes.
Pa. Qui scís? *Da.* Scio.
Túos pater modo *hic* me prendit: aít tibi uxorém dare
Hódie, item alia múlta, quae nunc nón est narrandí locus.
Cóntinuo ad te próperans percurro ád forum, ut dicám tibi haec. 355
Vbi te non inuénio, ibi ascendo ín quendam excelsúm locum.
Círcumspicio; núsquam. forte ibi húius uideo Býrriam;
Rógo: negat uidísse. mihi moléstum. quid agam cógito.
Rédeunti interea éx ipsa re mi íncidit suspítio 'hem,
Paúlulum obsoni: ípsus tristis: de ímprouiso núptiae: 360
Nón cohaerent.' *Pa.* Quórsum nam istuc? *Da.* Égo me continuo ád Chremem.
Quom íllo aduenio, sólitudo ante óstium: iam id gaúdeo.
Ch. Récte dicis. *Pa.* Pérge. *Da.* Maneo: intérea intro ire néminem
Vídeo, exire néminem: matrónam nullam in aédibus,

Níl ornati, níl tumulti: accéssi: intro aspexí.
Pa. Scio: 365
Mágnum signum. *Da.* Núm uidentur cónue-
nire haec núptiis?
Pa. Nón opinor, Dáue. *Da.* ' Opinor ' nárras? non
recte áccipis.
Cérta res est. étiam puerum inde ábiens
conuení Chremis:
Hólera et pisciculós minutos férre obolo in
cenám seni.
Ch. Líberatus sum hódie, Daue, túa opera. *Da.*
Ac nullús quidem. 370
Ch. Quíd ita? nempe huic prórsus illam nón dat.
Da. Ridiculúm caput,
Quási necessus sít, si huic non dat, té illam
uxorem dúcere:
Nísi uides, nisi sénis amicos óras, ambis. *Ch.*
Béne mones:
Íbo, etsi hercle saépe iam me spés haec frustra-
tást. uale.
Pa. Quíd igitur sibi uólt pater? quor símulat? *Da.*
Ego dicám tibi. 375
Si íd suscenseát nunc, quia non dét tibi uxorém
Chremes,
Príus quam tuom ut sese hábeat animum ad
núptias perspéxerit:
Ípsus sibi esse iniúrius uideátur, neque id
iniúria.

Séd si tu negáris ducere, íbi culpam in te tráns-
　　　feret:
Túm illae turbae fíent. *Pa.* Quiduis pátiar.
　　　Da. Pater est, Pámphile.　　　　　　　　380
Difficilest. tum haec sólast mulier. díctum
　　　ac factum inuénerit
Aliquam causam, quam óbrem cïciat óppido.
　　　Pa. Ëiciát? *Da.* Cito.
Pa. Cédo igitur quid fáciam, Daue? *Da.* Díc
　　　te ducturum. *Pa.* Hém. *Da.* Quid
　　　est?
Pa. Egon dícam? *Da.* Quor non? *Pa.* Númquam
　　　faciam. *Da.* Né nega.
Pa. Suadére noli. *Da.* Ex eá re quid fiát, uide.　385
Pa. Vt ab ílla excludar, húc concludar. *Da.* Nón
　　　itast
Nempe hóc sic esse opínor: dicturúm patrem
'Ducás uolo hodie uxórem:' tu 'ducam'
　　　ínquies:
Cedo quíd iurgabit técum? hic reddes ómnia,
Quae núnc sunt certa ei cónsilia, incerta út
　　　sient,　　　　　　　　　　　　　　　　390
Sine omní periclo: nam hóc haud dubiumst,
　　　quín Chremes
Tibi nón det gnatam. \néc tu ea causa mínueris
Haec quaé facis, ne is mútet suam senténtiam.
Patrí dic uelle: ut, quóm uelit, tibi iúre irasci
　　　nón queat.

Nam quód tu speres, própulsabo fácile. uxo-
       rem his móribus   395
*   *   *   *   *   *   *   *
Dabit némo. Inueniet ínopem potius, quám te
       corrumpí sinat.
Sed sí te aequo animo férre accipiet, négle-
       gentem féceris:
Alia ótiosus quaéret: interea áliquid acciderít
       boni.

Pa. Itau crédis? *Da.* Haud dubium íd quidemst.
       Pa. Vide quó me inducas. *Da.* Quín
       taces?
Pa. Dicám. puerum autem né resciscat míhi esse
       ex illa caútiost: 400
Nam póllicitus sum súscepturum. *Da.* O
       fácinus audax. *Pa.* Hánc fidem
Sibi me óbsecrauit, quí se sciret nón deserturum,
       út darem.
Da. Curábitur. sed páter adest. caue té esse tris-
       tem séntiat.

SIMO. DAVOS. PAMPHILVS.

Si. Reuíso quid agant aút quid captent cónsili.
Da. Hic núnc non dubitat, quín te ducturúm neges. 405
Venít meditatus álicunde ex soló loco:
Orátionem spérat inuenísse se,
Qui dífferat te: proín tu fac apud te út sies.
Pa. Modo ut póssim, Daue. *Da.* Créde inquam
       hoc mihi, Púmphile,

Numquam hódie tecum cómmutatúrúm patrem 410
Vnum ésse uerbum, sí te dices dúcere.

BYRRIA. SIMO. DAVOS. PAMPHILVS.

Erus mé relictis rébus iussit Pámphilum
Hodie óbseruare, quíd ageret de núptiis.
[Scirem: id proptereá nunc hunc uenientem
    sequor.]
Ipsum ádeo praesto uídeo cum Dauo: hóc
    agam. 415
Vtrúmque adesse uídeo. *Da.* Hem, serua.
    Si. Pámphile.
Quasi de ínprouiso réspice ad eum. *Pa.* Ehém
    pater.
Probe. *Si.* Hódie uxorem dúcas, ut dixí, uolo.
Nunc nóstrae timeo párti, quid hic respóndeat.
Neque istíc neque alibi tíbi erit usquam in mé
    mora. *By.* Hem. 420
Obmútuit. *By.* Quid díxit? *Si.* Facis ut té
    decet,
Quom istúc quod postulo ínpetro cum grátia.
Sum uérus? *By.* Erus, quantum aúdio, uxore
    éxcidit.
I núnciam intro, ne ín mora, quom opus sít,
    sies.
Eó. *By.* Nullane in ré esse quoiquam hominí
    fidem! 425
Verum íllud uerbumst, uólgo quod dicí solet,

Omnís sibi malle mélius esse quam álteri.
Ego íllam uidi : uírginem formá bona
Meminí uidere : quo aéquior sum Pámphilo. 430
Renúntiabo, ut pro hóc malo mihi dét malum.
Da. Hic núnc me credit áliquam sibi falláciam
Portáre et ea me hic réstitisse grátia.
Si. Quid Dávos narrat? *Da.* Aéque quicquam
  núnc quidem.
Si. Nilne? hém. *Da.* Nil prorsus. *Si.* Átqui
  expectabám quidem. 435
Da. Praetér spem euenit : séntio : hoc male habét
  uirum.
Si. Potiu és mihi uerum dícere? *Da.* Nil fácilius.
Si. Num illí molestae quídpiam haec sunt núptiae
Huiúsce propter cónsuetudinem hóspitae?
Da. Nil hércle : aut, si adeo, bíduist aut trídui 440
Haec sóllicitudo : nósti? deinde désinet.
Etenim ípsus secum eám rem reputauít uia.
Si. Laudó. *Da.* Dum licitumst éi dumque actás
  tulit,
Amáuit : tum id clam : cáuit, ne umquam in-
  fámiae
Ea rés sibi esset, út uirum fortém decet : 445
Nunc úxore opus est : ánimum ad uxorem
  ádpulit.
Si. Subtrístis uisus ést esse aliquantúm mihi.
Da. Nil própter hanc rem, séd est quod suscensét
  tibi.

Si. Quid námst? *Da.* Puerilest. *Si.* Quíd *id* est?
   Da. Nil. *Si.* Quin díc, quid est?
Da. Ait nímium parce fácere sumptum. *Si.* Méne?
   Da. Te.   450
   'Vix' ínquit 'drachumis ést obsonatús decem:
   Num fílio uidétur uxorém dare?
   Quem' inquít 'uocabo ad cénam meorum aequá-
      lium
   Potíssumum nunc?' Ét, quod dicendum híc
      siet,
   Tu quóque per parce nímium. Non laudó.
      Si. Tace: 455
Da. Commóui. *Si.* Ego istaec récte ut fiant uídero.
   Quid nam hóc est rei? quid híc uolt ueteratór
      sibi?
   Nam si híc malist quicquam, hém illic est huic
      reí caput.

Mysis. Simo. Davos. Lesbia. Glycerivm.

My. Ita pól quidem res est, út *tu* dixti, Lésbia:
   Fidélem haud ferme múlieri inueniás uirum.   460
Si. Ab Ándriast ancílla haec. *Da.* Quid narrás?
   Si. Itast.
My. Sed hic Pámphilus. *Si.* Quid dícit? *My.*
      Firmauít fidem. *Si.* Hem.
Da. Vtinam aút hic surdus aút haec muta fácta sit.
My. Nam quód peperisset, iússit tolli. *Si.* O
   Iúppiter,

3 — Ter.

Quid ego aúdio? actumst, síquidem haec uera
praédicat. 465
Le. Bonum ingénium narras ádulescentis. *My.*
Óptumum.
Sed séquere me intro, ne ín mora illi sís. *Le.*
Sequor.
Da. Quod rémedium nunc huíc malo inueniám?
Si. Quid hoc?
Adeón est demens? éx peregrina? iám
scio: ah
Vix tándem sensi stólidus. *Da.* Quid hic sen-
sísse aït? 470
Si. Haec prímum adfertur iám mi ab hoc fallácia:
Hanc símulant parere, quó Chremetem abstér-
reant.
Hui, tám cito? ridículum: postquam ante
óstium
Me audíuit stare, adpróperat. non sat cóm-
mode 475
Diuísa sunt tempóribus tibi, Daue, haéc. *Da.*
Mihin?
Si. Num inmémores discipuli? *Da.* Égo quid
narres néscio.
Si. Hic ínparatum mé si in ueris núptiis
Adórtus esset, quós mihi ludos rédderet?
Nunc huíus periclo fít, ego in portu náuigo. 480

LESBIA. SIMO. DAVOS.

Le. Per ecástor scitus púer est natus Pámphilo.
　Deos quaéso ut sit supérstes, quandoquidem ípsest ingenió bono,
　Quomque huíce ueritust óptumae adulescénti facere iniúriam.
Si. Vel hoc quís non credat, quí te norit, ábs te esse ortum? *Da.* Quíd nam id est?
Si. Non ínperabat córam, quid facto ésset opus puérperae:　　　　　　　　　490
　Sed póstquam egressast, íllis quae sunt íntus clamat dé uia.
　O Dáue, itan contémnor abs te? aut ítane tandem idóneus
　Tibi uídeor esse, quém tam aperte fállere incipiás dolis?
　Saltem áccurate, ut métui uidear cérte, si rescíuerim.
Da. Certe hércle nunc hic se ípsus fallit, haúd ego.
　　　　Si. Edixí tibi,　　　　　　　　495
　Intérminatus súm, ne faceres: núm ueritu's? quid ré tulit?
　Credón tibi hoc nunc, péperisse hanc e Pámphilo?
Da. Teneó quid erret, ét quid agam habeo. *Si.* Quid taces?
Da. Quid crédas? quasi non tíbi renuntiáta sint haec síc fore.

Si. Mihin quísquam? *Da.* Eho an tute íntellexti
    hoc ádsimulari? *Si.* Inrídeor.   500
Da. Renúntiatumst: nám qui tibi istaec íncidit
    suspítio?
Si. Qui? quía te noram. *Da.* Quási tu dicas,
    fáctum id consilió meo.
Si. Certe énim scio. *Da.* Non sátis me pernosti
    étiam, qualis sím, Simo.
Si. Egon té? *Da.* Sed siquid tíbi narrare occépi,
    continuó dari
    Tibi uérba censes fálso: itaque hercle níl iam
        muttire aúdeo.   505
Si. Hoc égo scio unum, néminem peperísse hic.
    Da. Intelléxti.
    Sed nílo setiús mox puerum huc déferent ante
        óstium.
    Id égo iam nunc tibi, ére, renuntió futurum, ut
        sís sciens,
    Ne tu hóc posterius dícas Daui fáctum consilio
        aút dolis:
    Prórsus a me opínionem hanc tuam ésse ego
        amotám uolo.   510
Si. Vnde id scis? *Da.* Audíui et credo: múlta
    concurrúnt simul,
    Quí coniecturam hánc nunc facio. iám primum
        haec se e Pámphilo
    Gráuidam dixit ésse: inuentumst fálsum.
        nunc, postquám uidet

Núptias domi ádparari, míssast ancilla ílico
Óbstetricem arcéssitum ad eam et púerum ut
    adferrét simul.   515
[Hoc nisi fit, puerum ut tu uideas, nihil mouen-
    tur nuptiae.]

Si. Quíd aïs?   quom intelléxeras
    Íd consilium cápere, quor non díxti extemplo
        Pámphilo?

Da. Quís igitur eum ab ílla abstraxit nísi ego?
    nam omnes nós quidem
    Scímus, hanc quam mísere amarit.   núnc sibi
        uxorem éxpetit.   520
    Póstremo id mihi dá negoti: tú tamen idem has
        núptias
    Pérge facere ita út facis: et id spéro adiuturós
        deos.

Si. Ímmo abi intro: ibi me ópperire et quód parato
    opus ést para.
    Non íupulit me, haec núnc omnino ut cré-
        derem.
    Atqui haúscio an quae díxit sint uera ómnia,   525
    Sed párui pendo: illúd mihi multo máxumumst,
    Quod míhi pollicitust ípsus gnatus.   núnc
        Chremem
    Conuéniam: orabo gnáto uxorem: id si ínpetro,
    Quid álias malim quam hódie has fieri núptias?
    Nam gnátus quod pollícitust, haud dubiúmst
        mihi,   530

Si nólit, quin eum mérito possim cógere.
Atque ádeo in ipso témpore eccum ipsum
óbuiam.

Simo. Chremes.

Si. Iubeó Chremetem. *Ch.* O te ípsum quaerebam.
Si. Ét ego te. *Ch.* Optato áduenis.
Aliquót me adierunt, éx te auditum qui aíbant,
hodie núbere
Meam fíliam tuo gnáto: id uiso tún an illi
insániant. 535
Si. Auscúlta paucis: ét quid te ego uelim ét tu
quod quaerís scies.
Ch. Auscúlto: loquere quíd uelis.
Si. Per té deos oro et nóstram amicitiám, Chremes,
Quae incépta a paruis cum aétate adereuít
simul,
Perque únicam tuám gnatam et gnatúm meum, 540
Quoius tíbi potestas súmma seruandí datur,
Vt me ádiuues in hác re, atque ita uti núptiae
Fuerúnt futurae, fíant. *Ch.* Ah, ne me óbsecra:
Quasi hóc te orando a me ímpetrare opórteat.
Alium ésse censes núnc me atque olim quóm
dabam? 545
Si in rémst utrique ut fíant, arcessí iube.
Sed si éx ea re plús malist quam cómmodi
Vtríque, id oro te ín commune ut cónsulas,
Quasi ílla tua sit Pámphilique ego sím pater.

Si. Immo íta uolo itaque póstulo ut fiát, Chremes: 550
Neque póstulem abs te, ni ípsa res moneát.
Ch. Quid est?
Si. Iraé sunt inter Glýcerium et gnatum. *Ch.*
Aúdio.
Si. Ita mágnae, ut sperem pósse auelli. *Ch.*
Fábulae.
Si. Profécto sic est. *Ch.* Síc hercle ut dicám tibi:
Amántium irae amóris integrátiost. 555
Si. Hem, id te óro ut ante cámus. dum tempús
datur,
Dumque eíus lubido occlúsast contuméliis,
Prius quam hárum scelera et lácrumae confictaé
dolis
Reddúcunt animum aegrótum ad misericórdiam,
Vxórem demus. spéro consuetúdine et 560
Coniúgio liberáli deuinctúm, Chremes,
Dein fácile ex illis sése emersurúm malis.
Ch. Tibi ita hóc uidetur: át ego non posse árbitror,
Neque illum hánc perpetuo habére neque me
pérpeti.
Si. Qui scís ergo istuc, nísi periclum féceris? 565
Ch. At istúc periclum in fília fierí grauest.
Si. Nempe íncommoditas dénique huc omnís redit,
Si euéniat, quod di próhibeant, discéssio.
At sí corrigitur, quót commoditatés uide:
Princípio amico fílium restítueris, 570
Tibi génerum firmum et fíliae inueniés uirum.

Ch. Quid istíc? si ita istuc ánimum induxti esse
    útile,
  Noló tibi ullum cómmodum in me claúdier.
Si. Meritó te semper máxumi fecí, Chremes.
Ch. Sed quíd aïs? *Si.* Quid? *Ch.* Qui scís eos
    nunc díscordare intér se?   575
Si. Ipsús mihi Dauos, qui íutumust eorúm consiliis,
    díxit:
  Et ís mihi suadet núptias quantúm queam ut
    matúrem.
  Num cénses faceret, fílium nisi scíret eadem
    haec uélle?
  Tute ádeo iam eius uerba aúdies. heus, euocate
    huc Dáuom.
  Atque éccum: uideo ipsúm foras exíre.

  DAVOS. SIMO. CHREMES.

Da. Ad te ibam. *Si.* Quíd namst?   580
Da. Quor úxor non arcéssitur? iam aduésperascit.
    Si. Aúdin?
  Ego dúdum non nil uéritus sum, Daue, ábs te,
    ne facerés idem,
  Quod uólgus seruorúm solet, dolís ut me delú-
    deres,
  Proptérea quod amat fílius. *Da.* Egon ístuc
    facerem? *Si.* Crédidi:
  Idque ádeo metuens uós celaui, quód nunc dicam.
    Da. Quíd? *Si.* Scies: 585

Nam própemodum habeo iám fidem. *Da.*
Tandém cognosti quí siem?

Si. Non fúerant nuptiaé futurae. *Da.* Quíd?
non? *Si.* Sed ea grátia
Simuláui, uos ut pértemptarem. *Da.* Quíd aïs?
Si. Sic res ést. *Da.* Vide:
Numquam ístuc quiui ego íntellegere. uáh
consilium cállidum.

Si. Hoc aúdi: ut hinc te intro íre iussi, oppórtune
hic fit mi óbuiam. *Da.* Hem,   590
Num nám perimus? *Si.* Nárro huic, quae tu
dúdum narrastí mihi.

Da. Quid nam aúdio? *Si.* Gnatam út det oro, uíx-
que id exoro. *Da.* Óccidi. *Si.* Hem,
Quid díxisti? *Da.* Optume ínquam factum.
Si. Núnc per hunc nullást mora.

Ch. Domúm modo ibo, ut ádparetur dícam, atque
huc renúntio.

Si. Nunc te óro, Daue, quóniam solus mi éffecisti
has núptias,   595

Da. Ego uéro solus. *Si.* Gnátum mihi corrígere
porro enítere.

Da. Faciam hércle seduló. *Si.* Potes nunc, dum
ánimus inritátus est.

Da. Quiéscas. *Si.* Age igitúr, ubi nunc est ípsus?
Da. Mirum ní domist.

Si. Ibo ád eum atque eadem haec, tíbi quae dixi,
dícam itidem illi. *Da.* Núllus sum

Quid caúsaest, quin hinc ín pistrinum récta
　　proficiscár uia?　　　　　　　　　　　　　600
Nil ést preci locí relictum: iám perturbaui
　　ómnia:
Erúm fefelli: in núptias coniéci erilem fílium;
Feci hódie ut fierent, ínsperante hoc átque inuito
　　Pámphilo.
Hem astútias: quod sí quiessem, níl euenissét
　　mali.
Sed éccum uideo ipsum: óccidi.　　　　　　605
Vtinám mihi esset áliquid hic, quo núnc me
　　praecipitém darem.

Pamphilvs. Davos.

Pa. Vbi illic est? scelús, qui me hodie .. *Da.*
　　Périi. *Pa.* atque hoc confíteor iure
Mi óbtigisse, quándoquidem tam inérs, tam nulli
　　cónsili sum:
Séruon fortunás meas me cómmisisse fúttili!
Ego prétium ob stultitiám fero: sed inúltum
　　numquam id aúferet.　　　　　　　　　610
Da. Posthác incolumem sát scio fore mé, si deuito
　　hóc malum.
Pa. Nam quíd ego nunc dicám patri? negábon
　　uelle mé, modo
Qui súm pollicitus dúcere? Qua *audácia* id
　　facere aúdeam?
Nec quíd me nunc faciám scio. *Da.* Nec mé
　　quidem, atque id ago sédulo.

Dicam áliquid me inuentúrum, ut huic malo
    áliquam productém moram. 615
Pa. Oh. *Da.* Vísus sum. *Pa.* Eho dum bóne uir,
    quid aïs? uíden me consiliís tuis
Miserum ínpeditum esse? *Da.* Át iam expe-
    diam. *Pa.* Expédies? *Da.* Certe,
    Pámphile.
Pa. Nempe út modo. *Da.* Immo mélius spero. *Pa.*
    Oh, tíbi ego ut credam, fúrcifer?
Tu rem ínpeditam et pérditam restítuas? hem
    quo frétus sim,
Qui me hódie ex tranquillíssuma re cóniccisti
    in núptias. 620
An non dixi esse hóc futurum? *Da.* Díxti.
    Pa. Quid meritú's? *Da.* Crucem.
Séd sine paululum ád me redeam: iam áliquid
    dispiciam. *Pa.* Eí mihi,
Quóm non habeo spátium, ut de te súmam sup-
    plicium, út uolo:
Námque hoc tempus praécauere míhi me, haud
    te ulciscí sinit.

ACTVS IV.

CHARINVS. PAMPHILVS. DAVOS.

Ch. Hócine crédibile aút memorábile, 625
 Tánta uecórdia innáta quoiquam út siet,
 Vt malis gaúdeant átque ex incómmodis
 Álteriús sua ut cómparent cómmoda? ah
 Ídnest uerum? ímmo id hominúmst genus
  péssumum,
 Dénegandi modo quís pudor paúlum adest: 630
 Póst ubi témpust promíssa iam pérfici,
 Túm coactí necessário se áperiunt:
 [Et timent, et tamen res cogit denegare]
 Íbi tum eorum ínpudentíssuma orátiost
 'Quís tu es? quis mihi es? quór meam tibi? 635
 Heus, próxumus sum egomét mihi.'
 At támen 'ubi f lés?' si rogés, nil pudént
  hic,
 Vbi opúst: illic úbi nil opúst, ibi ueréntur.
 Séd quid agam? adeamne ád eum et cum eo
  iniúriam hanc expóstulem?

Íngeram mala múlta? atqui aliquis dícat 'nil
promóueris :' 640
Multúm : molestus cérte ei fuero atque ánimo
morem géssero.

Pa. Charíne, et me et te inprúdens, nisi quid dí respiciunt, pérdidi.

Ch. Itane 'inprudens'? tándem inuentast caúsa.
soluistí fidem.

Pa. Quíd 'tandem'? *Ch.* Etiam núnc me ducere
ístis dictis póstulas?

Pa. Quíd istuc est? *Ch.* Postquám me amare díxi,
complacitást tibi. 645
Heú me miserum, quí tuom animum ex ánimo
spectauí meo.

Pa. Fálsus es. *Ch.* Non sátis tibi esse hoc sóli-
dumst uisum gaúdium,
Nísi me lactassés amantem et fálsa spe prodú-
ceres.
Húbeas. *Pa.* Habeam? ah néscis quantis ín
malis uorsér miser,
Quantásque hic consiliís mihi confláuit sollici-
túdines 650
Meus cárnufex. *Ch.* Quid istúc tam mirumst,
dé te si exemplúm capit?

Pa. Haud ístuc dicas, sí cognoris uél me uel
amorém meum.

Ch. Scio: cúm patre altercásti dudum, et ís nunc
proptereá tibi

Suscénset nec te quíuit hodie cógere illam ut
  dúceres.
Pa. Immo étiam, quo tu mínus scis acrumnás meas, 655
  Hacc núptiae non ádparabantúr mihi:
  Nec póstulabat núnc quisquam uxorém dare.
Ch. Scio: tú coactus tuá uoluntate és. Pa. Mane:
  Non dúm scis. Ch. Scio equidem íllam ductu-
    rum ésse te.
Pa. Quor me énicas? hoc aúdi. numquam dé-
    stitit   660
  Instáre, ut dicerém me ducturúm patri:
  Suadére, orare usque ádeo donec pérpulit.
Ch. Quis homo ístuc? Pa. Dauos . . . . Ch.
    Dauos? Pa. Intertúrbat. Ch. Quam
    obrem? Pa. Néscio,
  Nisi mihi deos sátis scio fuisse irátos, qui au-
    scultáuerim.
Ch. Factum hóc est, Daue? Da. Fáctum. Ch.
    Hem, quid aís, scelus?   665
  At tíbi di dignum fáctis exitiúm duint.
  Eho, díc mihi, si omnes húnc coniectum in
    núptias
  Inimíci uellent, quód nisi consilium hóc darent?
Da. Decéptus sum, at non défetigatús. Ch. Scio.
Da. Hac nón successit, ália adgrediemúr uia: 670
  Nisi si íd putas, quia prímo processít parum,
  Non pósse iam ad salútem conuorti hóc malum.
Pa. Immo étiam: nam satis crédo, si aduigiláueris,
  Ex únis geminas míhi conficies núptias.

Ego, Pámphile, hoc tibi pró scruitio débeo, 675
Conári manibus pédibus noctisque ét dies,
Capitís periclum adíre, dum prosím tibi :
Tuomst, síquid praeter spem éuenit, mi ignó-
scere.
Parúm succedit quód ago : at facio sédulo.
Vel mélius tute réperi, me missúm face. 680
Cupió : restitue quem á me accepistí locum.
Faciam. *Pa.* Át iam hoc opus est. *Da.*
Hem . . . . sed mane : concrepuit a
Glycerio óstium.
Nil ád te. *Da.* Quaero. *Pa.* Hem, núncin
demum ? *Da.* At iam hóc tibi inu-
entúm dabo.

Mysis. Pamphilvs. Charinvs. Davos.

Iam ubi úbi erit, inuentúm tibi curábo et
mecum addúctum
Tuom Pámphilum : modo tu, ánime mi, nolí te
maceráre. 685
Mysís. *My.* Quis est ? ehem Pámphile, op-
tumé mihi te offers. *Pa.* Quíd *id* est ?
Oráre iussit, sí se ames, era, iám ut ad sese
uénias :
Vidére aït te cúpere. *Pa.* Vah, perii : hóc
malum integráscit.
Sicín me atque illam operá tua nunc míseros
sollicitári !

Nam idcírco arcessor, núptias quod mi ádparari
sénsit. 690
Ch. Quibus quídem quam facile pótuerat quiésci,
si hic quiésset!
Da. Age, si híc non insanít satis sua spónte, instiga.
My. Atque édepol
Ea rés est: proptereáque nunc misera ín mae-
rorest. *Pa.* Mýsis,
Per omnís tibi adiuró deos, numquam eám me
desertúrum,
Non, sí capiundos míhi sciam esse inimícos
omnis hómines. 695
Hanc mi éxpetiui, cóntigit: conuéniunt mores:
uáleant
Qui intér nos discidiúm uolunt: hanc nísi mors
mi adimet némo.
Ch. Resipísco. *Pa.* Non Apóllinis magis uérum
atque hoc respónsumst.
Si póterit fieri, ut né pater per mé stetisse
crédat,
Quo mínus haec fierent núptiae, uoló. sed si
id non póterit, 700
Id fáciam, in procliuí quod est, per mé stetisse
ut crédat.
Quis uídeor? *Ch.* Miser, aeque átque ego. *Da.*
Consílium quaero. *Ch.* Forti's.
Pa. Scio quid conere. *Da.* Hoc égo tibi profécto
effectum réddam.

Pa. Iam hoc ópus est. *Da.* Quin iam habeó. *Ch.*
　　　Quid est? *Da.* Huic, nón tibi habeo,
　　　ne érres.
Ch. Sat hábeo. *Pa.* Quid faciés? cedo. *Da.* Dics
　　　híc mi ut satis sit uércor　　　　　　　705
　　Ad agéndum: ne uacuom ésse me nunc ád
　　　narrandum crédas:
　　Proinde hínc uos amolímini: nam mi ínpedi-
　　　mento éstis.
Pa. Ego hanc uísam. *Da.* Quid tu? quo hínc te
　　　agis? *Ch.* Verúm uis dicam? *Da.*
　　　Immo étiam
　　Narrátionis íncipit mi inítium. *Ch.* Quid me
　　　fíet?
Da. Eho tu ínpudens, non sátis habes, quod tíbi die-
　　　culam áddo,　　　　　　　　　　　　710
　　Quantum huíc promoueo núptias? *Ch.* Daue,
　　　át tamen. *Da.* Quid érgo?
Ch. Vt dúcam. *Da.* Ridiculum. *Ch.* Húc face ad
　　　me ut uénias, siquid póteris.
Da. Quid uéniam? nil habeo. *Ch.* Át tamen
　　　siquíd. *Da.* Age, ueniam. *Ch.* Sí-
　　　quid,
　　Domi éro. *Da.* Tu, Mysis, dum éxeo, parúmper
　　　opperíre hic.
My. Quaprópter? *Da.* Ita facto ópus est. *My.* At
　　　matúra. *Da.* Iam inquam hic ádero. 715

4—Ter.　　　　　E

MYSIS. DAVOS.

My. Nilne ésse proprium quoíquam! di uostrám
fidem :
Summúm bonum esse eraé putaui hunc Pám-
philum,
Amícum, amatorém, uirum in quouís loco
Parátum : uerum ex eó nunc misera quém capit
Labórem! facile hic plús malist quam illíc
boni. 720
Sed Dáuos exit. mí homo, quid istuc óbse-
crost?
Quo pórtas puerum? *Da.* Mýsis, nunc opus
ést tua
Mihi ad hánc rem exprompta málitia atque
astútia.
My. Quid nam íncepturu's? *Da.* Áccipe a me hunc
ócius
Atque ánte nostram iánuam adpone. *My.*
Óbsecro, 725
Humíne? *Da.* Ex ara hinc súme uerbenás
tibi
Atque eás substerne. *My.* Quam óbrem id tute
nón facis?
Da. Quia, sí forte opus sit ád erum iura*tó* mihi
Non ádposisse, ut líquido possim. *My.* Intél-
lego :
Noua núnc religio in te ístaec incessít. cedo. 730

Da. Moue ócius te, ut quíd agam porro intéllegas.
   Pro Iúppiter. *My.* Quid est? *Da.* Spónsae
      pater intérueuit.
   Repúdio quod consílium primum inténderam.
My. Nescióquid narres. *Da.* Égo quoque hinc ab
      déxtera
   Veníre me adsimulábo: tu ut subséruias   735
   Orátioni, ut quómque opus sit, uerbís uide.
My. Ego quíd agas nil intéllego: sed síquid est,
   Quod méa opera opus sit uóbis, ut tu plús uídes,
   Manébo, nequod uóstrum remorer cómmodum.

   CHREMES. MYSIS. DAVOS.

Ch. Reuórtor, postquam quae ópus fuere ad núptias 740
   Gnataé paraui, ut iúbeam arcessi. séd quid
      hoc?
   Puer hérclest. mulier, tu ádposisti hunc? *My.*
      V́bi illic est?
Ch. Non míhi respondes? *My.* Núsquam est. uae
      miseraé mihi,
   Relíquit me homo atque ábiit. *Da.* Di uostrám
      fidem,
   Quid túrbaest apud forúm? quid illi hominum
      lítigant?   745
   Tum annóna carast. quíd dicam aliud, néscio.
My. Quor tu óbsecro hic me sólam? *Da.* Hem,
      quae haec est fábula?
   Eho Mýsis, puer hic úndest? quisue huc áttulit?

My. Satin sánu's, qui me id rógites? *Da.* Quem
Ego igitúr rogem,
Qui hic néminem aliuṁ uídeam? *Ch.* Miror,
únde sit. 750
Da. Dictúra es quod rogo? *My.* Aú. *Da.* Con-
cede ad déxteram.
My. Delíras: non tute ípse? *Da.* Verbum sí mihi
Vnúm praeter quam quód te rogo . . faxís
caue.
Male dícis? undest? díc clare. *My.* A nobis.
Da. Háhae:
Mirúm uero, inpudénter mulier sí facit 755
Meretríx? *Ch.* Ab Andriást haec, quantum
intéllego.
Da. Adeón uidemur uóbis esse idónei,
In quíbus sic inludátis? *Ch.* Veni in témpore.
Da. Propera ádeo puerum tóllere hinc ab iánua :
Mané: caue quoquam ex ístoc excessís loco. 760
My. Di te éradicent : íta me miseram térritas.
Da. Tibi égo dico an non? *My.* Quíd uis? *Da.*
At etiám rogas ?
Cedo, quóium puerum hic ádposisti? díc mihi.
My. Tu néscis? *Da.* Mitte id quód scio : die quód
rogo.
My. Vostrí. *Da.* Quoius nostri? *My.* Pámphili.
Ch. Hem. *Da.* Quid? Pámphili? 765
My. Eho, an nón est? *Ch.* Recte ego sémper fugi
has núptias.

Da. O fácinus animaduórtendum. *My.* Quid clá-
          mitas?
Da. Quemne égo heri uidi ad uós adferri uésperi?
My. O hóminem audacem. *Da.* Vérum: uidi Cán-
          tharam
     Suffárcinatam. *My.* Dís pol habeo grátiam,   770
     Quom in páriundo aliquot ádfuerunt líberae.
Da. Ne illa íllum haud nouit, quóius causa haec
          íncipit:
     'Chremés si *ad*positum púerum ante aedis
          uíderit,
     Suam gnátam non dabít:' tanto hercle mágis
          dabit.
Ch. Non hércle faciet. *Da.* Núnc adeo, ut tu sís
          sciens,   775
     Nisi púerum tollis, iám ego hunc in mediám
          uiam
     Prouóluam teque ibídem peruoluam ín luto.
My. Tu pól homo non es sóbrius. *Da.* Fallácia
     Alia áliam trudit. iám susurrari aúdio,
     Ciuem Átticam esse hanc. *Ch.* Hém. *Da.*
          'Coactus légibus   780
     Eam uxórem ducet.' *My.* Óbsecro, an non
          cíuis est?
Ch. Ioculárium in malum ínsciens paene íncidi.
Da. Quis hic lóquitur? o Chremés, per tempus
          áduenis:

Auscúlta.   *Ch.* Audiui iam ómnia.   *Da.* Anne
   haec tu ómnia?
Ch. Audíui, inquam, a princípio.   *Da.* Audistin,
   óbsecro? hem   785
   Scelera, hánc iam oportet ín cruciatum hinc
      ábripi.
   Hic est ílle: non te crédas Dauom lúdere.
My. Me míseram: nil pol fálsi dixi, mí senex.
Ch. Noui ómnem rem.   est Simo íntus?   *Da.* Est.
      My. Ne me áttigas,
   Seceléste.   si pol Glýcerio non ómnia haec . .   790
Da. Eho inépta, nescis quíd sit actum?   *My.* Quí
      sciam?
Da. Hic sócer est.   alio pácto haud poterat fíeri,
   Vt scíret haec quae uóluimus.   *My.* Praedí-
      ceres.
Da. Paulum ínter esse cénses, ex animo ómnia,
   Vt fért natura, fácias an de indústria?   795

CRITO. MYSIS. DAVOS.

Cr. In hác habitasse plátea dictumst Chrýsidem,
   Quae sése inhoneste optáuit parere hic dítias
   Potiús quam in patria honéste pauper uíueret:
   Eius mórte ea ad me lége redierúnt bona.
   Sed quós perconter uídeo.   saluete.   *My.*
      Óbsecro,   800
   Quem uídeo? estne hic Critó sobrinus Chrý-
      sidis?

Is ést. *Cr.* O Mysis, sáluc. *My.* Saluos sís,
Crito.
Cr. Itan Chrýsis? hem. *My.* Nos quídem pol
miseras pérdidit.
Cr. Quid uós? quo pacto hic? sátine recte? *My.*
Nósne? sic:
Vt químus, aiunt, quándo ut uolumus nón licet. 805
Cr. Quid Glýcerium? iam hic suós parentis rép-
perit?
My. Vtinam. *Cr.* Án non dum etiam? haud aú-
spicato huc me áttuli:
Nam pól, si id scissem, númquam huc tetulissém
pedem:
Sempér enim dictast ésse haec atque habitást
soror:
Quae illíus fuerunt, póssidet: nunc me hóspitem 810
Litís sequi, quam id míbi sit facile atque útile,
Alióram exempla cómmonent: simul árbitror,
Iam aliquem ésse amicum et défensorem ei:
nám fere
Grandícula iam proféctast illinc. clámitent
Me sýcophantam, heréditatem pérsequi 815
Mendícum: tum ipsam déspoliare nón lubet.
My. O óptume hospes, pól Crito antiquom óbtines.
Cr. Duc me ád eam, quando huc uéni, ut uideam.
My. Máxume.
Da. Sequar hós: me nolo in témpore hoc uideát
senex.

ACTVS V.

CHREMES. SIMO.

Ch. Satis iam satis, Simó, spectata ergú te ami-
    citiáíst mea: 820
  Sátis pericli incépi adire: orándi iam finém face.
  Dúm studeo obsequí tibi, paene inlúsi uitam
    fíliae.
Si. Ímmo enim nunc quom máxume abs te póstulo
    atque oró, Chremes,
  V́t beneficium uérbis initum dúdum nunc re
    cómprobes.
Ch. Víde quam iniquos sís prae studio: dúm id
    efficias quód cupis,   825
  Néque modum benígnitatis néque quid me ores
    cógitas:
  Nám si cogités, remittas iám me onerare iniúriis.
Si. Quíbus? *Ch.* At rogitas? pérpulisti me, út
    homini adulescéntulo
  Ín alio occupáto amore, abhórrenti ab re uxória,
  Fíliam ut darem ín seditionem átque in incertas
    núptias,   830

Eíus labore atque eíus dolore gnáto ut medi-
    carér tuo :
Ínpetrasti : incépi, dum res tétulit. nunc non
    fért : feras.
Íllam hinc ciuem esse áiunt : puer est nátus :
    nos missós face.
Si. Pér ego te deos óro, ut ne illis ánimum inducas
    crédere,
Quíbus id maxume útilest, illum ésse quam
    detérrumum. 835
Núptiarum grátia haec sunt fácta atque incepta
    ómnia.
V́bi ea causa, quam óbrem haec faciunt, érit
    adempta his, désinent.
Ch. Érras : cum Dauo égomet uidi iúrgantem an-
    cillám. *Si.* Scio.
Ch. Véro uoltu, quom íbi me adesse neúter tum
    praesénserat.
Si. Crédo, et id factúras Dauos dúdum praedixít
    mihi : 840
Ét nescio qui tíbi sum oblitus hódie, ac uolui,
    dícere.

DAVOS. CHREMES. SIMO. DROMO.

Da. Ánimo nunciam ótioso esse ímpero. *Ch.* En
    Dauóm tibi.
Si. V́nde egreditur ? *Da.* meó praesidio atque
    hóspitis. *Si.* Quid illúd malist ?

Da. Égo commodiorem hóminem aduentum témpus
non uidí. *Si.* Scelus,
Quém nam hic laudat? *Da.* Ómnis res est iam
in uado. *Si.* Cesso ádloqui? 845
Da. Érus est: quid agam? *Si.* O sálue, bone uir.
Da. Éhem Simo, o nostér Chremes,
Ómnia adparáta iam sunt íntus. *Si.* Curastí
probe.
Da. Úbi uoles, arcésse. *Si.* Bene sane: íd enim
uero hinc núnc abest.
Étiam tu hoc respóndes, quid istic tíbi negotist?
Da. Míhin? *Si.* Ita.
Da. Míhin? *Si.* Tibi ergo. *Da.* Módo *ego* intro
iui. *Si.* Quási ego quam dudúm
rogem. 850
Da. Cúm tuo gnato una. *Si.* Ánne est intus Pámphilus? cruciór miser.
Eho, non tu dixti ésse inter eos ínimicitias, cárnufex?
Da. Súnt. *Si.* Quor igitur híc est? *Ch.* Quid illum
cénses? cum illa lítigat.
Da. Ímmo uero indígnum, Chremes, iam ˙fácinus
faxo ex me aúdias.
Néscio qui senéx modo uenit: éllum, confidéns,
catus: 855
Quóm faciem uideús, uidetur ésse quantiuís
preti:
Tristís seueritás inest in uóltu atque in uerbís
fides.

Si. Quíd nam adportas? *Da.* Níl equidem, nisi
quód illum audiui dícere.
Si. Quíd aït tandem? *Da.* Glýcerium se scíre
ciuem esse Atticam. *Si.* Hem,
Dromó, Dromo. *Da.* Quid ést? *Si.* Dromo.
Da. Audi. *Si.* Vérbum si addide-
rís . . Dromo. 860
Da. Audi óbsecro. *Dr.* Quid uís? *Si.* Sublimem
íntro hunc rape, quantúm potes.
Dr. Quem? *Si.* Dáuom. *Da.* Quam obrem? *Si.*
Quía lubet. rape ínquam. *Da.* Quid
fecí? *Si.* Rape.
Da. Si quícquam inuenies mé mentitum, occídito.
Si. Nil aúdio:
Égo iam te commótum reddam. *Da.* Támen
etsi hoc uerúmst? *Si.* Tamen.
Cura ádseruandum uínctum, atque audin? quá-
drupedem constríngito. 865
Age núnciam: ego pol hódie, si uiuó, tibi
Osténdam, erum quid sít pericli fállere,
Et illí patrem. *Ch.* Ah ne saéui tanto opere.
Si. Ó Chremes,
Pietátem gnati! nónne te miserét mei?
Tantúm laborem cápere ob talem fílium? 870
Age Pámphile, exi Pámphile: ecquid té pudet?

PAMPHILVS. SIMO. CHREMES.

Pa. Quis mé uolt? perii, páter est. *Si.* Quid aïs,
ómnium .. ? *Ch.* Ah,

Rem pótius ipsam díc, ac mitte mále loqui.

Si. Quasi quícquam in hunc iam gráuius dici póssiet.

Ain tándem, ciuis Glýceriumst? *Pa.* Ita praédicant. 875

Si. 'Ita praédicant'? o ingéntem confidéntiam!

Num cógitat quid dícat? num factí piget?

Vide num eíus color pudóris signum usquam índicat.

Adeo ínpotenti esse ánimo, ut praeter cíuium

Morem átque legem et suí uoluntatém patris 880

Tamen hánc habere stúdeat cum summó probro!

Pa. Me míserum! *Si.* Hem, modone id démum sensti, Pámphile?

Olim ístuc, olim, quom íta animum induxtí tuom,

Quod cúperes aliquo pácto efficiundúm tibi:

Eodém die istuc uérbum uere in te áccidit. 885

Sed quíd ego? quor me excrúcio? quor me mácero?

Quor meám senectutem huíus sollicito améntia?

An ut pro huíus peccatis égo supplicium súfferam?

Immo hábeat, ualeat, uíuat cum illa. *Pa.* Mí pater.

Si. Quid 'mí pater'? quasi tu húius indigeús patris. 890

Domus, úxor, liberi ínuenti inuitó patre.
Addúcti qui illam cíuem hinc dicant: uíceris.
Pa. Patér, licetne paúca? *Si.* Quid dicés mihi?
Ch. Tamén, Simo, audi. *Si.* Ego aúdiam? quid aúdiam,
Chremés? *Ch.* At tandem dícat. *Si.* Age, dicát sino. 895
Pa. Égo me amare hanc fáteor: si id peccárest, fateor íd quoque.
Tíbi, pater, me dédo. quiduis óneris inpone, ínpera.
Vís me uxorem dúcere? hanc uis míttere? ut poteró, feram.
Hóc modo te obsecro, út ne credas á me adlegatum húnc senem:
Síne me expurgem atque íllum huc coram addúcam. *Si.* Adducas? *Pa.* Síne, pater. 900
Ch. Aéquom postulát: da ueniam. *Pa.* Síne te hoc exorém. *Si.* Sino.
Quíduis cupio, dúm ne ab hoc me fálli comperiár, Chremes.
Ch. Pró peccato mágno paulum súpplici satis ést patri.

CRITO. CHREMES. SIMO. PAMPHILVS.

Cr. Mítte orare. una hárum quaeuis caúsa me ut faciám monet,

F

Vél tu uel quod uérumst uel quod ípsi cupio
    Glýcerio.   905
Ch. Ándrium ego Critónem uideo? cérte is est.
    Cr. Saluos sís, Chremes.
Ch. Quíd tu Athenas ínsolens?   *Cr.* Euénit. sed
    hicinést Simo?
Ch. Híc.   *Cr.* Simo, men quaéris?   *Si.* Eho tu,
    Glýcerium hinc ciuem ésse aïs?
Cr. Tú negas?   *Si.* Itane húc paratus áduenis?   *Cr.*
    Qua ré?   *Si.* Rogas?
    Túne inpune haec fácias? tune hic hómines
        adulescéntulos   910
    Ínperitos rérum, eductos líbere, in fraudem ín-
        licis?
    Sóllicitando et póllicitando eorum ánimos lac-
        tas?   *Cr.* Sánun es? -
Si. Ác meretricíos amores núptiis conglútinas?
Pa. Périi, metuo ut súbstet hospes.   *Ch.* Sí, Simo,
    hunc norís satis,
    Nón ita arbitrére: bonus est híc uir.   *Si.* Hic
        uir sít bonus?   915
    Ítane attemperáte euenit, hódie in ipsis núptiis
    Vt ueniret, ántehac numquam? est uéro huic
        credundúm, Chremes.
Pa. Ní metuam patrem, hábeo pro illa re íllum quod
        moneám probe.
Si. Sýcophanta.   *Cr.* Hem.   *Ch.* Síc, Crito, est hic:
    mítte.   *Cr.* Videat quí siet.

Sí mihi pergit quaé uolt dicere, éa quae non
  uolt aúdiet. 920
Égo istaec moueo aut cúro? non tu tuóm malum aequo animó feres?
Nam égo quae dico uéra an falsa audíerim, iam
  scirí potest.
Átticus quidam ólim naui frácta ad Andrum
  eiéctus est
Ét istaec una párua uirgo.   túm ille egens forte
  ádplicat
Prímum ad Chrysidís patrem se.   *Si.* Fábulam
  inceptát.   *Ch.* Sine. 925
Cr. Ítane uero obtúrbat?   *Ch.* Perge tu.   *Cr.* Ís
  mihi cognatús fuit,
Qui eúm recepit.   íbi ego audiui ex íllo sese
  esse Átticum.
Ís ibi mortuóst.   *Ch.* Eius nomen?   *Cr.* Nómen
  tam citó tibi?   *Pa.* Hem,
Perii.   *Cr.* Verum hercle opínor fuisse Phá-
  niam: hoc certó scio,
Rhamnúsium se aiébat esse.   *Ch.* O Iúppiter.
  Cr. Eadem haéc, Chremes, 930
Multi álii in Andro audíuere.   *Ch.* Vtinam id
  sít, quod spero.   eho, díc mihi,
Quid cúm tum? suamne esse aíbat?   *Cr.* Non.
  Ch. Quoiam ígitur?   *Cr.* Fratris
  fíliam.
Ch. Certé meast.   *Cr.* Quid aïs?   *Si.* Quid tu aïs?
  Pa. Árrige auris, Pámphile.

Si. Qui crédis? *Ch.* Phania íllic frater méus fuit.
Si. Noram ét scio.
Ch. Is béllum hinc fugiens méque in Asiam pérse-
quens proficíscitur: 935
Tum illám relinquere híc est ueritus. póst i*bi*
nunc primum aúdio
Quid illó sit factum. *Pa.* Víx sum apud me:
ita ánimus commotúst metu
Spe gaúdio, mirándo hoc tanto tám repentinó
bono.
Si. Ne istám multimodis tuam ínueniri gaúdeo.
Pa. Credó, pater.
Ch. At mi únus scrupulus étiam restat, quí me male
habet. *Pa.* Dígnus es 940
Cum tuá religione, ódium . . nodum in scírpo
quaeris. *Cr.* Quíd istuc est?
Ch. Nomén non conuenít. *Cr.* Fuit hercle huic
áliud paruae. *Ch.* Quód, Crito?
Numquíd meministi? *Cr.* Id quaéro. *Pa.*
Egon huius mémoriam patiár meae
Voluptáti obstare, quóm ego possim in hác re
medicarí mihi?
Non pátiar. heus, Chremés, quod quaeris, Pási-
*phi*last. *Ch.* Ipsúst. *Cr.* East. 945
Pa. Ex ípsa miliéns audiui. *Si.* Omnís nos gaudere
hóc, Chremes,
Te crédo credere. *Ch.* Íta me di ament, crédo.
Pa. Quid restát, pater?

Si. Iam dúdum res reddúxit me ipsa in grátiam.
Pa. O lepidúm patrem!
De uxóre, ita ut possédi, nil mutát Chremes?
Ch. Causa óptumast:
Nisi quíd pater aït áliud. *Pa.* Nempe id? *Si.*
Scílicet. *Ch.* Dos, Pámphile, est   950
Decém talenta. *Pa.* Accípio. *Ch.* Propero ad
fíliam. eho mecúm, Crito:
Nam illám me credo haud nósse. *Si.* Quor non
íllam huc transferrí iubes?
Pa. Recte ádmones: Dauo égo istuc dedam iám
negoti. *Si.* Nón potest.
Pa. Qui? *Si.* Quía habet aliud mágis ex sese et
máius. *Pa.* Quid nam? *Si.* Vínctus
est.
Pa. Patér, non recte uínctust. *Si.* Haud ita iússi.
Pa. Iube solui óbsecro.   955
Si. Age fíat. *Pa.* At matúra. *Si.* Eo intro. *Pa.*
O faústum et felicém diem!

CHARINVS. PAMPHILVS.

Ch. Prouíso quid agat Pámphilus: atque éccum.
Pa. Aliquis me fórsitan
Putet nón putare hoc uérum: at mihi nunc síc
esse hoc uerúm lubet.
Égo deorum uítam eapropter sémpiternam esse
árbitror,

5—Ter.   F 2

Quód uoluptates córum propriae súnt: nam mi
  inmortálitas   960
Pártast, si nulla aégritudo huic gaúdio intercés-
  serit.
Séd quem ego mihi potíssumum optem, quoí
  nunc haec narrém, dari?
Ch. Quíd illud gaudist? *Pa.* Dáuom uideo. némost,
  quem malim ómnium :
Nam húnc scio mea sólide solum gáuisurum
  gaúdia.

DAVOS. PAMPHILVS. CHARINVS.

Da. Pámphilus ubi nam híc est? *Pa.* Daue. *Da.*
  Quís homost? *Pa.* Ego sum. *Da.* O
  Pámphile.   965
Pa. Néscis quid mi obtígerit. *Da.* Certe: séd quid
  mi obtigerít scio.
Pa. Ét quidem ego. *Da.* More hóminum euenit, út
  quod sum nanctús mali
Príus rescisceres tu, quam ego illud quód tibi
  euenít boni.
Pa. Méa Glycerium suós parentis répperit. *Da.*
  Factúm bene. *Ch.* Hem.
Pa. Páter amicus súmmus nobis. *Da.* Quís? *Pa.*
  Chremes. *Da.* Narrás probe.   970
Pa. Néc mora ullast, quín iam uxorem dúcam.
  Ch. Num ille sómniat
Éa quae uigilans uóluit? *Pa.* Tum de púero,
  Daue .. *Da.* Ah désine.

Sólus est quem díligant di.   *Ch.* Sáluos sum, si
   haec uéra sunt.
Cónloquar. *Pa.* Quis homóst? Charine, in
   témpore ipso mi áduenis.
Ch. Béne factum. *Pa.* Audisti? *Ch.* Ómnia. age,
   me in tuís secundis réspice.   975
Túos est nunc Chremés: facturum quaé uoles
   scio esse ómnia.
Pa. Mémini: atque adeo lóngumst illum me éxpec-
   tare dum éxeat.
Séquere hac me intus ád Glycerium núnc *tu*.
   tu, Daue, ábi domum,
Própera, arcesse hinc qui aúferant eam.   quíd
   stas? quid cessás?   *Da.* Eo.
Ne éxpectetis dum éxeant huc: íntus despondé-
   bitur: 980
Íntus transigétur, siquid ést quod restet.
   Cantor. Plaúdite.

P. TERENTI
ADELPHOE.

GRAECA · MENANDRV · ACTA · LVDIS · FVNE-
RALIBVS · LVCIO · AEMILIO · PAVLO · QVOS
FECERE · Q · FABIVS · MAXVMVS · P · COR-
NELIVS · AFRICANVS · EGERE · L · ATILIVS
PRAEN · L · AMBIVIVS · TVRPIO · MODOS
FECIT · FLACCVS · CLAVDI · TIB · SERRANIS
TOTA · FACTA · SEXTA · M · CORNELIO
CETHEGO · L · GALLO · COS

PERSONAE.

MICIO...............................*senex.*
DROMO.............................*servos.*
DEMEA.............................*senex.*
CTESIPHO........................*advlescens.*
AESCHINUS.....................*advlescens.*
SYRUS.............................*servos.*

PAMPHILA.......................*virgo.*
SOSTRATA......................*matrona.*
CANTHARA.....................*nutrix.*
GETA..............................*servos.*
HEGIO.............................*senex.*

SANNIO..........................*leno.*

PROLOGVS.

Postquám poëta sénsit scripturám súam
Ab iníquis obseruári, et aduorsários
Rapere ín peiorem pártem quam acturí sumus:
Indício de sese ípse erit, uos iúdices,
Laudín an uitio dúci id factum opórteat.   5
Synápothnescontes Díphili comoédiast:
Eam Cómmorientis Plaútus fecit fábulam.
In Graéca adulescens ést, qui lenoni éripit
Meretrícem in prima fábula: cum Plautús locum
Relíquit integrum. eum híc locum sumpsít sibi   10
In Adélphos, uerbum dé uerbo expressum éxtulit.
Eam nós acturi súmus nouam: pernóscite
Furtúmne factum exístumetis án locum
Reprénsum, qui praetéritus neglegéntiast.
Nam quód isti dicunt máliuoli, homines nóbilis   15
Eum ádiutare adsídueque una scríbere:
Quod illí maledictum uémens esse exístumant,
Eam laúdem hic ducit máxumam, quom illís placet,
Qui uóbis uniuórsis et populó placent,
Quorum ópera in bello, in ótio, in negótio   20
Suo quísque tempore úsust sine supérbia.
Dehinc ne éxpectetis árgumentum fábulae:
Senés qui primi uénient, ei partem áperient,
In agéndo partem osténdent. facite aequánimitas
*   *   *   *   *   *   *   *   *
Poëtae ad scribendum aúgeat indústriam.   25

ACTVS I.

MICIO.

Storáx! Non rediit hác nocte a cena Aéschinus
Neque séruolorum quísquam, qui aduorsum ferant.
Profécto hoc uere dícunt: si absis úspiam,
[Aut ibi si cesses] éuenire ea sátius est
Quae in te úxor dicit [et quae in animo cogitat]
Iráta quam illa quaé parentes própitii.
Vxór, si cesses, aút te amare cógitat
Aut téte amari aut pótare atque animo óbsequi.
[Et tíbi bene esse, sóli sibi quom sít male.]
Ego quía non rediit fílius quae cógito!
Quibus núnc sollicitor rébus! ne aut ille álserit
Aut uspiam céciderit aut praefrégerit
Aliquid. Uah, quémquamne hominem in ánimum instituere aút
Paráre quod sit cárius quam ipse ést sibi!
Atque éx me hic natus nón est, sed éx fratre meo.

Dissímili is studiost iam índe ab adulescéntia.
Ego hánc cleméntem uítam urbanam atque ótium
Secútus sum et, quod fórtunatum istí putant,
Vxórem numquam habui. ílle contra haec
    ómnia:
Ruri ágere uitam: sémper parce ac dúriter   45
Se habére: uxorem dúxit: nati fílii
Duo: índe ego hunc maiórem adoptauí mihi:
Edúxi a paruolo, hábui, amaui pró meo;
In eó me oblecto: sólum id est carúm mihi.
Ille út item contra me hábeat facio sédulo: 50
Do, praétermitto: nón necesse habeo ómnia
Pro meó iure agere: póstremo, alii cláncnlum
Patrés quae faciunt, quaé fert adulescéntia,
Ea né me celet cónsuefeci fílium.
Nam quí mentiri aut fállere insuerít patrem,   55
Fraudáre tanto mágis audebit céteros.
Pudóre et liberálitate líberos
Retinére satius ésse credo quám metu.
Haec frátri mecum nón conueniunt néque pla-
    cent.
Venit ád me saepe clámans 'quid agis, Mício?   60
Quor pérdis adulescéntem nobis? quór amat?
Quor pótat? quor tu his rébus sumptum súg-
    geris?
Vestítu nimio indúlges: nimium inéptus es.'
Nimium ípsest durus praéter aequomque ét
    bonum:

Et érrat longe meá quidem senténtia, 65
Qui inpérium credat gráuius esse aut stábilius,
Vi quód fit, quam illud quód amicitia adiúngitur.
Mea síc est ratio et síc animum inducó meum:
Maló coactus quí suom officiúm facit,
Dum id réscitum iri crédit, tantispér pauet: 70
Si spérat fore clam, rúrsum ad ingeniúm redit.
Ille quém beneficio adiúngas ex animó facit,
Studet pár referre, praésens absensque ídem erit.
Hoc pátriumst, potius cónsuefacere fílium
Sua spónte recte fácere quam alienó metu: 75
Hoc páter ac dominus ínterest: hoc quí nequit,
Fateátur nescire ínperare líberis.
Sed éstne hic ipsus, dé quo agebam? et cérte is est.
Nescio quid tristem uídeo: credo iam, út solet,
Iurgábit.   saluom te áduenire, Démea, 80
Gaudémus.

Demea. Micio.

De. Ehem opportúne: te ipsum quaérito.
Mi. Quid trístis es? *De.* Rogás me? ubi nobis
    Aéschinust?
Scin iám quid tristis égo sim? *Mi.* Dixin hóc
    fore?
Quid fécit? *De.* Quid ille fécerit? quem néque
    pudet
Quicquám, nec metuit quémquam, neque legém
    putat 85

Tenére se ullam. nam ílla quae antehac fácta sunt
Omítto : modo quid désignauit ? *Mi.* Quíd nam id est ?
De. Forís ecfregit átque in aedis ínruit
Aliénas : ipsum dóminum atque omnem fámiliam
Mulcáuit usque ad mórtem : eripuit múlierem   90
Quam amábat.· clamant ómnes indigníssume
Factum ésse : hoc adueniénti quot mihi, Mício,
Dixére ! in orest ómni populo. dénique,
Si cónferendum exémplumst, non fratrém uidet
Reí dare operam rúri parcum ac sóbrium ?   95
Nullum húius simile fáctum. haec quom illi, Mício,
Dicó, tibi dico : tú illum corrumpí sinis.
Mi. Homine ínperito númquam quicquam iniústiust,
Qui nísi quod ipse fécit nil rectúm putat.
De. Quorsum ístuc ? *Mi.* Quia tu, Démea, haec male iúdicas.   100
Non ést flagitium, míhi crede, adulescéntulum
Scortári, neque potáre : non est : neque foris
Ecfríngere. haec si néque ego neque tu fécimus,
Non síit egestas fácere nos. tu núnc tibi
Id laúdi ducis, quód tum fecisti ínopia ?   105
Iniúriumst : nam si ésset unde id fíeret,
Facerémus. et illum tú tuom, si essés homo,

Sinerés nunc facere, dúm per aetatém licet,
Potiús quam, ubi te expectátum eiecissét foras,
Aliéniore aetáte post facerét tamen.   110
De. Pro Iúppiter, tu homo ádigis me ad insániam.
Non ést flagitium fácere haec adulescéntulum?
    Mi. Ah,
Auscúlta, ne me obtúndas de hac re saépius.
Tuom fílium dedísti adoptandúm mihi:
Is méus est factus: síquid peccat, Démea,   115
Mihi péccat: ego illi máxumam partém feram.
Obsónat, potat, ólet unguenta: dé meo;
Amat: dábitur a me argéntum, dum erit cóm-
    modum.
Vbi nón erit, fortásse excludetúr foras.
Forís ecfregit: réstituentur; díscidit   120
Vestém: resarciétur. et (dis grátia)
Est únde haec fiant, ét adhuc non molésta sunt.
Postrémo aut desine aút cedo quemuis árbi-
    trum:
Te plúra in hac re péccare ostendam. *De.* Eí
    mihi,
Pater ésse disce ab íllis, qui ueré sciunt.   125
Mi. Natúra tu illi páter es, consiliís ego.
De. Tun cónsulis quicquam? *Mi.* Áh, si pergis,
    ábiero.
De. Sicíne agis? *Mi.* An ego tótiens de eadem re
    aúdiam?
De. Curaést mihi. *Mi.* Et mihi cúraest. uerum,
    Démea,

Curémus aequam utérque partem: tu álterum, 130
Ego item álterum. nam cúrare ambos própe-
   modum
Repóscere illumst quém dedisti. *De.* Ah,
   Mício.
Mi. Mihi síc uidetur. *De.* Quíd istic? si tibi istúc
   placet,
Profúndat perdat péreat, nil ad me áttinet.
Iam sí uerbum ullum pósthac . . *Mi.* Rursum,
   Démea, 135
Iráscere? *De.* An non crédis? repeton quém
   dedi?
Aegrést: alienus nón sum: si obsto . . em,
   désino.
Vnúm uis curem, cúro. et est dis grátia,
Quom ita út uolo est; isté tuos ipse séntiet
Postérius: nolo in íllum grauius dícere. 140
Mi. Nec níl neque omnia haéc sunt quae dicít:
   tamen
Non níl molesta haec súnt mihi: sed osténdere
Me aegré pati illi nólui: nam itást homo:
Quom pláco, aduorsor sédulo et detérreo;
Tamen uíx humane pátitur: uerum si aúgeam 145
Aut étiam adiutor sim éius iracúndiae,
Insániam profécto cum illo. etsi Aéschinus
Non núllam in hac re nóbis facit iniúriam.
Quam hic nón amauit méretricem? aut quoi
   nón dedit

Aliquíd? postremo núper (credo iam ómnium 150
Taedébat) dixit uélle uxorem dúcere.
Sperábam iam deféruisse adulescéntiam:
Gaudébam. ecce autem de íntegro: nisi quíd-
  quid est
Volo scíre atque hominem cónuenire, si ápud
  forumst.

ACTVS II.

SANNIO. AESCHINVS. (PARMENO. PSALTRIA.)

Sa. Óbsecro, populáres, ferte mísero atque inno-
    cénti auxilium :   155
    Súbuenite inopi.   *Ae.* Ótiose, núnciam ilico híc
    consiste.
    Quíd respectas ? níl periclist : númquam, dum
    ego adero, híc te tanget.
Sa. Égo istam inuitis ómnibus.
Ae. Quamquámst scelestus, nón committet hódie
    umquam iterum ut uápulet.
Sa. Aéschine, audi, né te ignarum fuísse dicas
    meórum morum,   160
    Léno ego sum.   *Ae.* Scio.   *Sa.* Át ita, ut
    usquam fuít fide quisquam óptuma.
    Tú quod te postérius purges, hánc iniuriám mihi
    nolle
    Fáctam esse, huius non fáciam.   credo hoc, égo
    meum ius pérsequar :

Néque tu uerbis sólues umquam, quód mihi re
    male féceris.
Nóui ego uostra haec 'nóllem factum: dábitur
    ius iurándum, indignum   165
Te ésse iniuria hác', indignis quom égomet sim
    acceptús modis.

Ae. Ábi prae strenue ác foris aperi. *Sa.* Céterum
    hoc nilí facis?
Ae. Í intro nunciam. *Sa.* Át enim non sinam. *Ae.*
    Áccede illuc, Pármeno:
Nímium istoc abísti: hic propter húnc adsiste:
    em, síc uolo.
Caue núnciam oculos á meis oculis quóquam
    demoucás tuos,   170
Ne móra sit, si innuerím, quin pugnus cóntinuo
    in mala haéreat.
Sa. Istúc uolo ergo ipsum éxperiri. *Ae.* Em, sérua;
    omitte múlierem.
Sa. O indígnum facinus. *Ae.* Nísi caues, gemina-
    bit. *Sa.* Ei miseró mihi.
Ae. Non ínnueram: uerum ín istam partem pótius
    peccató tamen.
    I núnciam. *Sa.* Quid hóc reist? regnumne,
        Aéschine, hic tu póssides?   175
Ae. Si póssiderem, ornátus esses éx tuis uirtúti-
    bus.
Sa. Quid tíbi rei mecumst? *Ae.* Níl. *Sa.* Quid?
    nostin quí sim? *Ae.* Non desídero.

Sa. Tetigín tui quicquam? *Ae.* Si áttigisses, férres
infortúnium.

Sa. Qui tíbi magis licét meam habere, pró qua ego
argentúm dedi?

Respónde. *Ae.* Ante aedis nón fecisse erit
mélius hic conuítium: 180

Nam sí molestus pérgis esse, iam íntro abripiere
átque ibi

Vsque ád necem operíere loris. *Sa.* Lóris
liber? *Ae.* Síc erit.

Sa. O hóminem inpurum: hicín libertatem áiunt
esse aequam ómnibus?

Ae. Si sátis iam debacchátus es, leno, aúdi si uis
núnciam.

Sa. Egon débacchatus sum áutem an tu in me?
Ae. Mítte ista atque ad rém redi. 185

Sa. Quam rém? quo redeam? *Ae.* Iámne me uis
dícere id quod ad te áttinet?

Sa. Cupio, aéqui modo aliquíd. *Ae.* Vah, leno
iníqua me non uólt loqui.

Sa. Lenó sum, perniciés communis, fáteor, adule-
scéntium,

Periúrus, pestis: támen tibi a me núllast orta
iniúria.

Ae. Nam hercle étiam hoc restat. *Sa.* Illuc quaeso
rédi, quo coepisti, Aéschine. 190

Ae. Minís uiginti tú illam emisti? *Sa.* Lóqueris.
Ae. Tibi uortát male.

6 — Ter.

Argénti tantum dábitur. *Sa.* Quid? si ego tíbi
 illam nolo uéndere,
Cogés me? *Ae.* Minume. *Sa.* Námque id
 metui. *Ae.* Néque uendundam cénseo,
Quae líberast: nam ego líberali illam ádsero
 causá manu.
Nunc uíde utrum uis: argéntum accipere an
 caúsam meditarí tuam. 195
Delíbera hoc, dum ego rédeo, leno. *Sa.* Pró
 supreme Iúppiter,
Mínume miror qui ínsanire occípiunt ex iniúria.
Dómo me eripuit, uérberauit: me ínuito abduxít
 meam :
Hómini misero plús quingentos cólaphos in-
 fregít mihi.
Ób malefacta haec tántidem emptam póstulat
 sibi trádier. 200
Vérum enim quando béne promeruit, fíat: suom
 ius póstulat.
Áge iam cupio, módo si argentum réddat. sed
 ego hoc háriolor :
Vbi me dixeró dare tanti, téstis faciet ílico,
Véndidisse mé, de argento sómnium: 'mox :
 crás redi.'
Íd quoque possum férre, modo si réddat, quam-
 quam iniúriumst. 205
Vérum cogito íd quod res est: quándo eum
 quaestum ocféperis,

Accipiunda et mússitanda iniúria adulescén-
tiumst.
Séd nemo dabít: frustra egomet mécum has
rationés puto.

SYRVS. SANNIO.

Sy. Tace, égomet conueniam ípsum : cupide accípiat
faxo atque étiam
Bene dícat secum ésse áctum.   quid istuc,
Sánnio, est quod te aúdio   210
Nescio quid concertásse cum ero? *Sa.* Núm-
quam uidi iníquius
Certátionem cómparatam, quam haéc hodie
inter nós fuit:
Ego uápulando, ille uérberando usque, ámbo
defessí sumus.
Sy. Tua cúlpa. *Sa.* Quid facerem? *Sy.* Ádule-
scenti mórem gestum opórtuit.
Sa. Qui pótui melius, quí hodie usque os praébui?
Sy. Age, scis quíd loquar?   215
Pecúniam in locó neglegere máxumum inter-
dúmst lucrum : hui,
Metuísti, si nunc dé tuo iure cóncessisses paú-
lulum
Atque ádulescenti mórigera*sses*, hóminum homo
stultíssume,
Ne nón tibi istuc faéneraret. *Sa.* Égo spem
pretio nón emo.

Sy. Numquám rem facies: ábi, inescare néscis
  homines, Sánnio. 220
Sa. Credo ístuc melius ésse: uerum ego númquam
  adeo astutús fui,
  Quin quídquid possem mállem auferre pótius in
  praeséntia.
Sy. Age nóui tuom animúm: quasi iam usquam tíbi
  sint uigintí minae,
  Dum huic óbsequare. praéterea autem te áiunt
  proficiscí Cyprum, *Sa.* Hem.
Sy. coemísse hinc quae illuc uéheres multa, náuem
  conductam: hóc scio, 225
  Animús tibi pendet. úbi illinc spero rédieris
  tamen hóc ages.
Sa. Nusquám pedem. perii hércle: hac illi spe hóc
  inceperúnt. *Sy.* Timet:
  Iniéci scrupulum hómini. *Sa.* O scelera: illúd
  uide,
  Vt in ípso articulo oppréssit. emptae múlieres
  Complúres et item hinc ália quae portó Cyprum. 230
  Nisi eo ád mercatum' uénio, damnum máxu-
    mumst.
  Nunc si hóc omitto ac túm agam ubi illinc
    rédiero,
  Nil óst; refrixerít res: 'nunc demúm uenis?
  Quor pássu's? ubi eras?' út sit satius pérdere
  Quam aut núnc manere tám diu aut tum pérse-
    qui. 235

Sy. Iamne énumerasti id quód ad te rediturúm
putes?
Sa. Hocíne illo dignumst? hócine incipere Aéschi-
num?
Per oppréssionem ut hánc mi eripere póstulet?
Sy. Labúscit. unum hoc hábeo : uide si sátis placet:
Potiús quam uenias ín periclum, Sánnio, 240
Seruésne an perdas tótum, diuiduóm face.
Minás decem conrádet alicunde. *Sa.* Eí mihi,
Etiám de sorte núnc uenio in dubiúm miser?
Pudét nil? omnis déntis labefecít mihi :
Practérea colaphis túber est totúm caput : 245
Etiam ínsuper defrúdet? nusquam abeo. *Sy.*
Vt lubet:
Numquíd uis quin abeam? *Sa.* Ímmo hercle
hoc quaesó, Syre,
Vt ut haéc sunt acta, pótius quam litís sequar,
Meum míhi reddatur, sáltem quanti emptást,
Syre.
Scio té non usum antehác amicitiá mea : 250
Memorém me dices ésse et gratum. *Sy.* Sédulo
Faciám. sed Ctesiphónem uideo : laétus est
De amíca. *Sa.* Quid quod te óro? *Sy.* Pau-
lispér mane.

CTESIPHO. SYRVS. (SANNIO.)

Ct. Abs quíuis homine, quómst opus, benefícium
accipere gaúdeas:

H

Verum énim uero id demúm iuuat, si quem
  aéquomst facere is béne facit. 255
O fráter frater, quíd ego nunc te laúdem? satis
  certó scio:
Numquam íta magnifice quícquam dicam, id
  uírtus quin superét tua.
Itaque únam hanc rem me habére praeter álios
  praecipuam árbitror,
Fratrem hómini nemini ésse primarum ártium
  magis príncipem.
Sy. O Ctésipho. *Ct.* O Syre, Aéschinus ubist? *Sy.*
  Éllum, te expectát domi. *Ct.* Hem. 260
Sy. Quid est? *Ct.* Quíd sit? illius ópera, Syre,
  nunc uíuo: festiuóm caput,
Qui ignóminias sibi póst putauit ésse prae meo
  cómmodo,
Maledícta, famam, meúm laborem et péccatum
  in se tránstulit:
Nil pótis supra. quid nám foris crepuit? *Sy.*
  Máne, mane: ipse exít foras.

AESCHINVS. SANNIO. CTESIPHO. SYRVS.

Ae. Vbist ílle sacrilegús? *Sa.* Me quaerit. númquid nam ecfert? óccidi: 265
Nil uídeo. *Ae.* Ehem opportúne: te ipsum
  quaéro: quid fit, Ctésipho?
In tútost omnis rés: omitte uéro tristitiém
  tuam.

Ct. Ego illam hércle uero omítto, qui quidem te
    hábeam fratrem : o mi Aéschine,
  O mí germane : ah uéreor coram in ós te lau-
    dare ámplius,
  Ne id ádsentandi mágis quam quo habeam
    grátum facere exístumes.   270
Ae. Age inépte, quasi nunc nón norimus nós inter
    nos, Ctésipho.
  Hoc míhi dolet, nos séro *rescisse* ét paene in
    eum *rem* locum
  Redísse, ut si omnes cúperent nil tibi póssent
    auxiliárier.
Ct. Pudébat.   *Ae.* Ah, stultítiast istaec, nón pudor:
    tam ob páruolam
  Rem paéne e patria ! túrpe dictu.   deós quaeso
    ut istaec próhibeant.   275
Ct. Peccáui.   *Ae.* Quid aït tándem nobis Sánnio?
    Sy. Iam mítis est.
Ae. Ego ád forum ibo, ut húnc absoluam : tu íntro
    ad illam, Ctésipho.
Sa. Syre, ínsta.   *Sy.* Eamus : námque hic properat
    ín Cyprum.   *Sa.* Ne tám quidem :
  Quamuís etiam maneo ótiosus híc.   *Sy.* Red-
    détur : né time.
Sa. At ut ómne reddat.   *Sy.* Ómne reddet : táce
    modo ac sequere hác.   *Sa.* Sequor.   280
Ct. Heus heús, Syre.   *Sy.* Quid est?   *Ct.* Óbsecro
    hercle te, hóminem istum inpuríssu-
    mum

Quam prímum absoluitóte, ne, si mágis inrita-
    tús siet,
Aliqua ád patrem hoc permánet atque ego túm
    perpetuo périerim.

Sy. Non fíet, bono animo és: tu cum illa te íntus
    oblecta ínterim
Et léctulos iube stérni nobis ét parari cétera.   285
Ego iám transacta ré conuortam mé domum
    cum obsónio.

Ct. Ita quaéso: quando hoc béne successit, hílare
    hunc sumamús diem.

ACTVS III.

SOSTRATA.   CANTHARA.

So. Míserám me, neminem hábeo, solae súmus:
   Geta autem hic nón adest:
   Néc quem ad obstetrícem mittam, néc qui
   arcessat Aéschinum.
Ca. Pól is quidem iam hic áderit: nam numquam
   únum intermittít diem,
— Quin sémper ueniat.   *So.* Sólus mearum míse-
   riarumst rémedium.
Ca. É re nata mélius fieri haud pótuit quam fac-
   túmst, era,   295
   Quándo uitium oblátumst, quod ad illum
   áttinet potíssumum,
   Tálem, tali *ingénio* atque animo, nátum ex tanta
   fámilia.
So. Íta pol est ut dícis: saluos nóbis deos quaeso
   út siet.

Geta. Sostrata. Canthara.

Ge. Nunc íllud est, quom, si ómnia omnes súa con-
    silia cónferant
  Atque huíc malo salútem quaerant, aúxili nil
    ádferant,   300
  Quod míhique eraeque fíliaeque erílist. uae
    miseró mihi:
  Tot rés repente círcumuallant, únde emergi
    nón potest:
  Vís egestas íniustitia sólitudo infámia.
  Hócine saeclum! o scélera, o genera sácrilega,
    o hominem ínpium,
So. Me míseram, quid namst quód sic uideo tími-
    dum et properantém Getam?   305
Ge. quem néque fides neque iús iurandum néque
    illum misericórdia
  Représsit neque refléxit neque quod pártus in-
    stabát prope,
  Quoi míserae indigne pér uim uitium obtúlerat.
    So. Non intéllego
  Satis quaé loquatur.   *Ca.* Própius obsecro ácce-
    damus, Sóstrata.   *Ge.* Ah
  Me míserum, uix sum cómpos animi, ita árdeo
    iracúndia.   310
  Nil ést quod malim quam íllam totam fámiliam
    dari mi óbuiam,
  Vt ego íram hanc in eos éuomam omnem, dum
    aégritudo haec ést recens.

Satís mihi habeam súpplici, dum illós ulciscar
    meó modo.
Seni ánimam primum extínguerem ipsi, qui
    íllud produxít scelus:
Tum autém Syrum inpulsórem, uah, quibus   315
    íllum lacerarém modis!
Sublímem medium arríperem et capite próñum
    in terram státuerem,
Vt cérebro dispergát uiam.
Adulescenti ipsi ériperem oculos, póst haec
    praecipitém darem.
Céteros ruerem ágerem raperem túnderem et
    prostérnerem.
Sed césso eram hoc malo ínpertiri própere?
        So. Reuocemús.   Geta.   320
Ge. Hem, quísquis es, sine me.   *So.* Égo sum Sos-
    trata.   *Ge.* Vbi east? te ipsam quaé-
    rito,
Te éxpecto: oppido ópportune te óbtulisti mi
    óbuiam,
Éra.   *So.* Quid est? quid trépidas?   *Ge.* Ei
    mi.   *Ca.* Quíd festinas, mí Geta?
Ánimam recipe.   *Ge.* Prórsus.   *So.* Quíd istuc
    'prórsus' ergost?   *Ge.* périimus:
Áctumst.   *So.* Eloquere, óbsecro te, quíd sit.
        Ge. Iam.   *So.* Quid 'iám', Geta?   325
Ge. Aéschinus   *So.* Quid is érgo?   *Ge.* alienus ést
    ab nostra fámilia.   *So.* Hem,

Périi. qua re? *Ge.* Amáre occepit áliam.
So. Vae miserae mihi.

Ge. Néque id occulte fért, ab lenone ípsus eripuít
palam.

So. Sátin hoc certumst? *Ge.* Cértum : hisce oculis
égomet uidi, Sóstrata. *So.* Ah
Me míseram. quid iam crédas? aut quoi
crédas? nostrumne Aéschinum? 330
Nostram ómnium uitam, ín quo nostrae spés
opesque omnés sitae?
Quí sine hac iurábat se unum númquam uic-
turúm diem?
Quí se in sui gremió positurum púerum dicebát
patris?
Ita óbsecraturum, út liceret hánc se uxorem
dúcere?

Ge. Era, lácrumas mitte ac pótius quod ad hanc
rem ópus est porro próspice : 335
Patiámurne an narrémus quoipiam? *Ca.* Aú
au, mi homo, sánun es?
An hoc próferendum tíbi uidetur úsquam?
Ge. Mihi quidem *haú* placet.
Iam prímum illum alieno ánimo a nobis ésse
res ipsa índicat.
Nunc si hóc palam proférimus, ille infítias ibit,
sát scio :
Tua fáma et gnatae uíta in dubium uéniet.
tum si máxume 340

Fateátur, quom amet áliam, non est útile hanc
    illí dari.
Quaprópter quoquo pácto tacitost ópus. *So.*
    Ah minume géntium :
Non fáciam. *Ge.* Quid ages? *So.* Próferam.
    Ca. Hem, mea Sóstrata, uide quám
    rem agas.
So. Pcióre res locó non potis est ésse quam in quo
    núnc sitast.
Primum índotatast : túm practerea, quaé
    secunda ei dós erat,   345
Periít : pro uirgine *ea* dari nuptum *haú* potest.
    hoc rélicuomst :
Si infítias ibit, téstis mecum est ánulus quem
    amíserat.
Postrémo quando ego cónscia mihi sum, á me
    culpam esse hánc procul,
Neque prétium neque rem ullam íntercessisse
    ílla aut me indignám, Geta,
Expériar. *Ge.* Quid istic? cédo ut melius
    dícas. *So.* Tu quantúm potest   350
Abi atque Hégioni cógnato huius rem énarrato
    omnem órdine :
Nam is nostro Simuló fuit summus ét nos coluit
    máxume.
Ge. Nam hercle álius nemo réspicit nos. *So.* Pró-
    pere tu, mea Cánthara,
Curre, óbstetricem arcésse, ut quom opus sit ne
    ín mora nobís siet.

DEMEA. SYRVS.

De. Dispérii: Ctesiphónem audiui fílium   355
    Vná fuisse in ráptione cum Aéschino.
    Id mísero restat míhi mali, si illúm potest,
    Qui aliquoí reist, etiam meum ád nequitiem ·
        addúcere.
    Vbi ego íllum quaeram? crédo abductum in
        gáneum
    Aliquó: persuasit ílle inpurus, sát scio.   360
    Sed eccúm Syrum ire uídeo: hinc scibo iam úbi
        siet.
    Atqui hércle hic de grege íllost: si me sénserit
    Eum quaéritare, númquam dicet cárnufex.
    Non óstendam id me uélle. *Sy.* Omnem rem
        módo seni
    Quo pácto haberet énarramus órdine.   365
    Nil quícquam uidi laétius. *De.* Pro Iúppiter,
    Hominís stultitiam. *Sy.* Cónlaudauit fílium:
    Mihi, qui íd dedissem cónsilium, egit grátias.
De. Disrúmpor. *Sy.* Argentum ádnumerauit ilico:
    Dedít praeterea in súmptum dimidiúm minae: 370
    Id dístributum sánest ex senténtia. *De.* Hem,
    Huic mándes, siquid récte curatúm uelis.
Sy. Ehem Démea, haud aspéxeram te: quíd agitur?
De. Quid agátur? uostram néqueo mirarí satis
    Ratiónem. *Sy.* Est hercle inépta, ne dicám
        dolo,   375

Absúrda. piscis céteros purgá, Dromo:
Congrum ístum maxumum ín aqua sinito lúdere
Tantísper: ubi ego rédiero, exossábitur:
Prius nólo.' *De.* Haecin flagítia! *Sy.* Mihi
    quidem *haú* placent,
Et clámo saepe. sálsamenta haec, Stéphanio,   380
Fac mácerentur púlchre. *De.* Di uostrám
    fidem,
Vtrúm studione id síbi habet an laudí putat
Fore, sí perdiderit gnátum? uae miseró mihi.
Vidére uideor iám diem illum, quom hínc egens
Profúgiet aliquo mílitatum. *Sy.* O Démea,   385
Istúc est sapere, nón quod ante pedés modost
Vidére, sed etiam ílla quae futúra sunt
Prospícere. *De.* Quid? istaec iám penes uos
    psáltriast?
Ellam íntus. *De.* Eho, an domíst habiturus?
    Sy. Crédo, ut est
Deméntia. *De.* Haecin fíeri! *Sy.* Inepta léni-
    tas   390
Patris ét facilitas práua. *De.* Fratris mé
    quidem
Pudét pigetque. *Sy.* Nímium inter uos, Dé-
    mea,
(Non quía ades praesens díco hoc) pernimium
    ínter est.
Tu, quántus quantu's, níl nisi sapiéntia es,
Ille sómnium. *num* síneres uero illúm tuom   395

Facere haéc? *De.* Sinerem illum? aut nón sex
totis ménsibus
Prius ólfecissem, quám ille quicquam coéperet?
Sy. Vigiliántiam tuam tú mihi narras? *De.* Síc
siet
Modo ut núnc est, quaeso. *Sy.* Vt quísque
suom uolt ésse, itast.
De. Quid eúm? uidistin hódie? *Sy.* Tuomne fí-
lium? 400
Abigam húnc rus. iam dudum áliquid ruri
agere árbitror.
De. Satin scís ibi esse? *Sy.* Oh, qui égomet pro-
duxi. *De.* Óptumest:
Metuí ne haereret híc. *Sy.* Atque iratum ád-
modum.
De. Quid aútem? *Sy.* Adortus iúrgiost fratrem
ápud forum
De psáltria istac. *De.* Aín uero? *Sy.* Ah, nil
réticuit. 405
Nam ut númerabatur fórte argentum, intéruenit
Homo de ínprouiso: coépit clamare 'o Aé-
schine,
Haecíne flagitia fácere te! haec te admíttere
Indígna genere nóstro!' *De.* Oh, lacrumo
gaúdio.
Sy. 'Non tu hóc argentum pérdis, sed uitám tuam.' 410
De. Saluós sit: spero, est símilis maiorúm suom.
Sy. Hui.

De. Syre, praéceptorum plénust istorum ílle. *Sy.*
    Phy:
Domi hábuit unde dísceret. *De.* Fit sédulo:
Nil praétermitto: cónsuefacio: dénique
Inspícere tamquam in spéculum in uitas om-
    nium   415
Iubeo átque ex aliis súmere exemplúm sibi.
'Hoc fácito.' *Sy.* Recte sáne. *De.* 'Hoc
    fugito.' *Sy.* Cállide.
De. 'Hoc laúdist.' *Sy.* Istaec rés est. *De.* 'Hoc
    uitió datur.'
Sy. Probíssume. *De.* Porro aútem . . *Sy.* Non
    hercle ótiumst
Nunc mi aúscultandi. píscis ex senténtia   420
Nactús sum: ei mihi ne córrumpantur caútiost:
Nam id nóbis tam flagítiumst quam illa, Démea,
Non fácere uobis, quaé modo dixti: et quód
    queo
Conséruis ad eundem ístunc praecipió modum:
'Hoc sálsumst, hoc adústumst, hoc lautúmst 425
    parum:
Illúd recte: iterum síc memento:' sédulo
Moneó, quae possum pró mea sapiéntia:
Postrémo tamquam in spéculum in patinas,
    Démea,
Inspícere iubeo et móneo quid facto úsus sit.
Inépta haec esse, nós quae facimus, séntio: 430
Verúm quid facias? út homost, ita morém geras.

Numquíd uis? *De.* Mentem uóbis meliorém dari.
Sy. Tu rús hinc ibis? *De.* Récta. *Sy.* Nam quid tu híc agas,
Vbi síquid bene praecípias, nemo obtémperet?
De. Ego uéro hinc abeo, quándo is, quam obrem huc uéneram, 435
Rus ábiit: illum cúro unum : ille ad me áttinet,
Quando íta uolt frater : de ístoc ipse uíderit.
Sed quís illic est, quem uídeo procul? estne Hégio
Tribúlis noster? sí satis cerno, is est hércle: uah,
Homo amícus nobis iam índe a puero : dí boni, 440
Ne illíus modi iam mágna nobis cíuium
Penúriast antíqua uirtute ác fide
Haud cíto mali quid órtum ex hoc sit públice.
Quam gaúdeo! ubi etiam húius generis réli- quias
Restáre uideo, uíuere etiam núnc lubet. 445
Oppériar hominem hic, út salutem et cónloquar.

HEGIO. GETA. DEMEA. PAMPHILA.

He. Pro di ínmortales, fácinus indignúm, Geta,
Quid nárras. *Ge.* Sic est fáctum. *He.* Ex illan fámilia
Tam inlíberale fácinus esse ortum! o Aéschine,
Pol haúd paternum istúc dedisti. *De.* Vídelicet 450

Sc. III. 78–IV. 24.] ADELPHOE.

De psáltria hac audíuit: id illi núnc dolet
Aliéno. pater eius níli pendit: eí mihi,
Vtinam híc prope adsit álicubi atque haec
    aúdiat.
He. Nisi fácient quae illos aéquomst, haud sic aú-
    ferent.
Ge. In té spes omnis, Hégio, nobís sitast: 455
Te sólum habemus, tú es patronus, tú pater:
Illé tibi moriens nós commendauít senex:
Si déseris tu, périimus. *He.* Caue díxeris:
Neque fáciam neque me sátis pie posse árbitror.
De. Adíbo. saluere Hégionem plúrimum   460
Iubeo. *He.* Óh, te quaerebam ípsum: salue,
    Démea.
De. Quid aútem? *He.* Maior fílius tuos Aéschinus,
Quem frátri adoptandúm dedisti, néque boni
Neque líberalis fúnctus officiúmst uiri.
De. Quid istúc est? *He.* Nostrum amícum noras
    Símulum   465
Aequálem? *De.* Quid ni? *He.* Fíliam eius
    uírginem
Vitiáuit. *De.* Hem. *He.* Mane: nón dum
    audisti, Démea,
Quod ést grauissumum. *De.* An quid est etiam
    ámplius?
He. Vero ámplius: nam hoc quídem ferundum
    aliquó modost:
Persuásit nox amór uinum adulescéntia: 470

Humánumst. ubi scit fáctum, ad matrem uírginis
Venit ípsus ultro lácrumans orans óbsecrans
Fidém dans, iurans sé illam ducturúm domum.
Ignótumst, tacitumst, créditumst.
Ille bónus uir nobis psáltriam, si dís placet, 476
Paráuit, quicum uíuat : illam déserit.
De. Pro cérton tu istaec dícis ? *He.* Mater uírginis
In médiost, ipsa uírgo, res ipsa, híc Geta
Praetérea, ut captus ést seruorum, nón malus 480
Neque inérs : alit illas, sólus omnem fámiliam
Susténtat : hunc abdúce, uinci, quaére rem.
Ge. Immo hércle extorque, nísi ita factumst, Démea ;
Postrémo non negábit : coram ipsúm cedo.
De. Pudét : nec quid agam néque quid huic respóndeam 485
Sció. *Pa.* Miseram me, dífferor dolóribus.
He. Hem :
Illaéc fidem nunc uóstram inplorat, Démea,
Quod iús uos cogit, íd uoluntate ínpetret. 490
Haec prímum ut fiant deós quaeso ut uobís decet.
Sin áliter animus uóster est, ego, Démea,
Summá ui defendam hánc atque illum mórtuom.
Cognátus mihi erat : úna a pueris páruolis
Sumus éducti : una sémper militiae ét domi 495
Fuimús : paupertatem úna pertulimús grauem.

Quaprópter nitar, fáciam, experiar, dénique
Animám relinquam pótius quam illas déseram.
Quid míhi respondes? *De.* Frátrem conue-
    niam, Hégio.
He. Sed, Démea, hoc tu fácito cum animo cógites, 500
  Quam uós facillume ágitis, quam estis máxume
  Poténtes dites fórtunati nóbiles,
  Tam máxume uos aéquo animo aequa nóscere
  Opórtet, si uos uóltis perhiberí probos.
De. Redíto: fient quaé fieri aequomst ómnia. 505
He. Decét te facere. Géta, duc me intro ad Sós-
    tratam.
De. Non me índicente haec fíunt: utinam hic sít
    modo
  Defúnctum: uerum nímia illaec licéntia
  Profécto euadit ín aliquod magnúm malum.
  Ibo ác requiram frátrem, ut in eum haec
    éuomam. 510

HEGIO.

Bono ánimo fac sis, Sóstrata, et istam quód
    potes
Fac cónsolere. ego Mícionem, si ápud forumst,
Conuéniam atque ut res géstast narrabo órdine:
Si est, *is* facturus út sit officiúm suom,
Faciát: sin aliter de hác re est eius senténtia, 515
Respóndeat mi, ut quíd agam quam primúm
    sciam.

ACTVS IV.

CTESIPHO. SYRVS.

Ct. Aín patrem hinc abísse rus? *Sy.* Iam dúdum.
   Ct. Dic sodés. *Sy.* Apud uillamst:
Núnc quom maxume óperis aliquid fácere
   credo. *Ct.* Vtinám quidem:
Quod cúm salute eius fíat, ita se défetigarít
   uelim,
Vt tríduo hoc perpétuo prorsum e lécto nequeat
   súrgere.   520
Sy. Ita fíat, et istoc síquid potis est réctius. *Ct.*
   Ita: nam húnc diem
Miseré nimis cupio, ut coépi, perpetuom ín lae-
   titia dégere.
Et íllud rus nulla ália causa tám male odi, nísi
   quia
Propést: quod si esset lóngius,
Príus nox oppressísset illic, quam húc reuorti
   pósset iterum.   525
Núnc ubi me illic nón uidebit, iam húc re-
   curret, sát scio:

Rogitábit me, ubi fúerim: 'ego hoc te tóto non
    uidí die:'
Quid dícam? *Sy.* Nilne in méntemst? *Ct.*
    Numquam quícquam. *Sy.* Tanto né-
    quior.
Cliéns amicus hóspes nemost uóbis? *Ct.* Sunt:
    quid póstea?
Sy. Hisce ópera ut data sit. *Ct.* Quaé non data
    sit? nón potest fierí. *Sy.* Potest.   530
Ct. Intérdiu: sed si híc pernocto, caúsae quid
    dicám, Syre?
Sy. Vah, quám uellem etiam nóctu amicis óperam
    mos essét dari.
Quin tu ótiosus és: ego illius sénsum pulchre
    cálleo.
Quom féruit maxumé, tam placidum quási
    ouem reddo. *Ct.* Quó modo?
Sy. Laudárier te audít lubenter: fácio te apud
    illúm deum: 535
Virtútes narro. *Ct.* Meás? *Sy.* Tuas: homini
    ílico lacrumaé cadunt
Quasi púero gaudio. én tibi autem. *Ct.* Quíd
    namst? *Sy.* Lupus in fábula.
Ct. Pater ést? *Sy. Is* ipsust. *Ct.* Sýre, quid agi-
    mus? *Sy.* Fúge modo intro, ego
    uídero.
Ct. Siquíd rogabit, núsquam tu me: audístin? *Sy.*
    Potin ut désinas?

DEMEA. CTESIPHO. SYRVS.

De. Ne égo homo infelix: prímum fratrem nús-
quam inuenio géntium: 540
   Praéterea autem, dum íllum quaero, a uílla
   mercennárium
   Vídi: is filiúm negat esse rúri: nec quid agám
   scio.
Ct. Sýre. *Sy.* Quid est? *Ct.* Men quaérit? *Sy.*
   Verum. *Ct.* Périi. *Sy.* Quin tu animó
   bono es.
De. Quíd hoc, malum, infelícitatis? néqueo satis
   decérnere:
   Nísi me credo huic ésse natum reí, ferundis
   míseriis.   545
   Prímus sentió mala nostra: prímus rescisco
   ómnia:
   Prímus porro obnúntio: aegre sólus, siquid fít,
   fero.
Sy. Rídeo hunc: primum aít se scire: is sólus nescit
   ómnia.
De. Núnc redeo: si fórte frater rédierit uisó. *Ct.*
   Syre,
   Óbsecro, uide ne ílle huc prorsus se ínruat. *Sy.*
   Etiám taces?   550
   Égo cauebo. *Ct.* Númquam hercle hodie ego
   ístuc committám tibi:
   Nám me iam in cellam áliquam cum illa cón-
   cludam: id tutíssumumst.

Sy. Áge, tamen ego hunc ámouebo.   *De.* Séd eccum
   sceleratúm Syrum.
Sy. Nón hercle hic qui uólt durare quísquam, si sic
   fít, potest.
   Scíre equidem uoló, quot mihi sint dómini:
   quae haec est míseria!   555
De. Quíd ille gannit? quíd uolt? quid aïs, bóne
   uir? est fratér domi?
Sy. Quíd malum 'bone uír' mihi narras? équidem
   perii.   *De.* Quíd tibist?
Sy. Rógitas? Ctesiphó me pugnis míserum et istam
   psáltriam
   Vsque occidit.   *De.* Hém, quid narras?   *Sy.*
   Ém, uide ut discidít labrum.
De. Quam óbrem?   *Sy.* Me inpulsóre hanc emptam 560
   esse aít.   *De.* Non tu eum rus hínc
   modo
   Próduxe aibas?   *Sy.* Fáctum: ucrum uénit
   post insániens:
   Níl pepercit. nón puduisse uérberare hominém
   senem!
   Quem égo modo puerúm tantillum in mánibus
   gestauí meis.
De. Laúdo: Ctesiphó, patrissas: ábi, uirum te
   iúdico.
Sy. Laúdas? ne ille cóntinebit pósthac, si sapiét,
   manus.   565
De. Fórtiter.   *Sy.* Perquám, quia miseram múlierem
   et me séruolum,

Quí referire nón audebam, uícit: hui, perfór-
titer.
De. Nón potuit meliús. idem quod ego sénsit te
esse huic reí caput.
Séd estne frater íntus? *Sy.* Non est. *De.* V́bi
illum inueniam cógito.
Sy. Scío ubi sit, uerum hódie numquam mónstrabo.
De. Hem, quid aïs? *Sy.* Ita. 570
De. Dímminuetur tíbi quidem iam cérebrum. *Sy.*
At nomen néscio
Íllius hominis, séd locum noui úbi sit. *De.* Dic
ergó locum.
Sy. Nóstin porticum ápud macellum hac deórsum?
De. Quid ni nóuerim?
Sy. Praéterito hac récta platea súrsum: ubi eo
uéneris,
Clíuos deorsum uórsum est: hac te praécipitato:
póstea 575
Ést ad hanc manúm sacellum: ibi ángiportum
própter est,
De. Quá nam? *Sy.* Illi ubi etiám caprificus mágna
est. *De.* Noui. *Sy.* Hac pérgito.
De. Íd quidem angipórtum non est péruium. *Sy.*
Verum hércle: uah,
Cénsen hominem me ésse? erraui: in pórticum
rursúm redi:
Sáne hac multo própius ibis ét minor est errátio. 580
Scín Cratini huius dítis aedis? *De.* Scío. *Sy.*
Vbi eas praetérieris,

Ád sinistram hac récta platea; ubi ád Dianae
    uéneris,
Íto ad dextram: príus quam ad portam uénias,
    apud ipsúm lacum
Ést pistrilla et éxaduorsum fábrica: ibist. *De.*
    Quid íbi facit?
Léctulos in sóle ilignis pédibus faciundós dedit. 585
Úbi potetis uós: bene sane. séd cesso ad eum
    pérgere?
Í sane: ego te exércebo hodie, ut dígnus es,
    silicérnium.
Aéschinus odióse cessat: prándium corrúm-
    pitur:
Ctésipho autem in amórest totus. égo iam pro-
    spiciám mihi:
Nám iam adibo atque únum quicquid, quód
    quidem erit bellíssumum,   590
Cárpam et cyathos sórbilans paulátim hunc pro-
    ducám diem.

Micio. Hegio.

Ego in hác re nil repério, quam obrem laúder
    tanto opere, Hégio.
Meum officium facio: quód peccatum a nóbis
    ortumst córrigo.
Nisi sí me in illo crédidisti esse hóminum
    numero, qui íta putant,
Sibi fíeri iniuriam últro, si quam fécere ipsi
    expóstules,   595

  Et últro accusant: íd quia non est á me factum,
    agis grátias?
He. Ah, mínume: numquam te áliter atque es ín
    animum induxí meum.
  Sed quaéso ut una mécum ad matrem uírginis
    eas, Mício,
  Atque ístaec eadem quaé mihi dixti túte dicas
    múlieri:
  Suspítionem hanc própter fratrem eius ésse et
    illam psáltriam   600
  * * * * * * * *
Mi. Si ita aéquom censes aút si ita opus est fácto,
    eamus. *He.* Béne facis:
  Nam et íllic animum iám releuaris, quaé dolore
    ac míseria
  Tabéscit, et tuom offícium fueris fúnctus. sed
    si alitér putas,
  Egomét narrabo quaé mihi dixti. *Mi.* Ímmo
    ego ibo. *He.* Béne facis:
  Omnés, quibus res sunt mínus secundae, mágis
    sunt nescio quó modo   605
  Suspítiosi: ad cóntumeliam ómnia accipiúnt
    magis:
  Proptér suam inpoténtiam se sémper credunt
    lúdier.
  Quaprópter te ipsum púrgare ipsi córam placa-
    bílius est.
Mi. Et récte et uerum dícis. *He.* Sequere me érgo
    hac intro. *Mi.* Máxume.

Aeschinvs.

Díscrucior auimi: hócine de inprouíso mihi
  mali óbici   610
Tántum, ut neque quid dé me faciam néc quid
  agam certúm siet!
Mémbra metu débilia súnt: auimus timore
Óbstipuit: péctore nil sístere consili quit.
Vah, quó modo hac me expédiam turba? tánta
  nunc
Suspítio de me íncidit: 615
Néque ea inmerito: Sóstrata
Crédit mihi me psáltriam hanc emísse: id anus
  mi indícium fecit.
Nám ut hinc forte ea ad óbstetricem erat míssa,
  ubi eam uidi, ílico
Accédo: rogito, Pámphila quid agát.
Illa exclámat 'abi, abi: iam, Aéschine, 620
Satis diú dedisti uérba: sat adhuc túa nos frus-
  tratást fides.'
"Hem, quíd istuc obsecro" ínquam "est?"
  'ualeas, hábeas illam quaé placet.'
Sensi ílico id illas súspicari: séd reprendi mé
  tamen,
Nequíd de fratre gárrulae illi dícerem ac fierét
  palam.
Núnc quid faciam? dícam fratris ésse hanc?
  quod minumést opus   625

K

Vsquam ecferri: ac mitto: fieri pótis est ut
    nequa éxeat.
Ípsum id metuo ut crédant: tot concúrrunt ueri
    símilia:
Égomet rapui: ipse égomet solui argéntum: ad
    me abductást domum.
Haéc adeo mea cúlpa fateor fíeri. non me hanc
    rém patri,
Vt ut erat gesta, índicasse! exórassem ut eam
    dúcerem.   630
Céssatum usque adhúc est: nunc porro, Aé-
    schine, expergíscere:
Núnc hoc primumst: ád illas ibo, ut púrgem
    me. accedam ád foris.
Périi: horresco sémper, ubi pultáre hasce occi-
    pió miser.
Heús heus: Aeschinús ego sum. aperite áliquis
    actutum óstium.
Pródit nescio quís: concedam huc.   635

Micio. Aeschinvs.

Mi. Íta uti dixi, Sóstrata,
Fácite: ego Aeschinúm conueniam, ut quó modo
    acta haec súnt sciat.
Séd quis ostium hóc pultauit? *Ae.* Páter hercle
    est, perii. *Mi.* Aéschine,
Ae. Quid huic híc negotist? *Mi.* túne has pepulistí
    foris?

Tacet. quór non ludo hunc áliquantisper? mélius est,
Quandóquidem hoc numquam mi ípse uoluit dícere. 640
Nil míhi respondes? *Ae.* Nón equidem istas, quód sciam.
Ita: nám mirabar, quíd hic negoti essét tibi.
Erúbuit: salua rés est. *Ae.* Dic sodés, pater,
Tibi uéro quid istic ést rei? *Mi.* Nil *est* míhi quidem.
Amícus quidam me á foro abduxít modo 645
Huc áduocatum síbi. *Ae.* Quid? *Mi.* Ego dicám tibi:
Habitánt hic quaedam múlieres paupérculae:
Vt opínor has non nósse te, et certó scio:
Neque ením diu huc commigrárunt. *Ae.* Quid tum póstea?
Virgo ést cum matre. *Ae.* Pérge. *Mi.* Haec uirgo orbást patre: 650
Hic méus amicus ílli generest próxumus:
Huic léges cogunt núbere hanc. *Ae.* Perií. *Mi.* Quid est?
Nil: récte: perge. *Mi.* Is uénit ut secum áuehat:
Nam habitát Mileti. *Ae.* Hem, uírginem ut secum áuehat?
Sic ést. *Ae.* Miletum usque óbsecro? *Mi.* Ita.
Ae. Animó malest. 655

Quid ipsaé? quid aiunt? *Mi.* Quíd illas censes?
   níl enim.
Comménta mater ést, esse ex alió uiro
Nesció quo puerum nátum: neque eum nóminat:
Priórem esse illum, nón oportere huíc dari.
Ae. Eho, nónne haec iusta tíbi uidetur póscere? 660
Mi. Non. *Ae.* Óbsecro non? án illam hinc abducét,
   pater?
Mi. Quid illám ni abducat? *Ae.* Fáctum a uobis
   dúriter
Inmísericorditérque atque etiam, si ést, pater,
Dicéndum magis apérte, inliberáliter.
Mi. Quam obrém? *Ae.* Rogas me? quíd illi tandem
   créditis 665
Fore ánimi misero, qui cum ea consueuít prior?
Qui infélix hauscio án illam misere núnc amat,
Quom hanc síbi uidebit praésens praesentem
   éripi,
Abdúci ab oculis? fácinus indignúm, pater.
Mi. Qua rátione istuc? quís despondit? quís dedit? 670
Quoi quándo nupsit? aúctor his rebús quis
   est?
Quor dúxit alienam? *Ae.* Án sedere opórtuit
Domi uírginem tam grándem, dum cognátus
   hinc
Illínc ueniret éxpectantem? haec, mí pater,
Te dícere aequom fúit et id deféndere. 675
Mi. Ridículum: aduorsumne íllum causam dícerem,

Quoi uéneram aduocátus? sed quid ista, Aé-
schine,
Nostra? aút quid nobis cum íllis? abeamús.
quid est?
Quíd lacrumas? *Ae.* Pater, óbsecro, ausculta.
Mi. Aéschine, audiui ómnia
Ét scio: nam té amo: quo magis quaé agis curae
súnt mihi. 680
Ae. Íta uelim me prómerentem amés, dum uiuas,
mí pater,
Vt me hoc delictum ádmisisse in me, íd mihi
uementér dolet
Ét me tui pudét. *Mi.* Credo hercle: nam ín-
genium nouí tuom
Líberale: séd uereor ne indíligens nimiúm sies.
Ín qua ciuitáte tandem te árbitrare uíuere? 685
Vírginem uitiásti, quam te nón ius fuerat tán-
gere.
Iam íd peccatum prímum magnum, *mágnum*, at
humanúm tamen:
Fécere alii saépe item boni. at póstquam id
euenít, cedo
Númquid circumspéxti? aut numquid túte pro-
spextí tibi,
Quíd fieret? qua fíeret? si te mi ípsum puduit
próloqui, 690
Quá resciscerem? haéc dum dubitas, ménses
abierúnt decem.

Pródidisti et te ét illam miseram et gnátum,
    quod quidem in té fuit.

Quíd? credebas dórmienti haec tíbi confecturós
    deos?

Et illam sine tua ópera in cubiculum íri deduc-
    túm domum?

Nólim ceterárum rerum té socordem eodém
    modo.   695

Bóno animo es, ducés uxorem hanc. *Ae.* Hém.
    Mi. Bono, inquam, animo és. *Ae.*
    Pater,

Óbsecro, num lúdis tu [nunc] me? *Mi.* Égo
    te? quam obrem? *Ae* Néscio:

Quía tam misere hoc ésse cupio uérum, eo uereór
    magis.

Mi. Ábi domum ac deos cómprecare, ut úxorem
    arcessás: abi.

Ae. Quíd? eam uxorem? *Mi.* Eám. *Ae.* Iam?
    Mi. Iam quantúm potest. *Ae.* Di mé,
    pater,   700

Ómnes oderínt, ni magis te quam óculos nunc
    ego amó meos.

Mi. Quíd? quam illam? *Ae.* Aeque. *Mi.* Pérbe-
    nigne. *Ae.* Quíd? ille ubist Milésius?

Mi. Ábiit, periit, náuem ascendit; séd quor cessas?
    Ae. Ábi, pater:

Tú potius deos cómprecare: nám tibi eos certó
    scio,

Quó uir melior múlto es quam ego, obtémpera-
    turós magis. 705
Mi. Égo eo intro, ut quae opus súnt parentur: tú
    fac ut dixi, sí sapis.
Ae. Quid hoc ést negoti? hoc ést patrem esse aut
    hóc est filium ésse? — .
    Si fráter aut sodális esset, quí magis morem
        géreret?
    Hic nón amandus? hícine non gestándus in
        sinúst? hem:
    Itaque ádeo magnam mi ínicit sua cómmoditate
        cúram: 710
    Ne fórte inprudens fáciam quod nolít, sciens
        cauébo.
    Sed césso ire intro, né morae meis núptiis
        egomét siem?

Demea. Micio.

De. Deféssus sum ambulándo: ut, Syre, te cúm tua
    Monstratióne mágnus perdat Iúppiter!
    Perréptaui usque omne óppidum: ad portam,
        ád lacum, 715
    Quo nón? neque illic fábrica erat neque frátrem
        homo
    Vidísse se aibat quísquam.   nunc ueró domi
    Certum ósbidere est úsque, donec rédierit.
Mi. Ibo, íllis dicam núllam esse in nobís moram.
De. Sed eccum ípsum: te iam dúdum quaero, Mício. 720

Mi. Quid nám? *De.* Fero alia flágitia ad te ingéntia
Boni illíus adulescéntis. *Mi.* Ecce autém noua.
De. Capitália. *Mi.* Ohe iam. *De.* Néscis qui uir
sít. *Mi.* Scio.
De. O stúlte, tu de psáltria me sómnias
Agere: hóc peccatum in uírginemst ciuém.
Mi. Scio. 725
De. Oho, scís et patere? *Mi.* Quíd ni pátiar? *De.*
Díc mihi,
Non clámas? non insánis? *Mi.* Non: malím
quidem —
De. Puer nátust. *Mi.* Di bene uórtant. *De.* Virgo
níl habet.
Mi. Audíui. *De.* Et ducenda índotatast. *Mi.*
Scílicet.
De. Quid núnc futurumst? *Mi.* Íd enim quod res
ípsa fert: 730
Illínc huc transferétur uirgo. *De.* O Iúppiter,
Istócine pacto opórtet? *Mi.* Quid faciam ám-
plius?
De. Quid fácias? si non ípsa re tibi istúc dolet,
Simuláre certe est hóminis. *Mi.* Quin iam
uírginem
Despóndi: res compósitast: fiunt núptiae: 735
Dempsí metum omnem: haec mágis sunt homi-
nis. *De.* Céterum
Placét tibi factum, Mício? *Mi.* Non, sí queam
Mutáre. nunc quom nón queo, animo aequó
fero.

Ita uítast hominum, quási quom ludas tésseris,
Si illúd quod maxume ópus est iactu nón cadit, 740
Illúd quod cecidit fórte, id arte ut córrigas.

De. Corréctor: nempe tua árte uigintí minae
Pro psáltria periére: quae quantúm potest
Aliquo ábiciendast, sí non pretio, grátiis.

Mi. Neque ést neque illam sáne studeo uéndere. 745

De. Quid ígitur facies? *Mi.* Dómi erit. *De.* Pro diuóm fidem,
Meretríx et mater fámilias una ín domo?

Mi. Quor nón? *De.* Sanumne crédis te esse? *Mi.* Equidem árbitror.

De. Ita mé di ament, ut uídeo tuam ego inéptiam,
Factúrum credo, ut hábeas quicum cántites. 750

Mi. Quor nón? *De.* Et noua nupta éadem haec discet. *Mi.* Scílicet.

De. Tu intér eas restim dúctans saltabís. *Mi.* Probe.

De. Probe? *Mi.* Ét tu nobiscum úna, si opus sit. *De.* Eí mihi.
Non te haéc pudent? *Mi.* Iam uéro omitte, Démea,
Tuam istam íracundiam, átque ita ut *hodié* decet 755
Hilarum ác lubentem fác te gnati in núptiis.
Ego hós conueniam: póst huc redeo. *De.* O Iúppiter,
Hancíne uitam! hoscin móres! hanc deméntiam!
Vxór sine dote uéniet: intus psáltriast:

Domus súmptuosa : aduléscens luxu pérditus : 760
Senéx delirans. ípsa si cupiát Salus,
Seruáre prorsus nón potest hanc fámiliam.

Syrvs. Demea.

Sy. Edepól, Syrisce, té curasti mólliter
Lautéque munus ádministrastí tuom.
Abi. séd postquam intus sum ómnium rerúm
    satur, 765
Prodeámbulare huc lúbitumst. *De.* Illud sís
    uide
Exémplum disciplínae. *Sy.* Ecce autem híc
    adest
Senex nóster. quid fit? quíd tu es tristis? *De.*
    Óh scelus.
Sy. Ohe iám : tu uerba fúndis hic, sapiéntia?
De. Tu sí meus esses . . *Sy.* Dís quidem esses, Démea, 770
Ac tuám rem constabilísses. *De.* Exemplo óm-
    nibus
Curárem ut esses. *Sy.* Quam óbrem? quid
    fecí? *De.* Rogas?
In ípsa turba atque ín peccato máxumo,
Quod uíx sedatum sátis est, potastí, scelus,
Quasi ré bene gesta. *Sy.* Sáne nollem huc
    éxitum. 775

DROMO. SYRVS. DEMEA.

Dr. Heus Sýre, rogat te Ctésipho ut redeás. *Sy.* Abi.
De. Quid Ctésiphonem hic nárrat? *Sy.* Nil. *De.* Eho, cárnufex,
Est Ctésipho intus? *Sy.* Nón est. *De.* Quor hic nóminat?
Sy. Est álius quidam, párasitaster paúlulus:
Nostín? *De.* Iam scibo. *Sy.* Quíd agis? quo abis? *De.* Mítte me. 780
Sy. Noli ínquam. *De.* Non manum ábstines, mastígia?
An tíbi iam mauis cérebrum dispergam híc? *Sy.* Abit.
Edepól commissatórem haud sane cómmodum,
Praesértim Ctesiphóni. quid ego núnc agam?
Nisi, dum haé silescunt túrbae, interea iu ángulum 785
Aliquo ábeam atque edormíscam hoc uilli. síc agam.

MICIO. DEMEA.

Mi. Paráta a nobis súnt, ita ut dixi, Sóstrata,
Vbi uís. quis nam a me pépulit tam grauitér foris?
De. Ei míhi, quid faciam? quid agam? quid clamem aút querar?

O caélum, o terra, o mária Neptuni. *Mi.* Ém
    tibi, 790
Rescíuit omnem rem : íd nunc clamat scílicet :
Parátae lites : súccurrendumst. *De.* Éccum
    adest
Commúnis corruptéla nostrum líberum.
Mi. Tandém reprime iracúndiam atque ad té redi.
De. Représsi, redii, mítto maledicta ómnia : 795
Rem ipsám putemus. díctum hoc inter nós
    fuit
(Ex te ádeost ortum), né tu curarés meum
Neue égo tuom ? respónde. *Mi.* Factumst, nón
    nego.
De. Quor núnc apud te pótat ? quor recipís meum ?
Quor émis amicam, Mício ? numquí minus 800
Mihi idém ius aequomst ésse quod mecúmst
    tibi ?
Quando égo tuom non cúro, ne curá meum.
Mi. Non aéquom dicis. *De.* Nón ? *Mi.* Nam uctus
    uerbum hóc quidemst,
Commúnia esse amícorum inter se ómnia.
De. Facéte : nunc demum ístaec nata orátiost. 805
Mi. Auscúlta paucis, nísi molestumst, Démea.
Princípio, si id te mórdet, sumptum fílii
Quem fáciunt, quaeso hoc fácito tecum cógites :
Tu illós duo olim pró re tollebás tua,
Quod sátis putabas túa bona ambobús fore, 810
Et mé tum uxorem crédidisti scílicet

Ductúrum : eandem illam rátionem antiquam
    óbtine :
Consérua, quaere, párce, fac quam plúrimum
Illís relinquas : glóriam tu istam óbtine.
Mea, quae praeter spem euénere, utantúr sine.   815
De súmma nil decédet : quod hinc accésserit,
Id dé lucro putáto esse omne.   haec sí uoles
In ánimo uere cógitare, Démea,
Et mi ét tibi et illis démpseris moléstiam.
De. Mittó rem : consuetúdinem ipsorúm.   *Mi.*
    Mane :   820
Scio : ístuc ibam.   múlta in homine, Démea,
Signa ínsunt, ex quibus cóniectura fácile fit,
Duo quóm idem faciunt, saépe ut possis dícere
'Hoc lícet inpune fácere huic, illi nón licet',
Non quó dissimilis rés sit, sed quo is quí facit.   825
Quae ego inésse in illis uídeo, ut confidám fore
Ita ut uólumus.   uideo eos sápere, intellegere,
    ín loco
Veréri, inter se amáre : scires líberum
Ingénium atque animum.   quó uis illos tú die
Reddúcas.   at enim métuas, ne ab re sínt tamen   830
Omíssiores paúlo.   o noster Démea,
Ad ómnia alia aetáte sapimus réctius :
Solum únum hoc uitium fért senectus hómini-
    bus :
Atténtiores súmus ad rem omnes, quám sat
    est :

Quod illós sat aetas ácuet. *De.* Ne nimiúm
    modo 835
Bonaé tuae istae nós rationes, Mício,
Et túos iste animus aéquos subuortát. *Mi.*
    Tace:
Non fíet. mitte iam ístaec: da te hodié mihi:
Expórge frontem. *De.* Scílicet ita témpus fert,
Faciúndumst: ceterúm rus cras cum fílio 840
Cum prímo luci ibo hínc. *Mi.* De nocte cénseo:
Hodié modo hilarum fác te. *De.* Et istam
    psáltriam
Vna ílluc mecum hinc ábstraham. *Mi.* Pug-
    náueris.
Eo pácto prorsum illi ádligaris fílium.
Modo fácito ut illam sérues. *De.* Ego istuc
    uídero 845
Atque íbi fauillae pléna, fumi ac póllinis
Coquéndo sit faxo ét molendo: praéter haec
Merídie ipso fáciam ut stipulam cólligat;
Tam excóctam reddam atque átram quam car-
    bóst. *Mi.* Placet:
Nunc míhi uidere sápere. atque equidem fílium 850
Tum etiám si nolit cógam ut cum illa uná cubet.
De. Derídes? fortunátu's, qui isto animó sies:
    Ego séntio. *Mi.* Ah, pergísne? *De.* Iam iam
    désino.
Mi. I ergo íntro, et quoi rei est, eí rei hunc suma-
    mús diem.

ACTVS V.

DEMEA.

Númquam ita quisquam béne subducta rátione
    ad uitám fuit,   855
Quín res aetas úsus semper áliquid adportét
    noui,
Áliquid moneat: út illa quae te scíre credas
    néscias,
Ét quae tibi putáris prima, in éxperiundo ut
    répudies.
Quód nunc mi euenít: nam ego uitam dúram,
    quam uixi úsque adhuc,
Própe iam excurso spátio mitto. id quam
    óbrem? re ipsa répperi   860
Fácilitate níl esse homini mélius neque cle-
    méntia.
Íd esse uerum ex me átque ex fratre quoíuis
    facilest nóscere.
Ílle suam egit sémper uitam in ótio, in conuíuiis,

Clémens, placidus, núlli laedere ós, adridere
  ómnibus :
Síbi uixit: sibi súmptum fecit ómnes bene
  dicúnt, amant.   865
Égo ille agrestis, saéuos, tristis, párcus, truculen-
  tús, tenax
Dúxi uxorem : quam íbi miseriam uídi ! nati
  fílii,
Ália cura : heia aútem, dum studeo íllis ut quam
  plúrimum
Fácerem, contriui ín quaerundo uítam atque
  aetatém meam :
Núnc exacta aetáte hoc fructi pró labore ab eís
  fero,   870
Ódium : ille alter síne labore pátria potitur
  cómmoda.
Íllum amant, me fúgitant : illi crédunt consilia
  ómnia,
Íllum diligúnt, apud illum súnt ambo, ego
  desértus sum :
Íllum ut uiuat óptant, meam autem mórtem
  expectant scílicet.
Íta eos meo labóre eductos máxumo hic fecít
  suos   875
Paúlo sumptu : míseriam omnem ego cápio, hic
  potitur gaúdia.
Áge age nunciam éxperiamur cóntra, ecquid
  ego póssiem

Blánde dicere aút benigne fácere, quando hoc
  próuocat.
Égo quoque a meís me amari et mágni pendi
  póstulo
Si íd fit dando atque óbsequendo, nón posteriorés
  feram.   880
Déerit : id mea mínume re fert, quí sum natu
  máxumus.

Syrvs. Demea.

Sy. Heus Démea, orat fráter ne abeas lóngius
De. Quis homo? ó Syre noster, sálue : quid fit?
  quíd agitur?
Sy. Recte. *De.* Óptumest. iam núnc haec tria
  primum áddidi
Praetér naturam : 'o nóster, quid fit? quíd
  agitur?'   885
Seruom haúd inliberálem praebes te, ét tibi
Lubéns bene faxim. *Sy.* Grátiam habeo. *De.*
  Atquí, Syre,
Hoc úerumst et re ipsa éxperiere própediem.

Geta. Demea. (Syrvs.)

Ge. Era, ego húc ad hos prouíso, quam mox uírginem
Arcéssant. sed eccum Démeam. saluós sies.   890
De. O quí uocare? *Ge.* Géta. *De.* Geta, hominem
  máxumi
Pretí te esse hodie iúdicaui animó meo :

Nam is míhi profectost séruos spectatús satis,
Quoi dóminus curaest, íta uti tibi sensí, Geta,
Et tíbi ob eam rem, síquid usus uénerit, 895
Lubéns bene faxim.   méditor esse adfábilis,
Et béne procedit.   *Ge.* Bónus es, quom haec existumas.

De. Paulátim plebem prímulum facio meam.

AESCHINVS.   DEMEA.   SYRVS.   GETA.

Ae. Occídunt me quidem, dúm nimis sanctas núptias
Student fácere: in adparándo consumúnt diem. 900
De. Quid ágitur, Aeschine?   *Ae.* Éhem, pater mi,
    tu híc eras?
De. Tuos hércle uero et ánimo et naturá pater,
Qui té amat plus quam hosce óculos.   sed quor nón domum
Vxórem arcessis?   *Ae.* Cúpio: uerum hoc míhi moraest:
Tibícina et hymenaéum qui cantént.   *De.* Eho, 905
Vin tu huíc seni auscultáre?   *Ae.* Quid?   *De.*
    Missa haéc face,
Hymenaéum turbas lámpadas tibícinas,
Atque húnc in horto máceriam iube dírui
Quantúm potest: hac tránsfer: unam fác domum:
Tradúce et matrem et fámiliam omnem ad nós.
    Ae. Placet, 910
Patér lepidissume.   *De.* Eúgae, iam lepidús uocor.

Fratri aédes fient péruiae, turbám domum
Addúcet, sumptu amíttet multa: quíd mea?
Ego lépidus ineo grátiam. iube núnciam
Dinúmeret ille Bábylo uigintí minas. 915
Syre, céssas ire ac fácere? *Sy.* Quid ego? *De.*
  Dírue.
Tu illás abi et tradúce. *Ge.* Di tibi, Démea,
Bene fáciant, quom te uídeo nostrae fámiliae
Tam ex ánimo factum uélle. *De.* Dignos árbi-
  tror.
Quid tú aïs? *Ae.* Sic opínor. *De.* Multo réc-
  tiust 920
Quam illám puerperam húc nunc duci pér uiam
Aegrótam. *Ae.* Nil enim uídi melius, mí pater.
De. Sic sóleo. sed eccum Mício egreditúr foras.

      MICIO. DEMEA. AESCHINVS.

Mi. Iubet fráter? ubi is est? tún iubes hoc, Démea?
De. Ego uéro iubeo et hác re et aliis ómnibus 925
  Quam máxume unam fácere nos hanc fámiliam,
  Colere ádiuuare adiúngere. *Ae.* Ita quaesó,
    pater.
Mi. Haud áliter censeo. *De.* Ímmo hercle ita nobís
    decet:
  Primum huíus uxorist máter. *Mi.* Est. quid
    póstea?
De. Proba ét modesta. *Mi.* Ita áiunt. *De.* Natu
    grándior. 930

Mi. Scio. *De.* Párere iam diu haéc per annos nón
    potest :
  Nec qui cám respiciat quísquam est : solast.
    Mi. Quam híc rem agit?
De. Hanc te aéquomst ducere, ét te operam ut fiát dare.
Mi. Me dúcere autem? *De.* Té. *Mi.* Me? *De.*
    Te inquam. *Mi.* Inéptis. *De.* Si tu
    sís homo,
  Hic fáciat. *Ae.* Mi patér. *Mi.* Quid tu autem
    huic, ásine, auscultas? *De.* Níl agis : 935
  Fieri áliter non potést. *Mi.* Deliras. *Ae.* Síne
    te exorem, mí pater.
Mi. Insánis : aufer. *De.* Áge, da ueniam fílio.
    Mi. Satin sánus es?
  Ego nóuos maritus ánno demum quínto et sexa-
    génsumo
  Fiam átque anum decrépitam ducam? idne éstis
    auctorés mihi?
Ae. Fac : prómisi ego illis. *Mi.* Prómisti autem?
    dé te largitór, puer. 940
De. Age, quíd siquid te máius oret? *Mi.* Quási non
    hoc sit máxumum.
De. Da uéniam. *Ae.* Ne grauére. *De.* Fac, pro-
    mítte. *Mi.* Non omíttitis?
Ae. Non, nísi te exorem. *Mi.* Vís est haec quidem.
    De. Áge prolixe, Mício.
Mi. Etsi hóc mihi prauom inéptum absurdum atque
    álienum a uitá mea

Vidétur: si uos tánto opere istuc uóltis, fiat.
  Ae. Béne facis.
Meritó *tuo* te amo. uérum .. *Mi.* Quid? *De.*
  Ego dícam, hoc quom fit quód uolo.
Quid núnc? quid restat? *De.* Hégio cognátus
  his est próxumus,
Adfínis nobis, paúper: bene nos áliquid facere
  illí decet.
Quid fácere? *De.* Agelli est híc sub urbe
  paúlum quod locitás foras:
Huic démus qui fruátur. *Mi.* Paulum id aú-
  temst? *De.* Si multúmst, tamen
Faciúndumst: pro patre huíc est, bonus est,
  nóster est, recté datur.
Postrémo non meum íllud uerbum fácio, quod
  tu, Mício,
Bene ét sapienter díxti dudum: 'uítium com-
  mune ómniumst,
Quod nímium ad rem in senécta attenti súmus'?
  hanc maculam nós decet
Ecfúgere: dictumst uére et re ipsa fíeri oportet.
  Ae. Mí pater.
Quid ístic? dabitur quándoquidem hic uolt.
  Ae. Gaúdeo.
Nunc míhi germanu's páriter animo et córpore.
Suó sibi gladio hunc iúgulo.
  9 — Ter.

SYRVS. DEMEA. MICIO. AESCHINVS.

Sy. Factumst quód iussisti, Démea.
De. Frúgi homo's. ergo édepol hodie meá quidem
  senténtia
Iúdico Syrum fíeri esse aequom líberum. *Mi.*
  Istunc líberum?   960
Quód nam ob factum? *De.* Múlta. *Sy.* O
  noster Démea, edepol uír bonu's:
Égo istos uobis úsque a pueris cúraui ambos
  sédulo;
Dócui, monui, béne praecepi sémper quae potui
  ómnia.
De. Rés apparet: ét quidem porro haec, óbsonare
  cúm fide,
Scórtum adducere, ádparare dé die conuíuium: 965
Nón mediocris hóminis haec sunt ófficia. *Sy.* O
  lepidúm caput.
De. Póstremo hodie in psáltria hac emúnda hic
  adiutór fuit,
Híc curauit: pródesse aequomst: álii melióres
  erunt:
Dénique hic uolt fíeri. *Mi.* Vin tu hoc fíeri?
  Ae. Cupio. *Mi.* Sí quidem
Tú uis, Syre, eho accéde huc ad me: líber esto.
  Sy. Béne facis: 970
Ómnibus gratiam hábeo, et seorsum tíbi prae-
  terea, Démea.

De. Gaúdeo. *Ae.* Et ego. *Sy.* Crédo: utinam hoc perpétuom fiat gaúdium,
Phrýgiam ut uxorém meam una mécum uideam líberam.
De. Óptumam quidem múlierem. *Sy.* Et quidem tuó nepoti huius fílio
Hódie prima mámmam dedit haec. *De.* Hércle uero sério, 975
Síquidem prima dédit, haud dubiumst quín emitti aequóm siet.
Mi. Ób eam rem? *De.* Ob eam: póstremo a me argéntum quantist súmito.
Sy. Dí tibi, Demea, ómnia omnes sémper optata ófferant.
Mi. Sýre, processisti hódie pulchre. *De.* Síquidem porro, Mício,
Tú tuom officium fácies, atque huic áliquid paulum praé manu 980
Déderis, unde utátur: reddet tíbi cito. *Mi.* Istoc uílius.
Ae. Frúgi homost. *Sy.* Reddam hércle, da modo.
 Ae. Áge, pater. *Mi.* Post cónsulam.
De. Fáciet. *Sy.* O uir óptume. *Ae.* O patér mi festiuíssume.
Mi. Quíd istuc? quae res tám repente móres mutauít tuos?
Quód prolubium? quaé istaec subitast lárgitas?
 De. Dicám tibi: 985

Vt id ostenderém, quod te isti fácilem et fes-
  tiuóm putant,
Íd non fieri ex uéra uita néque adeo ex aequo
  ét bono,
Séd ex adsentando índulgendo et lárgiendo,
  Mício.
Núuc adeo si ob eám rem uobis méa uita inuisa,
  Aéschine, est,
Quía non iusta iniústa prorsus ómnia omnino
  óbsequor, 990
Míssa facio: ecfúndite, emite, fácite quod uobís
  lubet.
Séd si id uoltis pótius, quae uos própter adules-
  centiam
Mínus uidetis, mágis inpense cúpitis, consulitís
  parum,
Haéc reprendere ét corrigere et óbsecundare ín
  loco:
Écce me, qui id fáciam uobis. *Ae.* Tíbi, pater,
  permíttimus 995
Plús scis quid facto ópus est. sed de frátre quid
  fiet? *De.* Sino
Hábeat: in istac fínem faciat. *Mi.* Ístuc recte.
  CANTOR. Plaúdite.

NOTES.

REFERENCES AND ABBREVIATIONS.

Grammars.		Editors and Commentators.	
A.,	Andrews & Stoddard's.	Don.,	Donatus.
Al.,	Allen & Greenough's.	Ds.,	Davies.
B.,	Bullions & Morris's.	Fn.,	Fleckeisen.
G.,	Gildersleeve's.	Kz.,	Klotz.
H.,	Harkness's.	Mt.,	Marriott.
M.,	Madvig's.	Pn.,	Papillon.
R.,	Roby's.	Py.,	Parry.
Z.,	Zumpt's.	Ps.,	Phillips.
		Uh.,	Umpfenbach.
		Wr.,	Wagner.

Arn., — *Arnold's* Introduction to Latin Prose Composition, Part II.
Dict. Antiqq., — *Smith's* Dictionary of Greek and Roman Antiquities.
Dict. Biog., — *Smith's* Dictionary of Greek and Roman Biography and Mythology.
D., — *Doederlein's* Latin Synonymes.
Lex., — *Andrew's Freund's* Latin Lexicon.
W. & R., — *White & Riddle's* Latin-English Dictionary.
Mom., — *Mommsen's* History of Rome.
Ry., — *Ramsay's* Manual of Roman Antiquities.
T., — *Teuffel's* History of Roman Literature.
s. v., — *sub voce*.

Other abbreviations the same as in the other works of this series.

NOTES

TO THE

ANDRIA AND ADELPHOE OF TERENCE.

INTRODUCTION.

The very little that is known of the life of Publius Terentius Afer is obtained chiefly from an extract from the *De Poetis* of Suetonius, preserved by the grammarian Aelius Donatus (fl. A. D. 350) in the introduction to his commentary on the comedies of this author.

According to this account, Terence was a native of Carthage, as would also be inferred from his *cognomen*, and was brought to Rome a slave in his childhood, having been perhaps taken prisoner at some inroad made by the Numidians into Carthaginian territory. There he came into the possession of Terentius Lucanus, a senator, who educated and then emancipated him, the freedman, according to custom, taking the gentilic name of his patron.

If the reading of Suetonius' text, now most approved, be correct, Terence was born B. C. 184, the year of Plautus's death — the only other Roman writer of comedies whose works are extant — and the first of Cato's censorship. Going to Greece for travel and study in B. C. 160, he died the next year, in Arcadia or Leucadia, of an illness caused by grief at the loss at sea of a number of his translations of Greek plays, or, according to another report, by shipwreck on his return-voyage to Italy. His brief life thus fell within the first half of the second century B. C., in the interval between the victory of the Romans over Antiochus the Great and their final struggle against Carthage — the period in which, by their wars against Perseus, the Ligurians, Spaniards, and Sardinians, they were completing that circuit of conquest which brought to the State and to individual citizens vast wealth, but in its train political corruption, a rapid deterioration of morals, and the decline of the nation's greatness.

Though the Greek language had been generally well known for a century, and the Greek dramatists were popular at Rome as early as the second Punic war, there was no prose literature in Latin prior to Terence's day, and the language had just been receiving its first real culture at the hands of Ennius, "the father and prince of Roman poetry." Even the drama, in its earliest rude form of translations of Greek plays by Livius Andronicus, had its beginning only about half a century before his birth; the first eminent tragedian, Pacuvius, was his contemporary, and but three writers of comedy had preceded him — Cn. Naevius, Plautus, and Caecilius Statius. To Caecilius, then at the head of his profession, Terence was referred by the curule aediles, on offering his first play to them for exhibition, at the age of sixteen. As the story ran, he began the reading of it seated near the table at which the critic and his friends were dining. He had not proceeded far, when Caecilius, delighted with the character of the work, invited him to join the party at the feast; and after it was over, the remainder of the play was read, highly approved by the audience, and recommended to the aediles. Though it was not acted for two years, copies of it were in circulation, and the author was very soon brought into intimate friendship with Scipio Aemilianus and Laelius, young men of about the same age with himself, and already enthusiastic students of Greek literature. Through them he also gained the acquaintance of the Aemilii, the Metelli, the Scaevolae, and other learned and influential families, as well as that of the principal literary men. A rumor soon started, and was circulated by his rivals, that he was aided in the composition of his plays by his patrons, and even that they were the real authors. Cicero (*ad Att.* VII. 3) and Quintilian (X. 1, 100) state, without, however, endorsing these reports, that they were generally supposed to refer to Scipio and Laelius; while Santra, a grammarian and contemporary of Cicero, is quoted as remarking that, if the poet had needed aid, he would not have applied to those noblemen, on account of their youth, but to such men as Q. Fabius Labeo, M. Popillius Laenas, or L. Sulpicius Galus, who were already distinguished for their learning. This entire supposition, however, is a mere conjecture, unsupported by a particle of proof. The argument against it, from internal evidence, is thus stated by Parry: "A careful consideration of Terence's plays leads us to the conclusion that they are the production of a writer not only thoroughly educated, but having a consistent theory of dramatic composition. Add to this the remarkable purity of the language, and we cannot, without a violent inconsistency, suppose that this was the result of the patchwork contributions of two or three dilettanti noblemen. These plays are so even and consistent throughout, individually and with one another, having the same neatness of language, the same attention to metre, the same quiet tone of good-natured humor and practical knowledge of the world, that we might well defy any critic to show where Terence left off and his friends began." The story can be explained by the fact of literary jealousy, the hostility of the conservative faction in literature led by Cato and the Fabii to every prominent writer in the opposite party, and, perhaps, in part also, by the strong prejudices of the Romans against freedmen and foreigners, which even Horace experienced. In his allusions to this accusation in the prologues of the *Hauton timorvmenos* (l. 22–25), and of the *Adelphoe* (l. 15–21), Terence does not indeed deny it, in the former leaving the question of its truth to the judgment of his hearers, and in the latter insisting that if it were true, he ought to feel proud of it rather than ashamed; but his evasion of the charge can be accounted for on the ground that it was impolitic for him to deny that which would be so creditable, and therefore flattering, to his patrons, while it would of course be readily admitted that he may have read his plays to them, and have availed himself of their criticisms.

The names of Terence's comedies in the order in which they are believed to have been written are: The *Andria* or Woman of Andros, The *Hecyra* or Mother-in-law, The *Eunuchus*, The *Hauton timorvmenos* or Self-Tormentor, The *Phormio* or Parasite, and the *Adelphoe* or Brothers. It has been the fashion to charge him with being a copyist in the preparation of these plays, but this charge has been pressed too closely. Even Mommsen admits that " by the literal adherence of his imitations to the originals we are not to understand a verbal translation in our sense." For these productions he did not indeed claim originality in the strict sense of that term. In common with all the playwrights of his day, it was simply his aim to reproduce in Latin the best works of the Attic comedy, or rather to construct plays independently out of the common Greek materials. Four of them are founded upon comedies of Menander, the most eminent of the poets of the New Comedy (whose works are not now extant), and the other two upon comedies of Apollodorus of Carystus in Euboea; and his indebtedness to these writers is distinctly and fully acknowledged in his prologues. He may, however, justly claim the merit of great art and some inventive power in the skill with which he combined two or more Greek plays into one, and in his treatment of his characters. The practice of *contaminating* plays, as it was called, was a common one with the early Roman poets, and Terence formed the plots of four of his plays in this way. But in this work he was no mere compiler. Parry, who has carefully examined all the extant fragments of Menander, expresses the opinion that Terence " cannot simply have dovetailed his new matter into the existing plot, but must, to a great extent, have recast the whole. The *known* variations from the original extend not only to minor differences of name and incident, but to a new conception in some instances of the plots of his plays and the characters he was reproducing. Availing himself of the whole of the Menandrian repertory, he worked up the old materials into a new and consistent creation. The number of fragments of unascertained plays of Menander which fit more or less closely with Terence, many of them quite as well as those passages directly quoted from the corresponding plays of Menander, leads us to the conclusion that Terence drew not only from the single play which he had before him, but also from his general knowledge of the works of Menander and the other authors of Greek comedy."

His excellence in the delineation of character has also been generally admitted. Varro's judgment was: *In ethesin Terentius poscit palmam*. "A close study," says Parry, "will verify that both in the grouping and the treatment of his characters, Terence is an original, as compared with Plautus; and from the hints we can glean from the scattered fragments of the Greek comedians, we may conclude that he was in a great measure original, even when compared with Menander." And Mommsen remarks that "while Plautus paints his characters with broad strokes, often after a stock model, Terence handles the psychological development with a careful and often excellent miniature painting."

The complaint has sometimes been made that Terence was deficient in *comic force*, and that he lacked the liveliness, freshness, and versatility of Plautus. Mommsen's language is that 'he reproduced the agreeableness without the merriment of Menander.' And in support of this allegation the famous epigram of Caesar, preserved by Suetonius, has been often quoted:

> *Lenibus atque utinam scriptis adiuncta foret uis,*
> *Comica ut aequato uirtus polleret honore*
> *Cum Graecis, neque in hac despectus parte iaceres:*
> *Vnum hoc maceror et doleo tibi deesse, Terenti.*

But it must always be remembered that Terence's plays are 'comedies of sentiment,' in which the *ris comica* has a subordinate place, and the distinguishing characteristics of which are humor and pathos. In these qualities he has been considered by scholars best qualified to pronounce an opinion, not deficient by the side of Menander. The conclusion of the writer in Smith's Dictionary, in his comparison of the two comedians, is: " Granting to Plautus the highest genius for exciting laughter, the eloquence Aelius Stilo ascribed to him, and a natural force — *virtus* — which Terence wanted, there will remain to the latter greater consistency of plot and character, closer observation of generic and individual distinctions, deeper pathos, subtler wit, and a wider command of the middle region between sport and earnest."

The purity and elegance of *the style* of Terence were heartily praised by the most competent judges among his countrymen. The first lines of Caesar's epigram are:

> Tu quoque tu in summis, O dimidiate Menander,
> Poneris et merito, puri sermonis amator.

Cicero's opinion is expressed in a fragment which has been preserved of a poem called *Limo:*

> Tu quoque, qui solus lecto sermone, Terenti,
> Conuersum expressumque Latina uoce Menandrum
> In medium nobis sedatis nocibus ecfers
> Quicquid come loquens atque omnia dulcia dicens.

And Quintilian's words are: *Terenti scripta sunt in hoc genere elegantissima.* Modern critics, also, have unanimously confessed that in correctness, refinement, and grace of expression, he was surpassed by no other Roman writer, declaring that 'although a foreigner, and a freedman, he divides with Cicero and Caesar the palm of pure latinity.' Mommsen is of the opinion that " it is perhaps justifiable to date a new era in Roman literature — the real essence of which lay not in the development of Latin poetry, but in the development of the Latin language — from the comedies of Terence, as the first artistically pure imitation of Hellenic works of art."

THE ANDRIA.

The *Andria* was the earliest of the plays of Terence, as the order of the words in the original title *Andria Terenti* proves. It takes its name from the heroine, who was from the island of Andros in the Aegean, and the plot turns upon her previous history.

Chremes, an Athenian, starting on a voyage to Asia, left his daughter Pasiphila with his brother Phania, who afterwards also sailed for Asia to escape a war, was shipwrecked with his niece upon Andros, and became a client of a citizen of that island. Upon Phania's death, this man adopted Pasiphila, and, changing her name to Glycerium, brought her up with his daughter Chrysis. On his death they removed to Athens, where Pamphilus became a lover of Glycerium, and promised her marriage; while Simo, without the knowledge of his son, had betrothed him to Philumena, another daughter of Chremes. His father's first suspicion of Pamphilus' opposition to this was awakened by observing his conduct at Chrysis' funeral; while Chremes, on learning the whole story of Pamphilus' connection with her, broke off the match.

The action of the play begins at this point. Simo announces to Pamphilus that he must marry Philumena at once, hoping that if he consents Chremes may be reconciled. This brings Pamphilus into great perplexity. But Davus, finding on investigation that the marriage is a pretence, advises Pamphilus to humor his father by professing to consent, and to keep up the suspicions of Chremes by his intimacy with Glycerium. Meanwhile, Charinus, a friend of Pamphilus and lover of Philumena, has heard of his proposed marriage to her, and urges him to defer it, if possible.

Just at this time, Simo, again negotiating with Chremes, secures his assent, and Charinus is now angry at the supposed treachery of Pamphilus, while Davus is reproached by his master for his untoward advice. As a last resort, he brings about an interview between Chremes and Mysis, whose story of Glycerium and her child occasions again a rupture between him and Simo. At this juncture, Crito, a citizen of Andros and next of kin to Chrysis, arrives, who clears up the history of Glycerium. She is recognized as Chremes' daughter, and his consent, with that of Simo, Pamphilus then obtains for their marriage.

The *Andrienne* of Michel Baron the French dramatist, and the *Conscious Lovers* of Steele, are close imitations of this play.

DIDASCALIA.

The now current text of the *didascaliae*, or *tituli*, prefixed to the plays of Terence is due to the *Emendationes* of Ant. Goveanus (Venice, 1567). In it various readings, both of the Bembine and the Calliopian text, are mixed up. Both are again founded on a more original and complete collection of notices, which seem to have been put together from stage-copies by grammarians of the seventh cent. u. c., who also, without doubt, availed themselves of the *commentarii magistratuum*, in which an accurate account was kept of all exhibitions made by the magistrates on the great annual festivals. T. The work of Varro, *De actionibus scenicis libri* (not now extant), was based on these critical labors of the grammarians, and is the real source of the *didascaliae* in their present form. That of the Andria is wanting in the best MSS., but has been preserved by Donatus in his preface to the play. Wr.

With the text of Fn., which is given here, that of Uh. and of Kz. agree. See *Jahrbücher*, 1865, p. 293; *Rheinisch. Museum*, xxi. 89.

LVDIS MEGALENSIBVS, a festival in honor of the great mother of the gods (Cybele, μεγάλη μήτηρ), whence it derived its name, celebrated for six days, beginning on the fourth of April. The statue of the goddess was brought to Rome from Pessinus in Phrygia, in 203 B. C.; but the regular celebration of the festival did not begin until the year 191, when a temple was dedicated to her. The third day was especially set apart for the performance of scenic plays, which were first introduced on this occasion, and were then exhibited on the Palatine in front of that temple, but afterwards also in the theatres. AEDILIB. CVRVLIB. The chief duties of the Aediles (whose office was established B. C. 494) were threefold: to act as police and sanitary commissioners, as inspectors of markets, and as superintendents of public lands, public buildings, and the public games. After the institution of the *curule* aedileship, B. C. 367, there were two *aediles plebeii* and two *aediles curules*, who had certain distinctive prerogatives; but, so far as is now known, there was no separation of duties between them, except that the charge of the celebration of the *Ludi Romani* and the *Ludi Megalesii* devolved upon the latter, and that of the *Ludi Plebeii* upon the former. EGERE, *brought out the play*, i. e. were the managers and actors. They contracted with the aediles for the performance of the play. L. AMBIVIVS TVRPIO, a celebrated *actor* mentioned by Cic. *De. Sen.*, 14, and Tac. *Dial. de Or.*, 20, and the manager of all the plays of Terence. L. ATILIVS of Praeneste is repeatedly mentioned in the *Didascaliae*; but it is almost certain that he belonged to a somewhat later period. Cf. *Havt. Didasc.* Wr. MODOS FECIT, *set the play to music.* The business of the *conductor* was to arrange the musical accompaniment so that a proper emphasis should be given to every part of the dialogue. Each kind of play had its proper accompaniment, and the intervals between the acts were also filled up with music. FLACCVS CLAVDI, sc. *servus* (not *libertus*, as is commonly assumed), of whom nothing is known, except that he wrote the music for all the plays of Terence. Wr. TIBIIS PARIBVS (also called *Serranis*. Cf. *Adelph. Didasc.*, note), i. e. pipes adapted to *the same mode.* These words depend on TOTA, sc. *fabula*. The principal modes were the Lydian, the Dorian, and the Phrygian, and they corresponded to the three species of tetrachord, or system of four sounds, which was the fundamental system in ancient music, the *species* of a system depending upon the order of succession of certain of its intervals. See Dict. Antiq., *s. Musica*. The TIBIA resembled the clarinet or flageolet, and the Romans generally employed a combination of two. Hence the terms *tibia dextra*, i. e. held in the right hand and playing the air, *tibia sinistra*, held in the left hand and used to play the bass. Ry. He, however, as well as other writers, admits that these phrases are involved in much obscurity, in consequence of our ignorance of the technical details of ancient music; and Wr. asserts that the exact meaning of this expression, *tibiis paribus*, is quite unknown. FACTA PRIMA, *holds the first place*, i. e. according to the usual order of Terence's plays. In the Bembine MS., which alone makes regular mention of the order, denoting it by *facta* I. (*prima* or *primo loco*), II., etc., it seems to be intended as *the order of composition*. T. M. Claudio MARCELLO, a grandson of the famous general of that name in the second Punic war, and himself three times consul; C. SVLPICIO Galo, distinguished for his Greek scholarship, his oratory, and his knowledge of astronomy, as well as in public life. Cos., i. e. in the year 166 B. C.

PROLOGVS.

1. Poeta. The term by which Terence designates himself in all his prologues, as an aesthetic poet in the spirit and sense of the Greeks. Kz. The first person occurs in **moneo**, in l. 22, because the advice tendered there is put into the mouth of the actor who spoke the prologue. **Quom.** Both **Quo**— and **Cu**— were in use from the later part of the republic till after the middle of the first century A. D., when quo began to give place to **quu**, the forms with c remaining also. **Quum** appears to be not earlier than the fourth century A. D. R. **Quom primum, etc.**, i. e. on making up his mind to write for the stage. Wr. On the tense of **adpulit**, see M. 338, b; Z. 506. For the use of **scribendum** in the sense of *composition*, especially of poetic composition, cf. Cic. *pro Archia*, 3; *Se ad scribendi studium contulit;* Hor. *Epist*. II. 1, 108: *Populus levis calet uno scribendi studio.* **2. Id negoti,** *so much of duty* only. Cf. l. 521, l. 953, and see M. 285, **b**; Z. 432. In the Augustan and prae-Augustan period substantives with stems in **io** formed the genitive singular in **i** single. R. 351; M. 37, Obs. 1; Al. 10, 4, **b**. **3. Quas — fabulas.** An instance of inverse attraction. Cf. l. 26, and see M. 319, Obs.; II. 445, 9; Al. 48, 3, *b;* A. 206, 4, b; B. 705, Exc. 3; G. 619, 2. **Fecisset,** i. e. any that *he might* hereafter *have written*. It does not imply that they had been already written at the time indicated by **credidit.** Pn. See M. 379; Z. 496, 5. **4. Intellegit** is one of the few compounds of *lego* which do not change the e into i. *Intelligo* is a form without authority. See R., p. 248. **5. In prologis, etc.** The prologues of Plautus (which, however, are prefixed to about half of his plays only, and the greater part of which are not genuine) generally included an explanation of the plot. This Terence gives in the first scene of each play, while his prologues are devoted to a defence of himself from the attacks of a rival. Wr. thinks *the Andria* was first brought out without any, and that this one was added for a second exhibition of the play (which may have been in B. C. 163). This view, however, is opposed by C. Dziatzko and others. The poet is evidently introducing his comedy for the first time to his audience, and the time which must have elapsed since its composition (for Caecilius, to whom it was first read, died B. C. 168) was sufficiently long for the play to become well known in literary circles, and to have received the adverse criticisms which occasioned the writing of this prologue. **Scribundis.** The older form of the gerundive (and the gerund), probably for an earlier in ond, which is common in inscriptions to the middle of the first century B. C.; in Plautus, Terence, and Sallust; and after i, and in *gerundus* and *ferundus*, in the MSS. of Caesar, Cicero, and Livy. R. **Operam.** The accusative is found, according to M., *occasionally*, according to Z. *frequently*, according to Wr. *ordinarily*, with *uti*, *frui*, and their compounds in archaic Latin, in the comic poets, and some few prose writers. M. 265, Obs. 2: Z. 466. Cf. Phorm., l. 413; *Ut meretricem ubi abusus sis;* Plaut. Bacch. II. 3, 126; Trin. III. 2, 56. *Utor* occurs with the accusative in Terence only once, in Adelph., l. 815; with the ablative at least ten times. Cf. Andr., l. 202; Havt., l. 217. For the usage with *fruor*, *fungor*, in Terence, see Adelph., l. 464, and note. *Potior* occurs in at least three instances with the accusative. Cf. Adelph., 871, 876; Cic. *Tusc.* Disp. II. 37. But Py. remarks that it is chiefly so used in later writers; once in Lucretius (III. 1038). M. 265, Obs. 2; Z. 466. For the more common use of the ablative with these verbs, see M. 265, Obs. 1. **Abutitur,** *wastes, consumes.* This compound may have either of two meanings, *uses up* or *misspends.* Py. and Pn. give it the former here, Ds. the latter. Wr. thinks a Roman would feel *the two* meanings at once in a passage like this. **6. Qui,** ablative = *quo*, and denotes purpose. Cf. M. 440, Obs. 5; H. 497; Al. 64, 1, a. For the use of this form in classic prose, see M. 86, Obs. 2; Z. 133, note. **7. Poetae,** sc. Luscius Lavinius, a comic poet, a contemporary and rival of Terence. The name of only one of his plays is known, and only two lines of his poetry are extant. He is referred to also in the prologue of the *Havt.*, the *Eunuchus*, and the *Phormio*, but never mentioned by name by Terence. **8. Attendite.** So Fn., Uh., and Wr., following Don. It occurs also in the prologues of the *Eunuchus*, *Phormio*, and *Hecyra.* The reading of the MSS., attested by Priscian and adopted by Kz., is *advortite;* and Wr. admits that in cases like this it is almost impossible to decide what the poet really wrote. **9. Menander,** b. B. C. 342, d. B. C. 291, at Athens. He wrote more than a hundred comedies, but only fragments of them are extant. See Introduction, p. 137. **10. Qui — nouerit, etc.** It is not improbable that Menander's Περινθία was only an earlier or later treatment of the same subject as the 'Ανδρία; in other words, the former was probably rewritten in the latter. Wr. **11. Non ita dissimili,** *not so very unlike.* **Ita** is elliptical, sc. *ut quis putet.* See Hand's Tursel., III., p. 491. **Argumento,** *the subject-matter* or *plot;* **oratione,** *the form* and elaboration of the thought; **stilo,** *expression,* the form in which the thoughts (*oratio*) are embodied in words. Kz. Cf. *Havt.,* Prol. 46; *Phormio,* Prol. 5: *Tenui oratione et scriptura levi.* **13. Quae conuenere, etc.** Don. states that Terence took the first scene of his *Andria* from the Περινθία of Menander; and Wr. and Ihne find evidence that the characters Charinus and Byrrhia were taken from the same play, and that therefore all the scenes in which they appear must have been inserted into the original plot of Menander's Andrian. Py. and others, however, think that the materials left are not sufficient for determining the comparative obligations of Terence to these two plays. **16. Contaminari,** *mingled together, blended;* here, as always in Terence, in its original sense. Cf. *Havt.,* Prol. 17; *Eunuchus* III. 5, 4. It does not occur in Plautus, and only once in Lucretius (III. 883). The meaning, *defile by contact,* is later. Py. **17. Faciuntne.** Most editors have considered **ne** the affirmative particle, but that stands only at the beginning of a sentence, and in the best writers is found only with the personal pronouns. Arn.; Z. 360. The sentence is interpreted as a question by Fn., Uh., Wr., and by Kz.,who quotes a similar instance of Oxymoron from Menander, in A. Meineke's *Fragm. comic. Graec.* **18. Naeuium — Ennium** are mentioned in the true chronological order, as Ritschl has proved. See Dict. Biog., PLAUTUS. Cn. **Naeuius,** who lived in the third century B. C., was both an epic and dramatic poet. Of his works, the earliest of which were written in B. C. 234, and among which were some of the species of comedy called *togata,* only short fragments are extant. Though his antiquated style did not suit the fastidious taste of the Augustan age, he was ever a favorite with the admirers of the old school of Roman poetry; and the fact that he was so largely copied by later poets, particularly Ennius and Virgil, is a proof of his genius and originality. Naevius belonged to the plebeian party, and to the conservative or *Italian* faction in literature, and was a personal friend of Cato the Censor, though considerably older. His attacks upon the aristocracy in his plays led to his exile to Utica, where he died B. C. 202. T. Maccius **Plautus**, b. about 254 B. C., and d. 184 B. C. His twenty comedies are the earliest productions of Latin literature extant. See Introduction, p. 136. **Ennius**, b. B. C. 239, d. B. C. 169, an intimate friend of Scipio Africanus Major, the greatest literary genius of his age, and by his countrymen regarded as the father and prince of Roman poetry; but of his writings, epic and dramatic, only fragments have been preserved. 19. **Auctores,** *models.* Cf. Cic. in Verr. II. 5, 26 : *Unum cedo auctorem tui facti ; Unius profer exemplum ;* Hor. Sat. I. 4, 122 : *Habes auctorem quo facias hoc.* 21. **Istorum.** On the contemptuous force of the pronoun, see M. 486; Z. 701. **Obscuram.** Here, not merely an *industry not securing publicity,* but also *obtaining no approbation from the public.* Kz. On the first meaning, cf. Cic. De Orat. I. 14, 59 : *Sed ex obscuriore aliqua scientia sit promendum.* 22. **Porro,** here in its original sense of *henceforth.* Cf. Havt., l. 159. The general idea is that of distance, here applied to time. Py. 23. **Noscant,** i. e. hear their misdeeds revealed in public. Wr. 24. **Fauete.** See Lex. s. v. II. A. ; and cf. Hor. O. III., 1, 2. **Adeste, etc.** Parry and others take these expressions in their technical juridical sense : *Be candid umpires and investigate the matter, that you may arrive at a correct decision.* Wr. finds in them an allusion to the treatment the *Hecyra* had received, on the first performance of which the audience left the theatre, thus condemning without even taking the trouble of seeing it. Hence, **adeste,** sc. during the performance; **cognoscite,** sc. before passing judgment upon it. 25. **Relicuom.** The vowel **O**, after **V** (consonant or vowel), was retained till the Augustan age, and later; though after other letters it had usually changed to **U**. R. 26. **De integro,** i. e. *hereafter.* See Lex. s. v. I. B. 27. **Exigendae.** See Lex. s. v. I. B. **Prius,** sc. *quam spectentur.*

ACTVS I.

This act explains the "situation" at the point where the real action begins, and in such a way that it appears to be part of the action itself. The chief character, Pamphilus, is introduced, and his connection with *the Andrian* hinted at in the narration by Simo to his freedman, Sosia, of Pamphilus' mode of life, of his accidental disclosure of an interest in Glycerium, and of his own plan for ascertaining his son's real intention respecting her, and for bringing about the marriage with Philumena. In accomplishing this, he desires Sosia's aid. The latter does not appear farther in the play at all. The art of this scene has been the admiration of ancient and modern critics alike. See Cic. *De Orat.* II. 80.

28. Vos — abite, addressed to the servants, who then withdraw. **Istaec,** sc. *obsonia,* just bought at the market. **29. Dum,** from *dium,* accusative of *dius,* lit. *the day long, a space of time, while;* but in colloquial lang. appended to certain imperatives and interjections as an intensive enclitic, *Now, Pray.* See Lex. *s. v.* The verb is sometimes omitted. See l. 184. **Paucis,** sc. *verbis.* Cf. l. 536. **Dictum puta,** i. e. I understand what you would say. **30. Curentur,** *prepared, cooked,* a very common use of this verb. Kz. **Haec,** i. e. things with which **mea ars,** sc. *as a cook,* has to do; sc. *istaec,* l. 28. **32. Istac arte,** i. e. *that skill of yours.* Notice the carefulness with which the demonstratives of each person are used throughout the play. M. 485, 486; Z. 127. That of the second person has here a contemptuous force. See l. 21, note. **33. Eis,** explained in the next line. **35. Ut,** here in its original meaning. See M. 372, **a,** Obs. **36. Clemens,** *mild, easy.* **38. Seruibas.** So Uh., Fn., Kz., and Wr., though the MS. reading is *seruiebas.* The e of the imperfect suffix **eba** is in most i verbs not unfrequently absent in the earlier language. R. See also M. 115, b; Al. 30, 4, *a;* H. 239, 1; A. 162, 2; B. 325; G. 191, 4. **Liberaliter.** See Lex. *s. r.* **40. Haud muto factum,** *I do not change what I have done,* i. e. do not regret the deed. **42. Gratum** (= *acceptum*) — **gratiam.** Notice the play upon the words which gives an additional point to the extreme politeness of Sosia's answer. Wr. **Aduorsum te,** *in your eyes.* **44. Inmemori.** A conjectural reading adopted by Fn., Uh., Kz., and Wr., instead of the MS. reading, *inmemoris.* Cf. Livy XXIII. 35: *Ne qua exprobratio cuiquam.* As to the construction, see M. 244, **b,** Obs. 5; H. 392, I.; Al. 51, 6, c; A. 222, Rem. 8; G. 355. **45. Quin.** For the etymology and meaning, see M. 375, Obs. 4; Z. 542. Its use with the imperative may be explained by an ellipsis, e. g. *Tell me, why don't you?* **Quid est.** The indicative sometimes occurs in dependent questions in Terence as well as in Plautus; in the later poets rarely. M. 356, Obs. 3; Z. 553. **46. Praedico,** i. e. before entering into further details. Wr. **47. Quas** = *quales,* here. **48. Quor** originated from *Qua re,* and was afterwards softened to *Cur.* Corssen. **51. Excessit.** For the tense, see M. 338, **b**; Z. 507, *b.* **Ephebis.** At Athens the young men were called Ἔφηβοι, from the age of eighteen to twenty, during which time, after passing an examination and taking an oath of allegiance to their country, they were employed as guards on the coast and frontier. They were then admitted to all the rights and duties of a citizen. Cf. Plaut. *Merc.,* l. 61: *Exire ex ephebis;* Cic. *Pro. Arch.* 3, *ex pueris excessit.* **52. Liberius,** sc. than before. **Antea** occurs only here in Terence, and never in Plautus. Wr. **53.**

Scire, *understand;* **Noscere,** *gain any acquaintance with.* **55. Quod, etc.** Simo had digressed to remark upon the condition of untried boyhood, and now resumes his story as if no interruption had occurred. **Plerique omnes,** *by far the greater number.* See Z. 109, Note. **Adulescentuli.** Notice the form, expressive of their inexperience. **57. Alere,** in apposition to **studium,** instead of the more common genitive of the gerund. M. 286, Obs. 2; 419; Z. 659. **Ad philosophos,** sc. *animum adiungant.* **58. Nil.** The accusative is always found with *studeo* in Terence. Py. Plautus also has *has res studeant* (*Mil. Glor.* 1437) and *illum student.* (*Truc.* II. 3, 16). Respecting the usage, see M. 229, a; Z. 385, and Lex. *s. Studeo,* I., β. **Praeter cetera** expresses essentially the same idea as **egregie,** but adds to the force of it. **60. Gaudebam,** *I began to rejoice.* **61. Ne quid nimis,** a translation of the proverb μηδὲν ἄγαν, ascribed by some to Pittacus, by Aristotle to Chilon. Py. **62. Omnes.** Nom., *all liked his ways.* Wr. But Kz. regards it as accusative, *omnis: He easily endured and agreed with all.* On the construction of the infinitives, see M. 392; Z. 599, Note. **63. Quibus erat quomque,** Tmesis. M. 87, Obs. 2; H. 704, IV. 3; A. 323, 4, (5); B. 1381; G. 693. **64. Aduorsus — illis,** repeats for emphasis in a negative form the idea already expressed. Kz. **65. Illis.** The reading of the MSS. Uh., Kz., and Py. *Aliis,* an emendation of Bentley, is preferred by Wr., who thinks **illis** almost without any sense at all. **68. Obsequium, etc.** Py. remarks that Sosia is a dealer in proverbs, and that this one has been laboriously traced to Bias. It is also quoted by Cic. *De Amicit.* 24, and Quintil. VIII. 5. **69. Abhinc.** Generally used of past time. It is also followed by the accusative in *Hecyra,* l. 822; *Phormio,* l. 421; Cic. *pro Rosc.* 13. See M. 235, Obs. 2; Z. 478. **70. Huc uiciniae.** So Uh., Fn., Wr., Py. For the construction, see H. 396, III. 4; Al. 50, 2, d; A. 212, Rem. 4, Note 3; G. 371, 4. Kz. prefers the MS. reading, *huic.* **71. Cognatorum,** used not in the strict sense attached to it by Roman law, but as a translation of ἀγκιστεύς, or *nearest* (unmarried) *kinsman,* whose duty it was, by the Athenian law, either to marry an orphan girl or provide her with a dowry. See Dict. Antiqq., *Matrimonium,* and Maine's *Ancient Law,* ch. v. Cf. a similar law in the Mosaic code: Numbers xxxvi. 8. **72. Aetate integra,** *in the bloom of youth.* **74. Primo,** preferred by Fn., Kz., and Wr., to the MS. reading, *Primum,* on the ground that it emphasizes the idea of time. See Hand, *Tursell.* iv., p. 556. **Duriter,** *with hard work.* **75. Uictum quaeritans,** *eking out a scanty livelihood.* Py. Notice the force of the frequentative. **77. Vnus — alter,** denotes a quite limited but indefinite number. Kz. **79. Condicionem.** See

Lex. *s. v.* II. **Quaestum,** here in a bad sense. See Lex. *s. v.* I., B.
81. **Esset,** *dine, feast,* from *Edo.* See l. 89. **82. Captus est,** may be
a metaphor derived from the contests of the *retiarii,* but is more probably a merely general expression. Py. **83. Habet,** *he has got a blow.*
See Lex. *s. v.* II., L. **Seruolos,** i. e. the small pages who used to wait
on parties at dinner. Wr. **85. Sodes** for *si audes;* the latter word
probably, not for *audies,* as the Lexicon gives it, but from *audeo* in its
primitive sense as formed from the root **av,** whence *aveo, avidum esse.*
Kz. See also Corssen I. 631, and cf. Cic. *Orat.* 45. **88. Sumbolam**
was the contribution paid by each guest to the common expenses of a
feast. The pure Latin term was *collecta.* **91. Quicquam,** *in any
respect,* adverbial accus. See M. 229; Z. 677, *in fin.* By some it is
taken with **nil** as a redundant expression = *nihil,* or *non quicquam,*
and as corroborative of this view, Eunuchus, l. 226, is referred to:

*Hoc nemo fuit
Minus ineptus, magis severus quisquam nec magis continens.*

But Pn. remarks that in this case the words are in parallel clauses,
i. e. *nemo quisquam* is not = *nemo,* but *nemo* is followed up and repeated
in (*non*) *quisquam.* **Spectatum,** tested; a metaphor from the use of
the word for testing gold. Cf. Cic. *De Off.* II. 11; Ovid *Trist.* I. 5, 25.
93. Conflictatur, *comes into collision with,* according to Wr. and Py.,
alludes to the same. But the passages quoted of its use point rather to
violent collision. **Ingeniis,** *characters,* put for "*hominibus tali ingenio
praeditis;*" *ita tamen ut ingenium ponatur pro indole, natura.* Drakenborch. **Eius modi,** sc. as Chrysis and her lovers. **94. Ea re,** i. e.
amore. **95. Habere — modum,** *to regulate.* See Lex. *s. Modus,* I., B. 1.
97. Dicere, laudare. See l. 62, note. **Fortunas,** *good fortune.*
100. Vltro, i. e. *over and above* what was expected or usual;
not only was willing, but took the initiative. It indicates that in
ordinary circumstances this was never done by the father of the
maiden. **102. Despondi,** is used of him through whose solemn promise
a betrothal is effected. Generally, this depended upon the consent of
the bride's father, but in this case upon the father of Pamphilus. Kz.
103. Quor — fiant. So Fn. and Wr. Cf. l. 529, 542. **Igitur** is omitted, and *verae* inserted, by Uh. and Kz., on the ground that this reading
has the best MS. authority, and that the other is too bald. **104. In
diebus paucis,** *within those few days.* M. 276, Obs. 4; II. 426, 2; Al.
55, 1, a; A. 253, Rem. 5; B. 951; G. 393. **106. Ei metui,** sc. *some
evil.* **107. Frequens.** M. 300, b; Z. 682. **109. Conlacrumabat,** in

the opinion of some editors here put for the simple *lacrumo*. The force of this preposition *is* often partially lost in compound verbs, though there is even then, perhaps, the general sense of completeness or abundance. Here, however, the word may mean *would weep together with* them. Py. **110. Consuetudinis,** *acquaintance.* **111. Tam familiaritur,** *with so much friendly feeling* (of sorrow). Ds. **112.** Cf. the lines in the opening scene of Shakspeare's *Twelfth Night*:

> "O, she that hath a heart of that fine frame
> To pay this debt of love but to a brother,
> How will she love, when the rich, golden shaft
> Hath killed the flock of all affections else
> That live in her!"

114. Multis, sc. *verbis.* **115. Eius causa,** i. e. *humani et mansueti animi,* sc. of Pamphilus. Pn. **116. Etiam,** *as yet, even now.* **117. Ecfertur. imus.** These words are often used in reference to funerals. See Lex. *s. Effero* I., B. 1, and cf. Cic. *ad* Attic. xvi. 1; Nep. *Attic.* 22, Livy I. 59; Hor. *Sat.* II. 5, 85. The dead were burned outside the city walls. On the elegant brevity of the expression here, cf. the remark of Cicero, *De Orat.* II. 80 : *Quamquam hoc ipsum 'ecfertur, imus,' concisum est ita ut non brevitati servitum sit, sed magis venustati. Quod si nihil fuisset nisi 'in ignem impositast,' tamen res tota cognosci facile potuisset,* etc. **118. Unam,** *one in particular.* Retaining the original signification of the singular, it serves to make prominent what is seen to be the only one of its kind. Cf. Plaut. *Pseud.* IV. 1, 38 : *Ibidem una aderit mulier lepida,* etc. Kz. So also with the superlative frequently. See M. 310, Obs. 2; Z. 691. Wr. asserts that it is here little more than the indefinite article of modern languages, as sometimes elsewhere in the conversational language of the Romans. But in a note in his *Aulularia,* he remarks that nearly all the Plautian passages would also admit of a more exact explanation, in which *unus* would still have some meaning beyond a mere indefinite article, e. g. *Aul.* 563 : *cadum unum, only one bottle.* **119. Forma** is *the shape* and general bearing ; **Uoltu,** *the countenance,* or expression. Simo does not allow himself to be hindered in the flow of his narrative by the interruption of his freedman, but goes on with his description of the lovely appearance of the young maiden. Kz. **122. Quae quom.** So Fn. and Wr. *Quia tum,* which has MS. authority, is preferred by Kz. In either case, Simo is represented as stating two reasons which induced him to inquire after the maiden. Uh. adopts still another MS. reading, *Quae tum,* with a colon after **Visast. 123. Liberali.** Cf. Eunuchus, 473 :

liberalis facies. **Pedisequas,** the lowest class of slaves; here used more loosely in the sense of followers. Py. **125. Percussit,** *made me suspicious,* sc. *id quod aiunt, sororem eam esse Chrysidis.* The repeated form **attat,** *ah, ah,* is used to mark a sudden discovery. Key, 1445, e. **Hoc** — **est,** *this explains that matter.* **126. Hinc** — **lacrumae,** passed into a proverb. Cf. Cic. *Pro Caelio,* 25; Horace *Epist.* I. 19, 41; Juv. 1, 168. **128. Sepulcrum,** here the place where the body was burned. *Sepelio,* like the Greek θάπτω, has a generic sense, and includes all the various modes of funeral, whether by burial or by burning. Py. **131. Ibi tum,** pleonastic. **134. Is perditum,** a form of expression not uncommon in the older writings, but later sparingly employed by the historians, and carefully avoided by the orators and grammarians of the classical period. It gives emphasis to the idea of intention. Kz. See Z. 669; H. 569; Al. 74, 1; A. 276, II., Rem. 2; G. 436. **136. Reiecit.** Wr. refers to Lucretius: *In gremium se reicit aeterno devictus volnere amoris.* **Quam familiariter,** an elliptical expression; in full — *tam fam. quam potuit.* Then the original construction being lost sight of, the *quam* becomes a mere intensive enhancing the meaning of the adverb. Pn. **138.** For the tense of **diceret,** see H. 486, 4; Al. 59, 3, c; A. 260, Rem. 2; G. 252. **141. Honesta,** *specious.* **143. Dederit.** The MS. reading, retained by Uh., Kz., and Wr. It states only a supposed case, while **tulit** states a fact. Fn., however, prefers *dedit.* **Damnum** originally is = *damenum, δαόμενον, what is paid as a fine,* hence *loss.* Wr. *Damnum dare* is the usual Latin of the old Jurisconsults. **Damnum** has alone in view the material loss — damage to property; **malum,** the bodily injury, as frequently in the language of the Jurists. So Don. correctly remarks: *Damnum rei est, malum ipsius hominis.* Kz. **145. Comperisse,** sc. *se.* The subject of the infin. is often omitted in the loose language of the comic poets wherever it may be easily understood. Wr. See M. 401. **146. Pro uxore habere,** *treats like his lawful wife.* Wr. **Peregrinam,** *courtesan.* **Sedulo,** *expressly, earnestly.* Wr. favors the meaning *with sincerity,* endorsing the etymology of Don. and Doed., *se* (= *sine*) *dolo.* But the origin of the word is doubtful, partly on account of the meaning of *sedulus* itself, partly because the old formula always was *se dolo malo.* W. & R. **149. Ibi,** here of time. Adverbs of time and place are frequently interchanged in Plautus and Terence. Py. **Gnatum.** See M. 479, d; Z. 774. The freedman very properly leaves the verb to be supplied, since it would not become him to suggest the manner in which his master should treat the son of the family. Kz. **150. Ad. obiurgandum,** a negligent construction, frequently used by Livy for the objective genitive. Wr. Cf. l. 158; M. 417, Obs. 3. The use of the case expressing motion towards, perhaps brings out more clearly the object or design. Pn. **Qui cedo?** Sosia is represented as egregiously stupid; he never understands the motive of an action except when he is expressly informed of it: but his stupidity gives the poet an excellent opportunity of unfolding to us the innermost thoughts of Simo's heart. At the same time, honest Sosia's stupidity invites us to compare it with the sharp wit and shrewdness subsequently displayed by Davus. Wr. **151.** Supply *diceret*. Cf. l. 138. **Praescripsti.** On the form, see M. 113, Obs. 3; Z. 160, 2; and Kz., note. **152. Adest,** sc. *tempus*. **155. Nolet.** So Fn., Uh., and Wr., on the ground that Simo firmly believes his son will refuse to marry, and that therefore the future is more appropriate than *nolit*. The latter, however, is the MS. reading, and is retained by Kz., who thinks Simo intends to intimate only the possibility of his son's unwillingness, and who refers to l. 165, 568. **156. Ea primum — iniuriast,** *that offence on his part is the first*, etc. For the use of **ab**, cf. Havt., l. 158. Livy XXVII. 5; lit. *from his direction.* **157. Id,** the object of **operam do** = *ago*, Wr.; adverbial accus. defining the manner of the verbal notion **operam do.** Pn. See M. 229, 2; Z. 385. **160. Consumat,** *may exhaust*. **164. Mala mens, etc.** The gradually increasing anger of the old Simo, not towards his son, but towards Davus, which is disclosed even in the harsh mode of expression in which his ill-humor only throws out words in a proverbial form, is capitally exhibited by the poet. Kz. **Quem — sensero.** A common aposiopesis in case of threats. Cf. Virg. *Aen.* 1, 135: *Quos ego—;* V. 195. See M. 479, Obs. 6; Z. 758. **167. Confore,** sc. *id.* This verb occurs only in the future infinitive. II. 297, III. 2; Al. 29, 1; A. 183, Rem. 1; B. 445. **171. Eamus — intro,** usually assigned to Sosia. But Wr. thinks more appropriately to Simo, as it would be fitting that *he* should declare the interview ended, while one of *inferior* station would more naturally *follow* than go in advance. **Nunciam.** In Plautus and Terence, the *i* of *iam* must always be pronounced as a pure vowel when following *nunc;* this shows that *nunciam* is actually one word, just as much as *etiam, quoniam, uspiam,* and sometimes we find *nunciam* written together in the MSS. Brix.

ACTVS II.

The beginning of the real action of the play, with Simo's re-appearance after directing the preparations for the pretended wedding-feast; his conversation with Davus respecting the suspected amour of Pamphilus; his own intention of a marriage for him immediately, and the punishment the slave may expect if he devises any scheme to prevent it. Soliloquy of Davus, perplexed between fear of the father and devotion to the son; his mention of the connection of Pamphilus with Glycerium, and of the story of her origin, which foreshadows the ultimate solution of the plot without actually disclosing it. Soliloquy of Pamphilus, in a strait between his father's unexpected command and Chremes' supposed consent to his marriage with Philumena, and his own betrothal to Glycerium. His interview with Mysis, who represents Glycerium's fear of desertion by him; reiteration of his pledge of fidelity to her, formerly made to Chrysis.

172. Nolit, sc. *ducere.* **175. Eri semper lenitas.** The sense of the passage, which refers not to the continual fear of Davus, but to the indulgent disposition of Simo, and the position of the adverb between two words closely connected grammatically, require that these words be regarded as one idea. Kz. Cf. Plautus *Pers.* III. 1, 57 : *Non tu nunc hominum mores vides ;* Cic. *in L. Pis.* 9, 21 : *Discessu tum meo, etc. ; Philipp.* III. 6, 15 : *Cujus etiam natura pater, etc. ;* Virg. Aen. I. 198; and see Nägelsbach *Latein-Stilistik.* Wr. also gives to **semper** the force of an adjective, like the Greek idiom. Py. and others think it more natural to connect it with **verebar.** See M. 301, c, Obs. 2 ; Z. 262, Note; H. 583. **178. Neque — tulit,** i. e. did not appear to. **179. Faciet,** sc. *verbum.* **Magno malo,** generally implies corporal punishment in the comic writers. Wr. **180. Nec,** here not the mere negative, but = *nihil etiam.* Kz. Cf. Havt., l. 186. **Duci.** See Lex., s. v. II., B. 2, b. **181. Oscitantis opprimi,** *should be caught off our guard.* The art by which Simo is made to hear enough to alarm him, and to irritate him against his son, is cleverly indicated here and in many other parts of the play. Py. **183. Carnufex,** i. e. *carnifice dignus.* Wr. **184. Dum.** See l. 29, note. **185. Scilicet,** used ironically. Z. 345, note. *Oh, no doubt the whole town is interested in that.* Cf. Cicero's quotation of the sentence, *Ad Att.* XIII. 34 : *De quo quae fama sit scribes : Id populus curat scilicet ! Non me hercule arbitror.* In order not to commit himself, Davus ridicules the idea that Pamphilus' love interested anybody but his father. Kz. Py. thinks this sentence was spoken aside, and that this is the reason why Simo asks : (186.) **Hocine agis?** For the meaning of this expression, see Lex. s. *Ago* III. 7. On the use of **istuc** instead of **hoc** in the reply, see l. 32, note. **188. Dum — tulit.** *While the proper time for that matter permitted it.* Py. Cf. *Eunuchus*, l. 621 : *Ad eam rem tempus non erat.* Pn. prefers to connect **ad eam rem** with **tulit. 189. Hic dies,** etc., sc. since it was the one assigned for the marriage. **190. Siue.** M. 442, b; with **Aequomst — oro,** a

sarcastic epanorthosis of **postulo**: *or if I may venture so far.* Pn.
Uiam, *the right way.* **191. Hoc quid sit,** sc. *miror.* Cf. *Phormio,* l.
106: *Miror quid siet.* Kz. supplies *quaero* or *dic mihi.* **192. Ita aiunt,**
denotes an unwilling assent. Kz., Py. Cf. *Hart.,* l. 211; a general
answer, as if he did not understand the special application of the general remark made by Simo. Wr. **Magistrum.** See Lex. s. v. II. **193.
Ad — adplicat,** *generally influences for the worse.* **194. Non: Dauos
— Oedipus.** The dissembling Davus pretends that Simo seems to him
to have spoken enigmatically. As to the meaning, cf. Plaut. *Poen.* I.
3, 34: *Nam isti quidem hercle orationi Oedipo Opus coniectorest, qui
Sphingi interpres fuit.* Kz. **195. Nempe.** M. 435, Obs. 4, *in fin.;* Z.
278. **196. Hodie** does not limit the threat to this day, but gives point
to it. Kz. **199. Pistrinum,** a *grist-mill* worked either by animals or
by slaves. For a description of it, see Dict. Antiqq., p. 765. **200. Ea
— omine,** *On this condition and with this good prospect.* Kz. **201.
Callide,** *thoroughly, excellently,* sc. *intellego.* **203. Passus sim.** For
the mood and tense, see Z. 527; M. 350, b. **204. Bona uerba,** *words
of good omen,* i. e. *abstain from words of ill omen;* a common formula
derived originally from sacrificial language. Kz. remarks: The phrase
is here used derisively, and Simo regards it so, as his reply shows.
Edico. So Fn. and Wr., who call it an *excellent emendation* of Guyetus,
receiving full confirmation from l. 495. The MS. reading, *Sed dico,* is
retained by Uh., and by Kz., who remarks that it gives good sense, and
is corroborated by the explicit testimony of Nonius. **205. Neque tu
haud dices.** Instead of **haud,** most MSS. have *hoc;* but Don., in two
different notes, refers to *haud dicas* (*dices*) as the true reading. This
is the only instance of this kind in Terence where the two negatives do
not cancel each other; in Plautus at least five passages occur. Kz.
See also M. 460, Obs. 2; Z. 754, Note, *in fin.;* Hand's *Tursell,* III.,
p. 32.

206. Enim uero introduces a firm conviction with great emphasis
and strong asseveration. Kz., Z. 348, note. **Segnitiae,** *ad agendum;*
socordiae, *ad considerandum.* Don. On the construction. M. 211.
210. Illum—huius. M. 485, a; Z. 700. **211. Uerba dare,** frequently
used in comic writers in this sense. See Lex. s. *Verbum* II., B. **212.
Seruat,** for the compound *observat.* Cf. *Hart.,* l. 592. **213.** Fn. and
Wr., following Bentley, omit **perii** and insert *quam* before **lubitum.**
The text follows the MS. reading retained also by Uh. and Kz. See
note of the latter on this line. The use of the tense, which represents
completed action in future time in these verbs, makes the narration
more vivid than the simple future. Pn. As to the frequency of this

usage and the occurrence of the tense in both clauses, see M. 340, Obs. 2 and 4; Z. 511. **214. Quo — iniuria** = *cuius causae iure aut iniuria.* **Quo** appears sometimes to have the meaning *or* = *ve.* Arn. **215. Ad haec — etiam** corresponds to **primum** above, instead of *Deinde.* **216. Si — siue** is the regular construction in the language of the comic poets, never *sive — sive.* Wr. **218. Amentium — amantium.** Similar instances of *paronomasia* are frequent in the comic poets, though much more so in Plautus than in Terence, and are occasionally found in other writers. They are employed to produce a comic effect, sometimes a poetic effect. Cf. 1. 378, 386, 431. **219. Tollere.** See Lex. s. v. I., A. 2. It was for the father of a child to determine whether it should be recognized as his own and brought up, which he did by the symbolical action of raising it from the ground. Py. **221. Ciuem Atticam esse hanc.** If this could be proved, Pamphilus would be legally bound to marry her. Cf. 1. 780. Citizenship at Athens depended on having been born in lawful wedlock of parents who were both citizens. See Dict. Antiqq., *s. Civitas.* **221. Hinc.** So Fn. and Wr., following Bentley; and Wr. considers it quite indispensable for the sense of the passage. Uh. and Kz. retain the MS. reading on the ground that the first part of the line renders the insertion of this word unnecessary. **223. Eiectam,** *cast ashore.* **224. Recepisse.** A return to the Oratio Obliqua. **225.** The rejection of this line by Bentley, as a superfluous gloss of the word **fabulae,** though it has full MS. authority, is endorsed by Wr. on metrical grounds. Uh., Kz., and others, however, retain it, finding no difficulty with the sense or the metre. **Atqui,** substituted for *atque,* the MS. reading, by Kz. See M. 437, **c,** Obs.; 433, Obs. 2; Z. 349. **226. Ab ea.** The name of a person or a pronoun is not unfrequently put for his or her residence. Cf. *Haut.,* l. 510. **Me,** sc. *conferam.* On the ellipsis of the verb, see M. 479, **d;** Z. 774. **Ad forum.** The usual lounging place of idle young men, where the news of the day was most likely to be heard. Cf. Plaut. *Captiv.* III. 1, 18: *Accessi ad adulescentes in foro.* **227. De hac re,** an adjunct of **imprudentem.** Kz. It is omitted by Fn. and Wr. on account of the supposed necessity of the metre.

234. Exanimatum, *out of breath.* **Siet,** the old form, frequently found in the comic poets and early inscriptions, of which *sit* is a contraction. The ie represents the modal suffix **ya** appended to the root es, thus: (e) s — ya — t (i). Peile, p. 50. **235. Numquid nam.** See M. 451, **b,** *in fin.;* Z. 351, Note. **Turba** = *perturbatio,* sc. exhibited by Pamphilus; a very rare use of the word. Pn. Cf. *Eunuchus,* l. 723. **236. Factu aut inceptu.** So Fn. and Wr., following Bentley.

Kz. thinks this reading logically untenable, because what it was inhuman to do, it was surely also inhuman to begin; while it might be left uncertain whether his father's procedure was to be regarded as an accomplished action or a mere beginning. He therefore, with Uh., retains the MS. reading *factum aut inceptum*. **237. Pro — fidem.** See Lex. s. *Fides*, II., B. 2, and on the construction, M. 236, Obs. 1; Z. 402, and cf. l. 240. **Hoc.** So Uh. and Fn.; *haec* is the reading of most MSS., and retained by Kz. and Wr. See M. 313, Obs.; Z. 371. **238. Decrerat.** The pluperfect gives a vigor to the narrative, and helps to throw back the events alluded to so as to allow the present perplexities of Pamphilus to stand out more prominently, and to make his father's concealment of his intention seem still worse. Py. **239. Communicatum,** sc. *ab illo esse.* See M. 373, Obs. 1; Z. 625. This clause adds to the preceding the idea that his father was under obligation not only to have notified, but also, according to the custom of the times, to have consulted him about the marriage. Kz. **242. Inmutatum,** *unchanged*, a kind of oxymoron. Kz. **245. Esse.** See M. 399; Z. 609. **Inuenustum,** *unfortunate in love*. **248. Facta — omnia,** *everything firmly concluded* ; a legal phrase. Pn. Cf. Cic. *in Cat.* III. 6, 15. **249. Repudiatus repetor.** See l. 218, note. **250. Aliquid monstri,** *some deformity*, far more expressive than *aliquid monstrum*. Wr. Cf. *Hart.*, l. 1061. **257. Ineptam saltem,** *though it were ever so inappropriate.* **258. Facerem.** For the tense, M. 347, b, Obs. 2; Z. 525. **259. Aliquid,** *something (however unavailing).* Wr. **262. Patris pudor.** *Respect for my father.* **263. Quae — quomque.** See l. 63, note. **Ego ut aduorser,** sc. *fieri potest?* Notice the emphatic position of the pronoun. H. 602, III. 1; Z. 356; A. 279, 3, b; G. 675. For the construction of the verb, see Z. 609 *in fin.;* H. 495, 2, 2); Al. 70, 4, c; A. 270, Rem. 2; G. 560. **265. Ipsa,** sc. Glycerium. **Aduorsum hunc,** i. e. *face to face with him.* Wr. **266. Momento,** *impulse;* lit. *a particle sufficient to turn the scale.* **267. Agit.** See Lex. s. v. III. 1, c. **268. Laborat e dolore,** *she is weighed down with grief.* If the reference were to *bodily pain*, the plural *dolores* would have been used. Py. The latter meaning, however, Kz. and Wr. think is required by the connection, and that the former is too vague, and render **atque** *and in addition.* **271. Propter me,** *through me.* **273. Habuerim.** Notice the change of mood in expressing his own feelings from the indicative in **credidit,** which states a fact external to himself. M. 350, b; Z. 528, Note 1. Pn., however, takes **habuerim** in a concessive sense, *though I have*, etc., on the ground that **quae credidit** and **quam habuerim** are not coordinate clauses, but the former an adjunct of **illam,** the latter of the whole sentence **ogo — sinam.** **274. Bene** has an intellectual, **pudice** a moral, reference. On the use of **eductum,** see Lex. *s. v.* **276. Uerear.** So Uh. and Fn. According to Kz. and Wr., the best MSS. read *Uercor.* **279.** The substantives of this line form a climax, and correspond in inverse order with the adjectives of the preceding. **Consuetudo,** lit. *the customary manners and usages of society, civilization.* So Py. renders it *common decency.* Others give it the other meaning of *intimacy.* **285.** Notice the asyndeton. See M. 434. **286.** Notice the transition from **huius,** *that belongs to me,* to **illi,** *that poor girl,* speaking of her as absent, or as soon to be left alone, then the return to the former pronoun, and finally, when commending her to Pamphilus, the use of **isti** (l. 295), which refers to Glycerium as his. Py. See l. 32, note. **287. Clam.** See Lex. s. v. 2, b; H. 437, 3; Al. 56, 2, c; A. 235, 5; B. 473; G. 417, Rem. 1. **Nunc utraeque inutiles.** So Uh., Kz., and Wr., following the best MSS. Fn. and Py. consider the reading *utraeque res nunc utiles* proved correct by the subjunctive **sient** in the next line, and the ironical meaning of *utiles* better suited to the spirit of the passage. But such irony seems less fitting in the words of the dying Chrysis than further on, where Crito speaks (l. 811). Kz. **288. Ad pudicitiam,** *propter formam dixit;* **ad rem tutandam,** *propter aetatem.* Don. **289. Quod,** i. e. *Propter quod,* a common use of the relative *quod* in entreaties. Cf. Virg. Aen. II. 141; VI. 363; Hor. Epist. I. 7, 94. **Genium.** A spiritual being who presided over the birth of man, and attended and watched over him, his inseparable companion through life. Every individual had a separate *Genius.* It represented his spiritual identity, and the character of the genius was the character of the man. Long. This is the reading of Uh., and Wr. following Don., though all the MSS. have *ingenium,* and Kz. sees no reason for abandoning it. **291. Obtestor,** denotes a passionate asking as a suppliant; **oro,** a request as the quiet utterance of a wish. D. s. *Rogare.* **293. Maxumi.** H. 402, III. 1; Al. 50, 1, i; A. 214, N. 3; B. 800; G. 379. **295. Uirum.** See Lex. s. v. II., A. **296. Fide.** For the form, see H. 119, 4; Al. 13, 3; A. 90, 2; B. 149. **297. In manum dat,** *gives into my charge.* The supposition of Don., that marriage *per conventionem in manum* is here intended, is not accepted by recent editors, who think a general expression would be more in keeping with the Greek coloring of the play than the introduction of a technicality of Roman law. See Dict. Antiqq., *Matrimonium.* Yet Kz. remarks that Chrysis has already indicated in what sense and with what design she uses this expression by the words *Te isti uirum do.* **298. Accepi — seruabo.** *I received her as a trust, and as a sacred trust I will keep her.*

Py. **Acceptam,** equivalent to *quoniam quidem semel accepi.* It is the foundation on which **seruabo** rests. Kz. **300. Verbum unum,** sc. *dicas.* M. 375, **a**, Obs. 1; Z. 624. **Morbum.** See l. 268, and note. **Hoc,** sc. *sit.* Py. Cf. *Haut.,* l. 207. Kz., however, supplies *accedat.*

ACTVS III.

Charinus, in love with Philumena, learns from Byrrhia of her proposed marriage to Pamphilus, and urges the latter at least to postpone it; which he asserts his eagerness to do. Davus relates to Pamphilus his discovery that the marriage was only pretended by his father; suggests that Simo's real object is to ascertain his intentions about Glycerium in order to know whom to blame for Chremes' refusal of his daughter; and persuades Pamphilus to feign consent to his father's wishes, as the best device for preventing any further efforts of Simo to bring about his marriage. Byrrhia, whom Charinus, still suspicious of Pamphilus, has sent to watch him, overhears him professing to his father his willingness to marry Philumena. On his withdrawal, Simo questions the slave respecting his son's interest in Glycerium, but Davus evades, and attributes Pamphilus' apparent sadness to the niggardly preparations for the wedding. Conversation of Mysis and Lesbia upon Pamphilus' honorable conduct towards Glycerium. Simo overhearing, though at first perplexed, thinks it a trick devised to deter Chremes, and is also persuaded by Davus that through his influence Pamphilus has really abandoned Glycerium. Chremes, again urged by Simo to permit his daughter's marriage, objects on account of Pamphilus' intimacy with Glycerium, but assured by Simo that this is now ended, reluctantly consents. Davus, summoned to confirm Simo's statement, urges the hastening of the marriage, is informed of Chremes' consent, dissembles his alarm, promises to do his best to keep Pamphilus straight, and soliloquizes over the blunder he has made. Pamphilus, informed of Chremes' consent, seeks revenge upon Davus for his ill-judged advice, who appeases him by undertaking to find some escape.

301. Quid ais Byrria expresses astonishment or indignation rather than mere inquiry. Don. **Nuptum.** H. 569, 1; A. 276, Rem. 1; B. 1363; G. 436. **303. Attentus,** *kept on the stretch,* to which **lassus,** *unstrung,* is opposed. **307. Qui** = *quo.* **309.** With this sentiment, that of Shakespeare in 'Much Ado about Nothing' has been often compared:

"No, no: 'tis all men's office to speak patience
To those that wring under the load of sorrow;
But no man's virtue, nor sufficiency,
To be so moral when he shall endure
The like himself."

O

310. Hic, regarded by Bentley and some recent editors as an adv. = *in my place;* but more probably a pronoun = *myself* (Wr.); = *talis qualis ego sum,* i. e. *tam aegrotus.* Kz. Cf. *Havt.,* l. 356. **Sis.** For the tense, see M. 347, b, Obs. 1; Z. 524, Note 1. **311. Omnia experiri,** *to leave nothing unattempted.* **Quid — agit** is said aside. **313. Prodat.** This use of the word of *postponing a period of time* instead of *an event* is rare, and belongs to the older latinity. Kz. Cf. l. 329. **315. Adeon — eum?** *Shall I approach him?* an emphatic use of the present for the future. M. 339. Obs. 2. **316. Vt — arbitretur,** sc. *impetrabis.* **317. Abin,** an interrogative form used imprecatorily. Ds. M. 6, Obs. 2. **In malam rem.** See Lex. *s. Malus.* **Scelus,** the abstract put for the concrete. See Lex. *s. v.* II., B. **320. Ad auxilium copiam.** So Uh., Kz., Fn., and Wr., who remarks that it seems to be sufficiently supported by the reading *ad auxiliandum* of three late MSS., though no other passage occurs where *ad* stands after *copia.* The MS. reading *auxili copiam,* retained by Py., is against the metre. **327. Principio** = *ante omnia,* like the Greek μάλιστα μὲν. Kz. **Potest,** sc. *fieri.* So Uh., Fn., and Wr., following most of the MSS. It is often impersonal in the comic poets; and even occurs so in Cicero, *Tusc. Disp.* I. 11 : *Si posset.* Wr. *Potes* is preferred by Kz. and Py. **328. Haec,** as nom. plural fem., is often found in archaic language, in Lucretius, and twice at least in Virgil. R. The demonstrative **ce,** which is united with the stem **ho,** is in most of the cases shortened to **c,** and in many lost. Al. 20, 1. **331. Gratiae.** See H. 390, 1, 2); Al. 51, 5; A. 227, Rem. 1; B. 850, Obs. 1; G. 350. **332. Apiscier.** So Fn., and Wr., who remarks that it is often found in early Latin instead of the compound *adipiscier,* which Uh. and Kz. retain, following the MSS. **334.** The asyndeton regularly occurs in such summons when the different verbs aim at one object which the speaker strives earnestly to accomplish. Kz. See l. 285, note. **335. Id agam,** *I will do my best.* See l. 186, note. **Optume,** *very opportunely.* **336. Tu,** sc. Byrrhia, the subject of some verb suggested by the preceding clause, e. g. *affers, nuntias.* **337. Opus sunt.** See M. 266; Z. 464. **Sciri,** preferred by Uh., Fn., and Wr. to *scire.* Cf. Cic. *ad Attic.* VII. 6: *Si quid forte sit quod opus sit sciri.* According to Py., it is added exegetically to the predicate. See M. 419; H. 552, 3; Cf. l. 490, note. Kz. rejects this form on the ground that elsewhere with the plural, *quae opus sunt,* an infinitive (at least as a verbal ablative) never occurs, and reads *scire,* which he considers as belonging to the first member of the sentence: *You know nothing for me except what is of no use,* adding that its use here, instead of a finite verb, is occasioned by his anger. The whole sentence expresses the strongest displeasure.

340. Nescio quid, equivalent to a pronoun in the accusative, and constructed according to M. 229, 1, a. See l. 157, note. Some regard it as an accus. of specification. **Dum**, *yet*. Cf. l. 29, note. **342. Quaerere**, predicate of **Quem. 343. Intendam**, here used absolutely. See Lex. *s. v.* II., B. **344. Habeo.** So Uh., Fn., and Wr., *I have it*. Py. considers that in the MSS. and ancient editions in which it is found here, it is put for *abeo* (like *holim* and *hostium* for *olim* and *ostium*); and he and Kz. prefer the latter form. **346. Quin.** See l. 45, note. **Interii** applies more to the soul, and so is a stronger expression than **perii**, which applies more to the body. See D. *s. Mors.* **348. Etsi scio**, sc. *tamen pergis dicere?* Kz. **Obtundis**, a metaphor from boxing. Py. See Lex. *s. v.* **349. Autem**, *on the other hand.* Wr. **350. Me uide**, *only look to me*, a common formula by which the speaker guarantees the truth of an assertion, or takes upon himself the fulfilment of a promise, and formally appears as security for the same. Kz. **351. Quam primum.** M. 310, Obs. 3; Z. 108. **352. Iam**, emphatic, *At length* it is clear that Chremes, etc. Py. **357. Huius**, sc. *seruum.* M. 280, Obs. 4; Z. 761. **359. Ex ipsa re**, *from the facts of the case.* **Hem — cohaerent.** Davus is relating the coincidences which struck him, and throws them into the form of a soliloquy. Py. **360. Paululum obsoni**, i. e. a very frugal meal. **Ipsus**, *my master*, sc. Simo. For the form, see H. 186, 3, 2); Al. 20, 1, c; A. 135, Rem. 2; B. 243, 3; M. 82, 4, Obs. **Tristis**, *out of spirits.* **361. Quorsum — istuc**, sc. *tendit.* **Ego me.** See l. 226, note. **364. Matronam**, sc. to act as *pronuba.* See Dict. Antiqq., *Matrimonium.* **365. Ornati — tumulti.** For the form, see M. 46, Obs. 2; H. 117, 3; Al. 12, 3; A. 89, 2; B. 139; G. 77. It is not uncommon in archaic latinity. Ritschl gives a list of words of this form from six of the early dramatic authors, from Lucretius, Cato, Sallust, and others, and among them *quaesti, fructi, aduenti,* from Terence. On such an occasion the posts of the house were adorned with flowers, and musicians accompanied the marriage procession. Cf. Adelph., l. 904. **367. Opinor narras?** *Think, do you say?* **368. Puerum**, *slave.* **Chremis.** So Uh., following the MSS. Cf. l. 247. Wr., Fn., and Kz. read *Chremi*, and refer to *Haut.* 1065, and other passages. See M. 42, 2; H. 92, 2; Al. 11, I. 4; A. 73, Rem.; B. 125; G. 72. **369. Ferre.** Historical infin. So Fn. and Wr. See l. 62, note. **370. Nullus**, *not at all*, is sometimes used in familiar writing and speaking, and in imitations of the same, in apposition to the subject, instead of *non*, occasionally with an intensive signification. M. 455, Obs. 5; Z. 688. **371. Ridiculum caput**, *silly fellow.* **372. Necessus.** So Fn. and Uh., following Lachmann; Wr. and

Kz. have *necesse*. **373. Nisi,** i. e. which will never come to pass *unless*. Wr. **Uides.** See Lex. s. v. II., B. 1. **Ambis,** properly an electioneering term, deriving its sense of 'canvassing' from its original meaning; hence *seek* or *sue urgently*. Py. **376. Suscenseat,** the correct spelling, since it is a compound of *subs* and *censeo ;* = *subirasci*. Kz. **377.** So Fn. and Wr. The next line is placed before this one by Uh., Kz., and Py. **Tuom — animum.** For the case, M. 439, Obs. 1; a kind of attraction natural in conversation, and very frequent in Plautus and Terence, and in the dialogues and letters of Cicero. **378. Sibi,** of course, limits **uideatur. Iniurius** is an archaic word, and in later times was replaced by *injustus* or *injuria*, though it occurs once in Cicero. It differs from *injuriosus* as *ebrius* from *ebriosus*, the former a single act, the latter an habitual act. Kz. **Iniuria.** See l. 218, note. **379. Ducere,** for *te ducturum esse*, a constr. inadmissible in good prose, but suited to the easy and loose style of comedy. Wr. See M. 395, Obs. 3; Z. 605. **380. Illae,** *those terrible*. **381. Solast,** i. e. without a protector. **Dictum ac factum,** *No sooner said than done*. **386. Excludar, concludar,** often used in certain special senses,— the former of lovers *shut out* from their mistresses, the latter of wild animals shut up in a cage; yet here, probably, in a general sense, and placed together partly, at least, for the play on their sound. Py. Cf. l. 218, note. **389. Hic,** i. e. *when this is the case*. **391. Omni,** where *ullo* would be expected; a usage peculiar to Plautus and Terence. M. 494, a, foot-note. Py. **392. Det.** On the tense, see M. 378, a, 2, Obs. **Minueris,** *do less vigorously*, Wr.; *alter, change*. W. & R. **393. Haec — facis,** *your present conduct*, sc. your intimacy with Glycerium. **Is,** sc. Chremes. **394. Uelle,** sc. *te*. **395. Propulsabo, etc.** The common interpretation is: *For I will easily set aside what you may hope, viz., 'no one will marry his daughter to a man of my character.'* But it is doubtful whether **propulsabo** will bear this rendering. Uh. reads:

Nam quod tu speres : "*propulsabo facile uxorem his moribus :*
Dabit nemo :" *inueniet inopem potius, etc.*

Fn. and Wr., on account of the difficulties of the passage, assume a gap after l. 395. **396. Inopem.** This would show the strength of Simo's feeling in the matter, since it was usually considered indispensable that a woman should bring something with her as a dowry on her marriage. **Corrumpi,** *to be ruined*, sc. by dissolute society. **398. Alia,** sc. *consilia, some other scheme*. So Wr. and Fn., following the MSS. *Aliam*, which Wr. thinks would be quite out of place after l. 396, is preferred by Uh., Py., and Kz. on the ground that **alia** is too vague and indefinite. **399. Quin,** interrogative, is always used in the sense of an earnest command: *Be silent, can't you?* and this use is very common in Terence. Cf. l. 45, note. **400. Cautiost,** the verbal noun put for the gerundive; a colloquialism. See Lex. s. v. 1, b. **401. Hanc fidem,** the object of **darem. 402. Qui** = *ut eo.* **406. Meditatus,** *prepared in his part;* originally of *conning over verses.* Cf. Virg. *Ecl.* I. 2; Plaut. *Trinum.* III. 3, 87. **408. Qui** may be used for the ablat. singular of all genders; here fem. sing. H. 187, 2; Al. 21, 1, c; A. 136, Rem. 1; B. 245, note; G. 103, Rem. **Differat,** *disconcert.* **Apud —sies,** *that you have your wits about you.* See Lex. s. *Apud,* 1, b. **410. Commutaturum — uerbum,** i. e. *will have nothing whatever to chide you with.* The phrase is generally used of quarrels. Py.

412. Relictis rebus, *laying aside everything else.* **414.** Wr., following Bentley, pronounces this line spurious on the ground that Pamphilus, to whom alone **hunc** could refer, had not left the stage since his conversation with Charinus. Fn. also brackets it. Uh., Kz., and Py. regard it as genuine, and refer **hunc** to Simo, now coming on the scene in hopes of thus overhearing something of importance. **Id** points to his design in following; **propterea,** to the reason why he pursues that design, viz., the command of his master. There is, therefore, no pleonasm here. Kz. **415. Ipsum adeo,** *the very man,* sc. Pamphilus. **416. Vtrumque,** sc. Pamphilus and Davus. **Serua.** See Lex. s. v. II., A. 1. **418. Uolo.** A term of imperiousness. Don. **421. Obmutuit,** sc. *Simo.* **422. Cum gratia,** *with a good grace.* **423. Sum uerus?** i. e. *Am I not a truth-telling man?* Davus refers to what he had asserted above in l. 409–411. **Uxore excidit,** *has lost his wife;* in allusion, perhaps, to its technical use in juridical language, but more probably adapted from the Greek ἐκπίπτειν. Pn. **424.** The ready acquiescence of Pamphilus apparently puzzles and disconcerts Simo, and, not knowing what to do with him, he sends him into the house. Wr. and Py. **427.** A proverbial expression; a close imitation of Euripides, *Med.* 84: ὡς πᾶς τις αὑτὸν τοῦ πέλας μᾶλλον φιλεῖ. **429. Uidere.** On the tense, see M. 408, b, Obs. 2. **431.** Notice the play upon the word: **malo,** *ill news;* **malum,** *a flogging.* Cf. l. 218, and note. It is often used of the corporal punishment of slaves. **433. Ea,** for *ejus,* by attraction, an ante-classical usage. See M. 257, Obs. 1. **434. Davos.** The MS. reading retained by Uh., Kz., and Wr. The question does not imply that Simo had overheard what Davus had just been saying, but serves merely to open the conversation in a conciliatory way. Fn., following Bentley, reads *Dave.* But Davus had remained upon the stage during the last scene, and consequently could not have spoken with Pamphilus upon the subject. Kz. **Aeque — quidem**, sc. *atque alio tempore*, i. e. *no more and no less now than at any other time*, Kz.; *nothing at all new*, a euphemism for *nil*, as the next line shows. Ds. **436. Uirum**, gives an ironical coloring to the remark, which would be lacking if merely *hominem* stood here. Kz. **438. Haec**. See l. 328, note. **440. Si adeo**, an elliptical expression, sc. *est*. See Lex. s. *Adeo*. B. 2, b. **442.** So Ub., Kz., and Wr. **Uia** = *consilio, ratione*. Don. See Lex. s. v. II., B. Others read *recta via* with the MSS., and omit *secum*. **445. Fortem**, probably like *Firmus*, from a root = *To hold fast*. Corssen; with **Uirum**, *a man of character* or *respectability*. Cf. Plaut. Trinum. V. 2, 9: *Fortem familiam*, and see Lex. s. *Fortis* II. **448. Hanc rem**, explained by l. 439. **Suscenset**. On the mood, see M. 365, Obs. 1; Z. 563. **451. Obsonatus**. So Wr. and Kz., on the ground that it is the reading of the best MSS.; that this verb occurs as a deponent in Plaut. And. 293; *Stich*. 681: that since the grammarian Pompeius speaks of the active voice occurring in *Adelph*. 117, and in only one other passage in Terence, and since it is found in *Adelph*. 964, he must have had reference to this line when he stated that it was *also* used as a deponent (in Terence); and that the personal reference is strongly favored by the context. Ph., Fn., and Py. prefer **obsonatum**. **453. Aequalium**, lit. *equal in age*; here, as often, *companion*. See Lex. s. v. 2. **454. Potissumum**, *in preference to the rest*, i. e. 'since, owing to the mean preparations, I cannot ask them all.' Ds. **Quod — siet**, *as far as it can be said by one in my place*; apologetic. See M. 364, Obs. 2; Z. 559. **455. Quoque** seems to be best expressed by emphasizing the verb, which is understood. Ds. **Per parce nimium**. Wr. regards this as a tmesis instead of *pernimium parce*. Kz. remarks that this would directly violate the universal rule that only an enclitic can stand between *per* and its adjective or adverb. But see M. 203, Obs. **458. Caput**, i. e. *author, contriver*.

460. Haud ferme, *scarcely ever*. **461. Ab Andriast** = *e domo Andriae*, not a mere periphrasis for the genitive. Wr. Simo here speaks doubtfully. Davus evades with the reply: *Quid narras? what do you mean?* Simo, then recognizing Mysis as she came nearer, speaks more confidently: **Itast**. **464. Tolli**. See l. 219, note. **465. Actumst**, originally a judicial phrase, used of a suit once ended, that could not be begun again. See Lex. s. v. III. 10. **469. Ex peregrina**, sc. *puerum jussit tolli?* (l. 464.) an aposiopesis. Pn. Such a child would be illegitimate in the eye of the law. **Iam scio**. He suddenly imagines that this conversation is all a trick to impose on him. **471. Adfertur**, etc. Cf. l. 432, et seq. **Hoc**, sc. Davus. Simo's self-delusion is the finest bit in the whole comedy, and produces a most ludicrous effect. Wr. 474. **Ridiculum.** See Lex. I. 2. b. 476. **Diuisa temporibus,** *distributed as to time,* a metaphor from the Drama. 477. **Num — discipuli,** the reading of the MSS. retained by Ch., Fn., Kz., and Wr. *Have your pupils forgotten your first setting?* i. e. 'Perhaps the fault is not yours, but they have been rather quicker than you intended.' Simo is still insinuating that Davus has pre-arranged this mock affair, and derides him for having made it too apropos. Py. 479. **Quos — redderet!** *what a game he would have played me!* 480. **In portu nauigo,** a translation of the Greek proverb: Ἐν λιμένι πλέω, i. e. *I am in perfect safety.* 486. **Per — scitus,** a case of tmesis. See l. 455, note. 487. **Superstes,** used in a general sense without reference to other persons. Kz. 489. **Vel** = etiam. Z. 734. 490. **Coram,** sc. of the women within. **Facto opus.** See M. 266. Obs.; Z. 464. Note 1: and cf. l. 337, note; l. 525; a construction very common in early Latin. Py. remarks that the participle of a transitive verb is then followed by the accusative. Fn. regards *quid* as an accus. of specification. But see M., as above. 492. **Tandem.** See l. 375, note. 493. **Incipias,** *are undertaking* or *attempting.* 494. **Saltem accurate,** sc. *facias, y u should at least do it carefully.* Py. Stallbaum and Wr. regard *accurate* as the second person plural of the imperative = *operam date.* 496. **Quid re tulit,** *what was the use of it.* M. 166, c; Z. 449. 497. **Credon — nunc** = *videone* (or *putasne me*) *tibi hoc nunc credere.* Kz. 498. **Teneo — erret,** *I comprehend wherein his mistake consists.* Kz. 503. **Enim,** here, as often, with an asseverative force, nearly = *quidem.* Arn. **Etiam.** See l. 116, note. 506. **Intellexti,** i. e. *you understand it all, I see.* Davus intends to frighten Chremes out of his consent to the marriage of Philumena to Pamphilus by letting him discover the connection of the latter with Glycerium; and, that he may do so without Simo's at the same time discovering it, he cunningly prepares Simo for disbelieving the story, by predicting that it will be got up as a fraud. Fn. 508. **Iam nunc,** here = *even now,* i. e. *beforehand; sometimes = now at last.* Arn. **Sciens** has an adjectival force. See M. 424, b; H. 575, 1; Al. 72, 2; A. 205, Note 2; B. 1343; G. 429. 512. **Qui,** all. = *ex quibus.* 513. **Inuentum,** here a substantive; *the story is false.* 516. Fn. and Ritter consider this line an interpolation, but it is found in all the MSS., and is retained by most editors. Kz. encloses it in quotation marks, as expressing the sentiment of the women. For the same reason Wr. reads *moueri nuptias,* which, however, also necessitates the change of fit to *fiat.* **Nihil mouentur,** *are not disturbed ;* i. e. *there's no* *impediment to the marriage.* Cf. Cic. *Philipp.* I. 7, 17; Livy XXV. 16, 4. **517. Intellexeras.** For the mood, see M. 358, 2d paragr.; Z. 579. **519. Illa** refers to Glycerium as formerly loved by Pamphilus, but not now; **hanc,** as being near at hand, for they were standing at her door. Py. See l. 32, note. **521. Idem.** See M. 488; Z. 697. **525. Atqui.** See l. 225, note. **Hauscio** is in archaic Latin one word, like *nescio.* Wr. So also Fn. Other editors read *haud scio.* **527. Chremem.** See M. 45, 2, e; Z. 71, and cf. l. 533, and l. 368, note. **529. Quid alias,** *Why at any other time.* **532.** The reading of most MSS. retained by Uh., Fn., and Kz. *Chremem* is added by Wr., following Don. and Bentley, on the ground that **ipsum** alone would almost necessarily denote Pamphilus. Yet after the words *Nunc Chremem conueniam,* etc., it cannot easily be doubted to whom Simo refers here. Kz.

533. Iubeo Chrometem, sc. *saluere.* **Optato,** used adverbially. See M. 198, a, Obs. 2; Z. 266. **535. Id.** *As to this.* **538. Per — oro.** A formula common in poetry, also found in prose; apparently an imitation of the Greek πρός σε τῶν θεῶν. **541. Quoius,** old form for *cujus,* from the stem **Quo.** **544. Quasi** is particularly used when, to correct an erroneous supposition, we state what is *not* the case: *As if you ought = you ought not.* Respecting this and **545. Atque,** see M. 444, a, Obs. 1, and b; 303 a; Z. 340, Note. **Dabam,** i. e. *was ready to give.* II. 469, II. 1; Al. 58, 3, c; A. 145, II. 4; G. 224. **546. In remst,** *it is for the interest.* **Fiant,** sc. *nuptiae.* **Arcessi,** the common expression for escorting the bride from the house of her father to that of her husband. Kz. **548. In — consulas,** *to consult our common interests.* **550. Itaque** = *et ita.* **552. Irae,** i. e. *repeated quarrels,* the plural more expressive than *ira.* Wr. Cf. Virg. Ecl. II. 14: *Tristes Amaryllidis iras.* **Audio** = *I concede this, yet it does not at all change the situation of affairs.* Kz. **553. Posse auelli,** sc. *eum,* the subject, as usually in the comic poets, omitted after **spero.** Wr. See M. 395, Obs. 3; Z. 605. **555.** With the sentiment, cf. Menander: ὀργὴ φιλούντων ὀλίγον ἰσχύει χρόνον, and Plaut. *Amphit.* III. 2, 60:

> *Verum irae si quae forte eueniunt huiusmodi*
> *Inter eos: rursum si reuentum in gratiamst,*
> *Bis tanto amici sunt inter se, quam prius.*

But there is no necessity for imagining that Terence borrowed from any one. *The idea is taken from common life, and Terence's expression has all the terseness of an original suggestion.* Py. **Est.** For the number, see M. 216; H. 462, 2; Al. 49, Rem.; A. 209, Rem. 9; B. 668;

G. 202, Rem. 1, Exc. 3. **556. Ante eamus,** *anticipate, forestall.* **557. Occlusast,** *is restrained.* **558. Harum,** sc. Glycerium and those around her. He wishes it to appear that Pamphilus is ensnared rather than in love. Kz. **560. Consuetudine et coniugio,** *by the intimacy arising from honorable wedlock.* Hendiadys. So Uh., Kz., and others, following the older MSS. Fn. and Wr. omit et, and the latter reads *conjugi* (gen.) *eum,* rendering (with **consuet.**) *the getting accustomed to living in honorable wedlock.* **561. Liberali,** i. e. with a free woman, in opp. to *peregrina.* Cf. l. 38, note, and 469. **564. Perpetuo habere,** i. e. be always faithful and true to her. **Perpeti,** sc. that his daughter should be led into such a marriage as that with Pamphilus would be. Kz. See l. 218, note. **567. Nempe** sometimes appends a *but* to an implied concession, and is often ironical. See also Z. 278. **Incommoditas,** a euphemism for *calamitas* or *malum* as **discessio** is for *divortium.* Simo naturally uses the mildest terms possible to express an unpleasant fact. **Denique,** *after all.* **Huc,** sc. *ut periclum faciamus.* Wr. **568.** Notice the use of the subjunctive in **eueniat** to express a mere supposition which is uncertain and improbable, and of the indicative in **corrigitur** to denote his confidence that all will turn out well. Cf. l. 570, 571. **572. Quid istic?** *Why* say all *that?* i. e. *Enough;* a common formula of concession after dispute. Py. **573. Tibi — claudier,** *that you should have any advantage obstructed.* Cf. *De Off.* II. 15. **In me,** *in my person,* i. e. *as far as I am concerned.* Kz. **575. Sed quid ais?** *But apropos.* Kz. **578. Censes,** parenthetical. **579. Tute adeo,** *You yourself* or *You too.* With pronouns, *adeo* has an intensive force. Arn.

581. Aduesperascit, sc. the time when it was customary to escort the bride to her new home. **Audin?** So Uh. and Fn. *Tu illum* is added by Kz., Wr., and others, on the ground that special importance had just been attached to the testimony of Davus. See l. 576, and cf. l. 342. **583. Uolgus,** *the common herd.* **Solet,** sc. *facere.* **586. Tandem — siem.** Simo, of course, understands these words as an expression of offended virtue; but the spectator, who is better acquainted with Davus' real character, will readily catch the sneer implied in them. Wr. **587. Ea gratia.** See l. 433, note. **592. Occidi.** This is also said aside; but Simo partly overhears it, and Davus replies to his question, substituting **Optume.** **593. Per hunc,** sc. Chremes. See Lex. *s.* **Per,** II., C. **594. Adparetur.** So Uh., Fn., Kz., and Wr., impers. Cf. *Eun.*, l. 583: *Dum adparatur virgo in conclari sedet, etc.* The MS. reading is *adparentur,* sc. *nuptiae,* but the marriage-feast would be prepared at Simo's house rather than at Chremes'. Cf. l. 450, *et seqq.* Kz. **596. Ego — solus.** *Yes, I alone indeed.* Davus speaks in a double sense, taking credit to himself for it with his master, while accusing himself internally of the whole mischief. Py. **598. Quiescas.** *You may be unconcerned about that.* **599. Nullus sum.** See Lex. s. v. II., C. **601. Preci** occurs only here and in *Phorm.*, 1. 547, in the dat. sing.; elsewhere only in the ablat. sing. and the plural. M. 55, 3; Z. 89. **602. In — conieci**, as if into a prison. Cf. l. 386. **603. Hoc,** sc. *Simone.* **604. Hem astutias,** *so much for my cunning.* **606. Quo** = *in quod;* i. e. either a sword or a deep ditch, as different editors have suggested.

607. Scelus. See l. 317, note. On the gender of **qui**, see M. 317, d; H. 445, 5; A. 206, 11; B. 698; G. 616, 3, I. **608. Nulli** here, as in one or two other instances, for *nullius.* R. **609. Futtili.** So Fn., Uh., Kz., and Wr. for the common form *futili.* **613. Audacia.** So Fn., Uh., and Wr., who says it is proved correct by *Eun.* 958: *Qua audacia Tantum facinus audet?* Kz. and others retain the MS. reading, *fiducia*, on the ground that the question refers chiefly to the inward feeling. **614. Me,** ablative. M. 267; Z. 491. **615. Productem.** So Fn., and Wr., who interprets it, with **moram,** *try to delay,* as implying far less certainty than *producam,* which, however, is retained by Uh., Kz., and Py. **616. Bone uir,** spoken ironically. **617. Impeditum,** *entangled.* **618. Ut credam.** See l. 263, note. **622. Ad — redeam,** *to recover myself.* **Iam,** *soon.* **623. Quom** = *eo quod* has now and then the indicative, but only when the ground of the action is an objective fact. Arn. See also M. 358, Obs. 2. **624. Praecauere,** sc. *monet;* or this may be regarded as a case of Zeugma. H. 704, I. 2; A. 323, 1, (2); B. 1378; G. 690.

ACTVS IV.

Pamphilus, accused of treachery by Charinus, with difficulty persuades him that the present dilemma is due to the ill-judged advice of Davus; who, on their reproaching him, admits that he has been at fault, but promises to extricate them from their troubles. Interview of Mysis with Pamphilus, who repeats his pledge of fidelity to Glycerium. Davus, having devised a new scheme, puts Charinus contemptuously one side, and directs Mysis, who is soliloquizing over the troubles of Glycerium, to place the child at Simo's door. On Chremes' approach to announce his readiness for the marriage, Davus appears not to see him, pretends to have just come from the forum, and by skilful questioning leads Mysis to assert the parentage of the child, professing himself to disbelieve her story. Chremes, overhearing, is convinced, and hastens to Simo to break off the marriage again. Crito of Andros, cousin of Chrysis, having heard of her death, appears to claim her property; meeting Mysis, he inquires respecting Glycerium, and is conducted to her.

626. Uecordia, *heartlessness, inhumanity.* Cf. Festus: *Vecors est turbati et mali cordis.* **627. Gaudeant.** For the number, M. 215; Z. 367. **629. Uerum,** *right.* See Lex. s. v. **630. Quis.** *Who feel some little shame only in refusing you.* H. 187, 1; Al. 21, 1, d; A. 136, Rem. 2; B. 245, Note; G. 103, Rem. **632. Se aperiunt,** *they reveal their true character.* **633.** Wr. thinks this line spurious, neither the metre nor the sense being able to stand a close examination. But Kz. finds neither internal nor external grounds for this opinion. It is in all the MSS. Instead of **cogit,** Uh. and Kz. read *premit.* **635.** The first question refers to *rank;* the second to *relationship.* Don. Others regard **mihi** as ethical dative. **Meam,** sc. *rem habes,* or *postulas,* i. e. *meddle in my concerns.* Pn. **637. Pudeat.** So Uh., Fn., and Wr., following Bentley, though the MSS. read *pudet.* Priscian teaches, *ex usu ueterum,* and on the authority of the grammarian Caper, that the impersonal verbs *pudet, piget, etc.,* were originally used personally. Wr. **640. Mala** = *maledicta.* Ds. **641. Multum,** sc. *promovero.* **Animo — gessero,** *indulge my anger.* Cf. l. 294. **642. Respiciunt,** properly used of the regard of a superior to an inferior. Py. **643. Itane, etc.,** and **soluisti** are used ironically. The *fides* is a pledge by which a person binds himself. Hence, by fulfilling his promise, he releases himself from his pledge. Py. See Lex. s. *Solvo.* I., B. 2. *b.* **644. Ducere,** *to deceive.* For the mood, H. 558, VI. 3; Al. 70, 3, a; A. 273, 2; B. 1153; G. 532. **647. Falsus** is here used in its original participial sense; with **es,** *you are deceived, in error.* **649. Habeas.** An angry concession. **650. Conflauit.** So Uh., Fn., and Wr., following Don. instead of the MS. reading, *confecit.* On the change of mood from **uorser,** see l. 273, note; also l. 568, note. Pn. considers that the dependent question ends at **miser,** and that Pamphilus, pausing a moment, starts afresh: *And as to the anxiety which, etc.,* but is interrupted by Charinus, and leaves the sentence unfinished. **655. Quo** = *et eo;* with **minus scis,** *and so little do you know.* **656. Haec.** See l. 328, note. **658. Scio.** Ironical, as also in l. 669. **663.** So Uh., Kz., and Py., following the oldest MSS. and the testimony of Don. Fn., after Bentley, omits *Ch.* **Dauos?** *Pa.* **Interturbat** and **scio** in the next line. **664. Nisi,** common in Terence for the more usual expression *nisi quod;* with **scio,** *only I am sure.* Cf. M. 442, c, Obs. 3; Z. 735. The MS. reading **scio,** after **satis,** is also retained by Uh. and Kz. **Deos, etc.** A common formula for insinuating that a person had lost his senses, or was unfortunate. Py. **666. At** is often used in execrations, as here, and in prayers. Arn. **671. Nisi si.** So Uh., Fn., and Wr. It is nearly equivalent to *nisi forte, unless perchance*. See M. 412, c, Obs. 1; Z. 526. **674. Unis.** For the plural, see H. 176, 1; Al. 18, 1, a; A. 118, Rem. 2; B. 203, 3. **675. Pro seruitio,** i. e. *in consideration of my being your slave.* See Z. 312. **679. Facio sedulo,** *I am doing my best.* See l. 146, note. **680. Melius,** sc. *consilium*. **Missum.** See Lex. s. v. II., D. **681. Restitue — locum.** So Uh., Fn., Kz., and Wr.: *Restore* my former *situation,* the charge of *which you received from me.* **Locum,** i. e. the condition of affairs before he promised his father that he would marry. **682. Hem — ostium.** So the MSS. and Kz. Instead of **Hem . . . sed,** Fn. reads *St;* and instead of **concrepuit,** which is used with **ostium** in two other places in Terence, Uh. and Fn. read *crepuit ostium,* which is not found elsewhere in this author. Fn. also inserts *hinc,* and Wr. substitutes *istac* for **Glycerio.** The doors in Greece opened outwards, and those who were coming out rapped upon the door inside to warn passers-by. Those who knocked from without were said *pultare.* **683. Nil ad te,** sc. *attinet,* i. e. your thoughts should be otherwise occupied. **Quaero,** sc. *consilium quo te expediam.* **Nuncin** for *nunc — ce — ne;* with **demum** = *Have n't you by this time devised some plan?* — the expression indicating impatience.

684. Ubi ubi = *ubicunque*. Z. 128. **688. Hoc malum,** sc. Davus' mismanagement, which is producing new trouble. Ds. **689. Sicin,** etc. See l. 245, note. Pamphilus turns upon Davus reproachfully, as Charinus also does in v. 691. Davus has an answer for him, while he takes his master's reproaches quietly. Py. **691. Quibus,** sc. *nuptiis.* **Quiesci,** used impersonally. The ablative with it (*to have rest,* i. e. *liberty, from* something) is a rare construction. Symmachus, *Epist.* I. 8, has the same, while Capitolinus, *Maxim.* 23. has the preposition *a*. Kz. Others consider it an ablat. of specification. **Quiesset.** On the mood, II. 512, 2; Al. 59, 3, e; A. 259, Rem. 3, *d;* B. 1272; G. 599, 3. **694. Tibi.** The dat. also occurs with *adjurare* in Plaut. *Cist.* II. 3, 27; Ovid, *Metam.* III. 659. Kz. **696. Ualeant.** See Lex. s. v. I., B. 2, b. **698. Resipisco.** Uh., Kz., and Wr. follow the MSS. in attributing this word to Charinus, whose hopes are revived by hearing Pamphilus speak so strongly of his attachment to Glycerium. **Atque.** See l. 545, note. **699. Ut ne.** See M. 456. Obs. 4. **702. Quis uideor?** *What do you think of me now?* Pamphilus expects a commendatory answer. But Charinus, depressed by the wretched situation of both, only replies: *You are as badly off as I am.* Encouraged, however, by Davus' remark, and continually inclined to rely on others, he praises *him* with **Forti's,** *you are a clever fellow.* **703. Scio — conere.** Pamphilus is still out of humor with Davus, and means to intimate, by this cool reception of his announcement, that his plan will not amount to much. Kz. Py. thinks this sentence, in Pamphilus' mouth, is frigid, and proposes to read *Scin quid cocre? Be sure you mind what you are about*, as a warning to Davus not to get him into any more scrapes. Fn. reads PA. *Forti's, Scio, quod cocre.* But this is not suited to the character of Pamphilus, nor to the situation. Kz. **707. Amolimini** expresses great disdain and superciliousness. Wr.; also Lex. s. v. Davus, having hit upon a plan, assumes the tone of a superior towards those who are dependent upon him for help. **708. Verum — dicam.** Without understanding Davus' second hint to be off, Charinus begins with these words to open his heart to the slave. Kz. **Immo etiam,** *Nay rather* (i. e. instead of a plain answer). **709. Narrationis,** *a long story.* **710. Dieculam,** *a respite,* occurs in a similar sense in Plaut. *Pseud.* I. 5, 88, and in Cic. *ad Att.* V. 21, where he alludes to a law of Caesar prolonging the period of payment for debtors. Py. Davus means by this line that Charinus' request (in l. 329) had now been sufficiently complied with. Wr. thinks he is deriding Charinus, who had formerly limited his request to this very thing. **711. Quantum,** i. e. *for the space for which,* used adverbially. **Quid ergo,** sc. *quaeris.* **712. Ducam,** sc. Philumena. **Ridiculum.** Nominative. Cf. l. 474. **715. Facto.** See l. 490, note. Davus now goes into the house of Glycerium. **716. Proprium,** lit. *nearer,* then *belonging to ;* here, the idea of perpetuity, constant, lasting. **Di — fidem.** See l. 237, note. **718. Amatorem,** often as here in an honorable sense. Mysis describes Pamphilus' connection with her mistress as advancing from friendship to *marriage,* (**virum.**) Kz. **720. Hic,** *now,* in her present sad situation. **Illic,** *then,* in their former untroubled connection. Kz. **723. Malitia,** *shrewdness.* Wr. So the best MSS. and Eugraphius, followed by Uh., Fn., Kz., and Wr. **726. Ara.** Two altars stood on the stage; one on the right, sacred to Apollo (in Comedy), the other on the left, to the presiding deity of the games — in this case Cybele. Py. thinks there may be a more general allusion to the altar of Apollo, which stood before Grecian houses. **728. Iurato.** So Uh., Fn., and Wr. For the construction, see l. 490, note. Kz. and others, following the MSS., read *jurandum* in the sense of *jus-jurandum,* though there are no other instances of such a use. **729. Adposisse,** from *adposivisse = adposuisse.* The oldest form of the perfect was POSEIVEI, and *posivi* is frequent in Plaut. Cf. l. 742. **Liquido,** *with a clear conscience.* Py. **730. In te.** So Uh., Wr., and Kz., following the MSS. Fn. and others read *unde.* **Cedo,** *Give* the child to me. **734. Ego quoque.** As Chremes was approaching from the right,

P

Davus slips away so as to come up a little later from the same direction. Kz. **736. Orationi**, sc. *meae*. **Ut quomque** = the later form *utcumque*. **Uerbis**, *by your words*. **738. Ut**, *since*. **740. Quae — fuere**. See l. 337, note. **745. Quid hominum**, lit. *what a quantity of men = quot homines*; hence the plural **litigant**, *are going to law*, Py.; according to others, lit., *quarrelling*. H. 461, 1; Al. 49, 1, c; A. 209, Rem. 11; B. 618, 2; G. 202, Rem. 1, Ex. 1. **Illi**, an archaic form for *illic*; a locative case used adverbially. R. **746. Quid — nescio**, said aside. **747. Quae — fabula?** *What a farce is this*; lit. *What kind of a comedy is this*. Kz. **751. Au.** Davus seems to have pushed Mysis roughly in order to hurry her to the right. He then added **Concede — dexteram** in a low tone, wishing to talk aside to her, and prompt her, if necessary, without being overheard by Chremes. So l. 752, **Verbum si, etc.**, l. 760 and l. 764, **Mitte, etc.**, are uttered in a low tone to her. **752. Tute ipse**, sc. *puerum dedisti*. **754. Male dicis?** So Ub., Fn., Kz., and Wr. Most of the MSS. assign this to Mysis, i. e. *Do you threaten me?* and Py. thinks it very characteristic of her in her amazement at the tone taken by Davus. **758. In quibus inludatis**. This construction seems to occur only here, but is attested by the grammarian Arusianus Mess. Wr. See M. 245, b; Z. 416. **760. Excessis**. See M. 115, f; Z. 161. **763. Quoium**. See H. 185, 3; Al. 21, 2, f; A. 139, 2; G. 104. *Cujus* was treated in prae-Augustan writers as a declinable genitive, i. e. an adjective with an o stem. R. **768. Quemne** = *cumne quem*, *What! the boy whom*, etc. Davus, by insinuating that the story of the birth is false, irritates Mysis into saying what he wishes. **769. Verum**, *It is true*, used like *ridiculum* (l. 474), *malum*, and other neuter adjectives. **771. Aliquot liberae**. According to Roman law, at least five *matronae*, or women of free birth, were required in order to establish the legitimate birth of a child. Wr. **Adfuerunt**. For the mood, see l. 623, note. **773. Chremes, etc.** Davus pretends, of course, that this is what Glycerium and Mysis expect. **780. Coactus — ducet**. By the laws of Athens, he who had seduced a free-born maiden was compelled to marry her. The law ran: Ἡ βιασθεῖσα ἢ γάμον ἢ θάνατον αἱρείσθω τοῦ βιασαμένου. **782. Iocularium malum**, is an evil which, with all the mischief contained in it, has, through the way in which it enters, its comic side. Kz. **783.** Davus here pretends suddenly to be aware of Chremes' presence. **783. Scelera**, *Here's villanies*. He counterfeits horror at the idea of Chremes' having heard this scandal against his master, Pamphilus. **In cruciatum**, sc. to extort the truth, and make her recant her opprobrious imputations. Ps. **787. Hic est ille**, *Here is the very man*; addressed to Mysis. Cf. l. 772. **Dauom**, i. e. a mere slave; far more expressive than *me*. Wr. **789. No — attigas**. As Chremes enters the door, Davus hastens to congratulate Mysis on the success of his manœuvre; but she, not understanding his conduct, is indignant, and bids him keep away. **Attigas**, old form for *attingas*. See II. 242, 1; Al. 30, 3, *a*, 3; R. 632; G. 152, III. **791. Actum**, *attained*, not the same as *factum*. **792. Socer**, i. e. *sponsae pater*. Cf. I. 732. **793. Praediceres.** M. 351, b; Obs. 4; II. 488, II. 2; Al. 57, 3, d; A. 260, Rem. 6, *d*; G. 256, 3. **794. Ex animo**, *from the heart, sincerely*. **795. De industria**, *of set purpose*.

797. Sese is pleonastic. Other editors read *sibi*. **Ditias**, shortened from *diritias*. **798. Uiueret.** For the mood, II. 496, 2; Al. 70, 4, b; A. 264, 4, Rem.; G. 556, 3. **799. Redierunt.** When there was no will, the property went to the next of kin, and *Redire* was the term commonly used in this case; *Venire*, when an inheritance was left by will. Py. See Dict. Antiqq. **803. Itan Chrysis?** sc. *mortua est*. Crito speaks with tenderness of feeling, only hinting at her death. Kz. **Perdidit**, expresses the effect upon the surviving friends: *Yes, we are undone by her death*. Py. **804. Satine recte?** sc. *agitis, tolerably well?* a common phrase in conversation, as **Sic**, *so, so* is also. **805. Aiunt**, i. e. *as the proverb goes;* an allusion to a line of Caecilius (which is, indeed, also imitated from a Greek proverb): *vivas ut possis, quando non quis ut velis*. The gentle expression of gratitude (on the part of Terence to Caecilius, who had recommended the exhibition of his play) is characteristic. Mom. In Menander occurs the line: ζῶμεν γὰρ οὐχ ὡς θέλομεν ἀλλ' ὡς δυνάμεθα. **807. Auspicato.** See M. 198, Obs. 2; Z. 266. **Attuli.** So Fn. and Wr. The oldest and most of the MSS. read *adpuli*, which is retained by Uh. and Kz. Wr. remarks that *se appellere* seems to occur nowhere else; while Kz. replies that the same is true of *se afferre* in Terence, and that *appellunt corpora* (= *se*) is found in Lucretius. **808. Tetulissem.** The reduplicated form is archaic. **811. Litis sequi**, *to bring an action-at-law*, which it would be necessary for Crito to do in order to recover the property, since Glycerium, professing to be the sister of Chrysis, would be looked upon as her next of kin. **Quam — utile**, ironical. **814. Grandicula**, a conjecture of Fn. adopted by Uh. and Wr. It is also found in Plaut., *Poen*. II. 35, (though in another sense.) The MS. reading is *grandiuscula*, in which the synizesis *iu*, Wr. remarks, would be quite unexampled. **Illinc**, sc. Andros. **817. Antiquom**, frequently used thus absolutely, though the fuller expression also occurs, as in *Hec*. V. 4, 20: *Tu morem antiquom atque ingenium obtines*. Cf. Shakespeare, As You Like It, II. 3, 56:

> "O good old man; how well in thee appears
> The constant custom of the antique world,
> When service sweat for duty, not for meed!"

818. Maxume. See Lex. *s. v.* B. 2. **819. Me nolo,** etc., sc. because he fears that his master will summon him to attest his own words (l. 576), and to assure Chremes that Glycerium and Pamphilus are estranged. Py.

ACTVS V.

Chremes, having overheard the altercation between Davus and Mysis, again declines to give his daughter in marriage to Pamphilus; and although Simo explains all that has happened as an artifice of Glycerium, of which Davus had warned him in advance, he urges the fulfilment of Chremes' promise in vain. Davus reappears, soliloquizing on the intelligence communicated by Crito, and Simo, overhearing him, demands an explanation of his story of the quarrel between Pamphilus and Glycerium. He evades, and tells the news of her Athenian parentage, but is supposed by Simo to be inventing a new story, and is sent away to punishment. Pamphilus, summoned by his father, is reproached for his conduct. Confessing his love, he places himself at his father's disposal, but entreats a hearing for Crito, to which Simo, at Chremes' request, consents. On Crito's giving the real history of Glycerium, Chremes recognizes her as his own daughter, Pasiphila, who had been shipwrecked at Andros, and consents to her marriage with Pamphilus. Simo is convinced and reconciled. Charinus finds Pamphilus communicating his good fortune to Davus, who has been released, and asks his aid in his own suit for Philumena. Davus pronounces the Epilogue.

820. Spectata. Cf. l. 91, note. **822. Uitam,** i. e. all that makes life dear. Cf. *Hart.*, l. 315. **823. Immo enim.** An elliptical expression: *No*, I will not cease *for*, etc. Py. According to Wr. and Kz., it has an asseverative force. **Quom maxume,** a strengthened *maxime* = *tam . . . quam quum maxime,* Arn.; with **nunc,** *now more than ever.* **825. Prae** is generally used in Terence with a negative phrase, as in *Haut.*, l. 308, 920; and in other passsages there is a negative idea implied under the affirmative form. Thus here: 'You see that your eagerness prevents your being fair.' Py. See M. 256, Obs. 1; Z. 310. **827. Onerare.** This use of the infinitive, which is taken from the language of conversation, is also found in Hor. O. II. 11, 3; Sall. *Jugurth.* 53, but never in Cicero or Caesar. Kz. But see M. 389. **829. Re uxoria,** *matrimony.* **830. Seditionem,** *domestic discords.* **Incertas,** sc. as to duration, because Pamphilus would be likely to prove inconstant, and a separation would follow. **832. Feras,** sc. *oportet.* **833. Hinc,** i. e. *ex hac urbe.* Cf. l. 221. **834. Credere.** On the mood, see M. 389; Z. 614. **838. Scio.** *Of course,* ironically. Cf. l. 552. **839. Vero uoltu,** *in earnest.* **840. Facturas,** sc. *eas.* **842. Tibi.** H. 389; Al. 51, 7, d;

A. 228, Note; B. 838; G. 351. **844. Scelus,** sc. Davus. See l. 317, note. **845. In uado,** i. e. *in safety,* a proverb. expr. Cf. l. 480. **846. Noster Chremes.** Davus, pretending to regard him still as the destined father-in-law of Pamphilus, addresses him as his master. **848. Arcesse,** sc. Philumena. See l. 546, note. **Id — abest.** *This is now a great way off;* i. e. it is something not to be thought of at present. Kz. **849. Etiam,** in conversational language, is often used in indignant questions. Arn. See Lex. *s. v.* II. 4. **851.** Davus, in his confusion, only involves Pamphilus in trouble without extricating himself. **853. Quid — censes,** sc. *facere.* **854.** Davus, taking advantage of Chremes' incredulity about Pamphilus' quarrel with Glycerium, tells his piece of news as if it were an unworthy trick by which Crito hoped to force Pamphilus into a marriage with Glycerium, and to account at the same time for Pamphilus' presence in her house. Py. **Audias.** So the best MSS. and Kz. *Audies* is the reading adopted by Uh., Fn., and Wr. After *faxo,* the usage varied in both Plautus and Terence. The indicative occurs in four passages in Ter.: *Eunuch.* 285 and 663, *Phorm.* 308 and 1055, and the subjunctive in two passages, *Adelph.* 209 and 847, besides this one. **855. Ellum.** For the form, see M. 83, Obs. 2; Z. 132. It has a descriptive force: *Here you have him.* Py. **Confidens,** here in a bad sense, as usually in the classic period. Cf. Cic. *Tusc. Disp.* III. 7: *Qui fortis est, idem est fidens: quoniam confidens mala consuetudine loquendi in vitio ponitur, ductum verbum a confidendo, quod laudis est.* It sometimes occurs in a good sense in the ante-classic period, as in Plaut. *Capt.* III. 5, 8. **Catus,** *cunning.* **857. Tristis,** *grave,* not necessarily in a bad sense. Cf. Cic. *Verr.* I. 10: *Judex tristis at integer.* **Seueritas.** So Uh. and Fn., following the MSS. Wr. and Kz. have *ueritas,* the reading of a quotation in Nonius; i. e. Crito's face bears the stamp of truth. **Fides,** i. e. that which *inspires confidence* in him. **858. Quid adportas?** i. e. *What new story are you bringing to us?* **861. Sublimem,** *uplifted,* i. e. *Up with him and.* **Quantum potes,** *as fast as you can.* So the MSS., Kz., and Wr., who remarks that other passages in Terence and Plautus prove that in this phrase the verb could be personal as well as impersonal. Uh. and Fn. read *potest.* **864. Te commotum** refers to Davus' remark in l. 842, which Simo had overheard. Py. renders: *I'll soon make you stir yourself.* **865. Quadrupedem constringito.** In the Athenian punishment called Κυφωτισμός, a wooden collar was placed round the neck, to which the hands and feet were tied. **866. Si uiuo,** *As sure as I live, By my life;* frequently found in Terence and Plautus. Wr. **868. Illi,** sc. Pamphilus. **870. Capere.** This and *facere,* Plaut. *Aul.* 336, are the only two instances known, in which the *first person* is used in this construction. The third person is very common. Wr. But see l. 245, note.

872. Omnium. Simo is interrupted by Chremes as he is about to break out with reproaches upon Pamphilus. Kz. **873. Mitte,** *forbear*. **874. Grauius,** *too severe*. **875.** Notice the idiomatic use of **tandem** to express indignation or impatience, and add force to the interrogation, which implies a disbelief in the assertion of Pamphilus. Z. 287. **876. Confidentiam,** *presumption, effrontery*. See l. 855, note. **879. Impotenti,** *lacking self-control*. **884. Aliquo pacto,** *somehow*, no matter how. Ds. **885. Istuc uerbum,** sc. *miserum*. **Accidit,** *was applicable*. **890. Huius.** Cf. l. 310, note. **891. Liberi.** The plural is often used where only one child is spoken of, as the singular is very rarely found, and never in the older authors. Py. Cf. *Haut.* 151. **892. Uiceris,** *Enjoy your victory, have it your own way*. Py. **898. Mittere.** So Ub. and Fn. Kz. and Wr. read *amittere*, and omit **uis**. **899. Adlegatum,** *suborned*. **900. Expurgem.** On the construction, see M. 372, b, Obs. 4.

904. Una quaeuis, *any one whatever*. **Ut faciam,** i. e. that I state the facts about Glycerium to Simo. **905. Cupio.** See Lex. s. v. II. **907. Athenas,** sc. *adrenisti*. **Insolens,** *contrary to your custom*. **Euenit,** *It has happened so*. **909. Paratus,** sc. like an actor in his part. Cf. l. 406, and note. **913. Nuptiis,** ablat. of means. **916. Euenit,** a sneering allusion to Crito's expression in l. 907. Wr. The next sentence, too, is ironical. **919. Hem.** Crito begins to be angry at this epithet, and Chremes seeks to appease him: **Sic — hic,** *It's his way, Crito*. Never mind him. **Mitte.** *Let it pass*. But Crito rejoins: **Videat — siet,** *Let him look to his ways*. Ds. **921. Moueo,** *set in motion*, i. e. *Am I the author of all this;* **curo,** *have I any concern in it*. Py. **922. Audierim,** sc. from Phania. **924. Adplicat — se,** i. e. *becomes his client;* the technical term for choosing a *patronus*. **927. Esse,** instead of *fuisse*, for the sake of vividness, though Phania was dead. Wr. **930. Rhamnusium.** Rhamnus was a well-known δῆμος of Attica. **932. Quoiam.** See l. 763, note. **933. Auris.** On the form, see H. 88, 3, 1; Al. 11, 3, c; A. 85, Ex. 1; B. 114; G. 60, 1. **934. Qui credis?** *Why do you believe so?* Wr. thinks these words are addressed to Pamphilus. **Noram,** sc. *Phaniam;* **Scio,** sc. *eum fratrem tuum fuisse*. **936. Post ibi.** So Ub., Fn., and Wr. Kz. has *Postilla*. **937. Illo.** See l. 614, note. **938. Mirando — bono,** *while I marvel, etc.* See M. 416, Obs. 1; Z. 643. **939. Tuam,** sc. *filiam*. **941. Odium** = *odiose homo*. Cf. l. 317, **scelus,** note. So Ub., Fn., and Wr., following Bentley, and making an aposiopesis after **Dignus es.** Kz., Py., and others make it dependent upon **Dignus es** taken as equivalent to *meritus*, and refer to *Phorm.* 1. 519: *Di tibi omnes id quod es dignus duint.* But in this case the relative may be the accusative by attraction into the case of the antecedent, and therefore it is not parallel. **Nodum,** etc. A proverb. See Lex. s. v. I. 5. 944. **Voluptati,** here, of course, in a good sense. 945. **Pasiphila.** The true form of the name, due to an emendation made simultaneously by G. Bezzenberger and K. Keil. The MSS. give *Pasibula*, which would be against the metre, as the u cannot be short; but Terence himself wrote *Pasipila*, according to the usage of his period, and hence arose the error. Wr. 948. **Res** — gratiam, *the discovery has reconciled me.* 949. **De uxore nil mutat,** i. e. *Does he confirm the marriage?* Cf. 1. 40, and note. **Ita** — **possedi,** *as she is mine.* She is a *possessio*, but not yet legally his, and he therefore appeals to Chremes to confirm their union. Py. In the case of a disputed claim, he who had actual possession was protected by the *Interdictum :* UTI POSSIDETIS till the legal question was settled. See Dict. Antiqq., s. *Interdictum.* 951. **Accipio,** the legal formula of acceptance, without which the dowry was not given. 953. **Potest,** sc. *fieri.* 954. **Magis ex sese,** *more directly concerning himself.* 955. **Haud** — **jussi,** i. e. *I ordered it to be done rightly enough.* In joke, he takes **recte,** which Pamphilus had used in the sense of *justly, fairly,* as = *suitably, thoroughly,* i. e. as applying not to the *cause,* but to the *manner* of the punishment.

958. **Uerum,** *real.* 960. **Propriae.** See l. 716, note. **Nam mi, etc.** Colman compares Shakespeare, *Othello,* II. 1:

"—— If it were now to die,
'T were now to be most happy: for I fear,
My soul hath her content so absolute,
That not another comfort like to this
Succeeds in unknown fate."

962. **Dari,** sc? *obviam.* 964. **Solide,** *thoroughly, sincerely.* The double alliteration in this line, and the use of a substantive and verb from the same stem, make the expression of Pamphilus' joy very intense. Kz. **Gaudia.** II. 371, 1, 3); Al. 52, 1, b; A. 232, 1; B. 713; G. 331. 965. **Pamphilus,** one of the rare instances in which the original long quantity of this ending is still visible in comic prosody. Wr. 973. **Solus** — **di,** i. e. He is especially favored by the gods, since all this ends in his being recognized as the legitimate son and heir. Pn. There seems no good reason for the supposition of many commentators that this sentence implies that the child was dead, and to bring in such an occurrence at the end of the play would be quite out of place in comedy.

976. Tuos, explained by what follows. **977. Longumst.** II. 475, 4, 1); Al. 60, 2, c; A. 259, Rem. 4, (2); G. 246, Rem. 1. **981.** *Cantor.* The MSS. here have Ω, which some have supposed to stand for 'Ωδὸς, but more probably for the person who appears *last of all*, and terminates the play. The *cantor* was a singer who had to recite all such parts as were set to music, while the actor himself performed only the necessary gestures and motions. Wr. **Plaudite.** Cf. Horace A. P. 155: *Donec cantor* VOS PLAUDITE *dicat.*

Some of the later MSS. give a second ending of the play of twenty-one lines, beginning after l. 976, in which Charinus' love-affair is concluded. In the opinion of Kz. and Wr., its metre, prosody, and language are such as not to forbid the presumption that Terence was the author, that it may have been the original conclusion of the Play, and that after the first performance Terence conformed to the popular taste by omitting this passage. Cf. the expression *longumst* in l. 977. Ritschl, however, thinks it was by a different author, and intended for a performance not long after Terence's death; and Py. finds no evidence of its genuineness except a notice by Donatus, and the fact that it was known also to Sulpicius Apollinaris and Eugraphius.

THE ADELPHOE.

The *Adelphoe*, the last, and usually considered the finest, of the plays of Terence, derives its name from the two pairs of brothers who are the chief characters, Micio, a bachelor of an easy and indulgent disposition, residing in town, Demea, a farmer, thrifty and strict in the training of his children, and the two sons of the latter. One of these, Ctesipho, living at home, was considered by his father a model of propriety; the other, Aeschinus, adopted by his uncle, had been allowed such freedom that he had fallen into all sorts of excesses. Ctesipho, however, had secretly become attached to a music-slave, whose owner was threatening to sell her at a higher price than he could pay, when Aeschinus, to put her in possession of his brother and shield him from exposure, took her by force from the slave-merchant's house to his own.

The play begins with a discussion between the elder brothers upon the proper mode of parental training, in which Demea, who has just heard of this affair, lays the blame of Aeschinus' wrong-doing upon Micio. At the same time, Sostrata, also learning of it, infers that he has deserted her daughter, Pamphila, whom he had promised to marry, and appeals to Hegio, an old friend of the family, to see that justice is done them. Demea soon after hears a rumor that Ctesipho participated in the abduction of the music-slave, but is assured by Syrus that he had only met his brother to rebuke his conduct, and had then returned to the farm. Demea on his way home is informed by Hegio of Aeschinus' connection with Pamphila, and ascertaining on his arrival there that Ctesipho is still absent, returns to town for another interview with his brother. After a fruitless search in various quarters of the town, occasioned by another fiction of Syrus, he finds that Micio has given his consent to Aeschinus' marriage with Pamphila, and that Ctesipho has been all the while at his uncle's. Further discussion with Micio ensues, when Demea suddenly changes his demeanor, and, to the astonishment of every one, becomes extremely courteous and complaisant, humoring and promoting the happiness of all parties concerned. Pamphila is married to Aeschinus, and Sostrata to Micio; Hegio is presented with a farm; and Syrus and his wife receive their freedom. The play ends with an explanation by Demea of the sudden alteration in his behavior, and some wholesome advice to his brother and sons.

Baron's *Ecole des Pères* and Garrick's Farce of the *Guardian* are among the modern imitations of this play.

ADELPHOE. So Uh., and Wr., who thinks there can be little doubt that Terence transcribed the Greek 'Αδελφόι by this form, since *Adelphe* is the reading of the Ambrosian MS. and *Adelphos* of the Bembine.

DIDASCALIA.

See *Didascalia* of the *Andria*, notes. LVDIS FVNERALIBVS. So Fn. and Wr., following the Bembine MS. The word does not occur elsewhere, except in the *Hecyra, Didasc.* The other MS. reading is *Funebribus*. Funeral games in honor of deceased relatives were not unfrequently celebrated at Rome, generally accompanied, after the year 265 B. C., by gladiatorial shows; but the practice of exhibiting plays in connection with them did not begin before the time of Terence. The second exhibition of the *Hecyra* was on the same occasion as that of the *Adelphoe.* LVCIO AEMILIO PAVLO, surnamed *Macedonicus* for his victory over Perseus, B. C. 168. Q. FABIVS MAXVMVS *Aemilianus*, the eldest son of Paulus, consul B. C. 145, adopted by Q. Fabius Maximus *Cunctator.* P. CORNELIVS Scipio AFRICANVS Minor, the second son of Paulus, adopted by the son of Scipio Africanus Major, the friend of Laelius and the patron of Terence. SERRANIS, *Tyrian.* So Fn. and Mt., following the Bembine MS.; *Sarranis*, the other MS. reading adopted by Wr. *Sarra* (which word the Romans obtained direct from Carthage) and *Tyrus* are both derived from the Phoenician *Tsur, a rock*, the latter through the Greek τύρ ός. Mt. Cos., i. c. in B. C. 160.

PROLOGVS.

1. **Postquam** = *Quoniam*. Cf. l. 765. **Scripturam.** See Lex. *s. v.* II. 2. 2. **Aduorsarios.** See *Andria, Prol.*, and Introd. 3. **Rapere in — partem**, sc. *cam*. See Lex. *s. Rapio* II., A. 4. **Indicio — erit**, *he will inform against himself*. M. 249. *Indicium profiteri* denoted *to turn state's evidence* against a fellow-criminal. Py. See Lex. *s. v.* 5. **Id factum**, sc. *quod indicaturus est.* 6. **Synapothnescontes.** The subject of this was the mutual attachment of two friends, who desired to die at one and the same hour, as life seemed insupportable to each without the other. Wr. See Meineke, *Hist. Crit. Com. Gr.*, p. 456. **Diphili**, a native of Sinope, one of the principal poets of the New Comedy, and a contemporary of Menander. The **Commorientes** of Plautus is not now extant. 9. **Prima fabula**, *the first part of the play*. M. 311. 10. **Reliquit integrum**, *left untouched*, i. e. did not translate *that passage*. **Eum — locum.** So Uh. and Fn., following the MSS.; *hic eum*, Wr. 11. **Uerbum — expressum**, *translated word for word.* 12. **Nouam**, *as a new play.* i. e. one never before exhibited. **Pernoscite.** See *Andr.*, l. 25, and l. 24, note. 13. **Furtumne factum**, i. e. whether this is a case of plagiarism from Plautus. The *Greek* comedies were regarded as mines from which the Roman playwrights might legitimately transfer whatever they would for their own use. Mt. See Introd., p. 137. 14. **Reprensum.** See Lex. *s. v.* II., A. **Praeteritus**, sc. by Plautus. 15. **Nam**, *Now*, is often used in transitions. Arn. **Isti maliuoli.** Cf. *Andria*, l. 6. 15 *et seqq.* **Homines nobilis**, sc. Scipio and Laelius. As to this accusation, see Introd., p. 136, and cf. *Hart.*, l. 22–26. For the form, see *Andr.*, l. 933, note. 16. **Eum.** So Uh. and Fn., following the MSS.; *hunc*, Suetonius, also Wr., on the ground that Terence always designates himself in his prologues by the pronoun *hic*. 19. **Uobis uniuorsis**, the spectators in the theatre; **populo**, the whole city. 20. **Otio**, *peace*. **Negotio**, *civil administration*. Wr. Don. refers the three words respectively to Scipio, Furius Publius, and Laelius — whether justly or not, Wr. thinks may be safely left an open question. Py. regards this as rather forced, and understands the words as a general compendium of the relations of life. 21. **Suo tempore**, i. e. when it suited his convenience. **Sine superbia**, *without any false pride*, i. e. he has not been too proud to accept their help. Py. Ruhnken and Wr. make it refer to the condescension of the *homines nobiles*, but both the collocation and the sense seem to forbid this. 23. **Ei.** For the form, see M. 83, Obs.

1; Z. 132. Don. remarks upon l. 24, "et deest *vestra ;*" and Bentley, Wr., Fn., and Uh. assume a gap after it; though Wr. thinks it not quite impossible that **poetae** is a gloss of an original *vostra huius* or *huic.*

ACTVS I.

Soliloquy of Micio expressing his anxiety on account of the absence of his adopted son, Aeschinus, and contrasting his own mode of parental training with that of his brother, Demea. Conversation between Demea and Micio, the former reporting, with much excitement, what he has just heard of the recent misconduct of Aeschinus, the latter making light of it, apologizing for him, acknowledging his own responsibility for, and claiming the exclusive right to control the conduct of, the youth; yet, after Demea's departure, disclosing his vexation at Aeschinus' conduct.

26. Storax! Micio is represented as calling him. Receiving no answer, he infers that Aeschinus, whom the slave had *gone to meet* and attend home, had not yet returned. **27. Aduorsum.** See Lex. *s. v.* A. Slaves thus employed were called *adversitores.* **29. Cesses,** *delay.* The clauses in brackets, in this and the following line, are thought by Ritschl, Wr., and Fn. to be interpolations. **34.** This line is wanting in the Bembine MS., and is bracketed by Uh. and Fn. **Tibi bene esse,** *that you are enjoying yourself.* **Soli,** i. e. left at home in solitude. **37.** The text gives the reading of Uh., which is that of the MSS. Variations from this are *crus fregerit,* Wr.; *aliqua atque aliquid.* Ritschl, Fn. **38. In animum instituere, etc.,** *should admit into his heart, and there set up an object, which, etc.* W. & R. On the construction, see *Andr.,* l. 245, note. Uh. reads *animo,* Fn. inserts *sibi* after **aut,** and Wr. omits both. **40.** The reading of the Bembine MS., and adopted by Wr. and Fn. **41. Is,** sc. *frater meus.* **42. Clementem.** Cf. *Andria,* l. 36, note. **43. Quod,** sc. *uxorem habere.* **Isti,** i. e. *qui a me dissentiunt.* Don., Py. **44. Contra** is always an adverb in Terence. Wr. **45. Parce ac duriter.** Cf. *Andria,* l. 74, and note. **47. Inde** = *ex iis.* **49. Id** refers to the preceding clause. **50. Sedulo.** See *Andr.,* l. 146, note. **51. Do,** *sc. sumptum ;* **praetermitto,** *delicta.* Don. **52. Pro meo iure,** lit. *in conformity with my authority.* Py. **53. Fert,** *prompts.* **56. Fraudare.** The emendation of Ritschl adopted by Fn. and Wr. The MSS. read *Aut audebit.* **57. Pudore,** *by their respect for others' principles.* Mt. **Liberalitate,** *liberal treatment,* sc. on the part of the father. This sentiment is adopted by Ben Jonson in *Every Man in his Humor :*

> There is a way of winning more by love,
> And urging of the modesty, than fear:
> Force works on servile natures, not the free.

59. **Haec — conueniunt.** *As to this, my brother and I do not agree.*
60. **Clamans.** The MSS., Don., and Cic. *De Inv.* I. 19, read *clamitans*, which Wr. adopts, and omits **agis.** 61. **Nobis.** Ethical dat. M. 248. **Quor.** See *Andr.*, l. 48, note. 63. **Vestitu,** explained by Wr. and others as an archaic form of the dat.; as ablat. of material, by Ds. and Py., who states that *indulgeo* in Terence is used with an accus. of the person, except in *Haut.* 861. See Lex. *s. v.* 64. **Que et.** M. 435, a, Obs. 1; Z. 338. It occurs only in the older poets, and in Livy and later prose writers. Cf. Livy XXI. 30. Wr. 66. **Qui.** See M. 366; Z. 564. 68. **Ratio.** See Lex. *s. v.* II., B. 2, c. 69. **Malo,** i. e. fear of *punishment*. Cf. Hor. *Epist.* I. 16, 53:

> *Tu nihil admittes in te formidine poenae:*
> *Sit spes fallendi, miscebis sacra profanis.*

Sall. Jugurth. 100: *Pudore magis quam malo exercitum coercebat.* Cic. *in Verr.* II., iii. 25. 70. **Pauet.** So Uh. and Fn.; *cavet*, Wr. and Py. 71. **Ingenium,** *his natural disposition.* Cf. *Andr.*, l. 77. 75. **Alieno,** *of others.* 76. **Hoc,** either abl. or accus., and it is difficult to decide which is the more probable. The construction is rare in Latin. Wr. The more usual form would be *Hoc interest inter patrem ac dominum.* 78. **Ipsus.** See *Andr.*, l. 360, note. 79. **Nescio quid.** See *Andr.*, l. 340, note. 81. **Opportune,** sc. *advenis.* 83. **Scin iam.** Ritschl's emendation adopted by Fn. and Wr.; *Siet*, the MSS. Uh. and Py. **Dixin fore,** said aside to the audience. 84. **Quid — fecerit,** sc. *rogas?* the indirect quest. only expressed. 85. **Quicquam.** See M. 218, a, Obs. 2; Z. 442. 87. **Designauit,** lit. means *to mark out,* then *to plan a scheme of action.* Mt. See Lex. *s. v.* II., B. 89. **Dominum,** *the master of the house.* **Familiam,** here in its primitive meaning. 93. **In orest.** *He's the talk of the town.* Cf. Cic. *Lael.* I. 95. **Rei,** *his business.* 96. **Huius** limits **simile.** **Illi** = *in illum.* Don. 97. **Corrumpi.** See *Andr.*, l. 396, note. 101. **Flagitium.** He does not deny that it is wrong, but maintains that it is not an *infamous crime.* Don. Cf. Cic. *Pro Coel.* 20. 104. **Siit** = *Sivit.* 106. **Iniurium.** See *Andr.*, l. 378, note. **Esset,** sc. in our youth. 107. **Faceremus,** *we should have done the same over and over again.* On the tense of these verbs, see M. 347, Obs. 2; Z. 525. **Esses homo,** i. e. *had the common sense of a man.* Py. and Ds. Cf. l. 579, 934. 108. **Dum — licet,** *while he has the excuse of youth.* Mt. 109. **Expectatum.** See Lex. *s. v.* and cf. l. 874; Plaut. *Mostell.* II. 2, 10:

Th. *Triennio post Aegypto advenio domum.*
Credo, expectatus veniam familiaribus.
Tr. *Nimis edepol ille potuit expectatior*
Venire qui te nuntiaret mortuum;

and Quintil. IX. 3, 68: "When Proculeius complained of his son that he was *wishing for* (*expectaret*) his death, and the son had said that he was not, the father rejoined: 'But I wish you may have to *wait for* (*expectes*) it.'" **Eiecisset** denotes the indecorous haste and want of ceremony of the burial. Wr. *Ecferre* was the term for a decent funeral. Cf. *Andr.*, l. 117. **110. Alieniore,** *more unfitting.* **111. Tu homo,** i. e. *you,* with your *common sense,* as you call it. Mt. See l. 107. **113. Obtundas.** See *Andr.*, l. 348, note. **116. Mihi,** i. e. *to my cost.* **Illi,** a locative adv. = *illic (illi ce), in that case.* **117. Unguenta.** H. 371, 3, 2); Al. 52, 1, c; A. 232, 2; B. 716; G. 329, Rem. 1. **De meo,** *at my expense.* **118. Dum — commodum,** sc. for me. **119. Excludetur.** See *Andr.*, l. 386, note. **123. Cedo,** corrupted by contraction from *ce — duto = hocce dato,* W. & R.; with **arbitrum,** = appeal to any one you please to decide between us. **125. Qui — sciunt,** sc. what it is to be a father. **127. Consulis.** So the MSS. For the sake of the play on the words, Uh. reads *consiliis;* while Wr. reads *consuliis* in l. 126. **Abiero.** *I'm off,* more emphatic than the Fut. H. 473, 1; Al. 58, 7, Rem.; A. 259, Rem. 1 (5); B. 1099; G. 236. **129. Curaest mihi,** i. e. *I'm anxious about the boy.* **130. Curemus.** M. 215, a; Z. 367. **Aequam partem,** i. e. his *fair share.* **133. Quid istic.** See *Andr.*, l. 572, note. **135. Ullum.** So Fn., after several MSS.; *unum,* the Bemb. MS. Uh. and Wr. On the whole sentence, see *Andr.*, l. 164, note. **136. Credis,** sc. *me irasci,* i. e. *Don't you think I have reason to be angry.* **137. Aegrest,** *I grieve over him.* Wr. and Ps. **Alienus,** *a stranger; mire quasi timeat iam dicere* '*pater sum.*' Don. **139. Quom** = *quoniam* or *quod* of later Latin. Wr. **Sentiet,** sc. *the consequences.* See Lex. *s. v.* I., B. **140. In illum,** etc. Cf. *Andr.*, l. 874. **141. Nec — dicit.**

'Though what he says be not entirely true,
There's something in it.' — Colman.

142. Nil. M. 455, Obs. 4; Z. 677. **144. Placo,** *try to appease.* **Aduorsor,** etc., *I steadily oppose and repel him from me.* **147. Cum illo,** i. e. *as much as he.* **150. Omnium,** sc. *meretricium.* **151 Dixit,** etc., illustrates the poet's art in preparing incidents, causing even ignorant persons to open the plot; e. g. here Micio shows that Aeschinus had mentioned to him his intention of marrying some one, though he had

Q

not entered into particulars. Ps. **153.** **De integro,** *the same thing over again.* Mt. Cf. *Andr.,* l. 26. **Nisi,** here = *sed,* as in many passages of Terence. Py. Cf. *Andr.,* l. 664, and note.

ACTVS II.

Dispute between Sannio and Aeschinus respecting a slave-girl the latter had taken from Sannio's house. Negotiations between Syrus and Sannio, who finally consents to Aeschinus' retaining the slave at cost-price. Ctesipho's laudation of his brother's self-sacrificing kindness to him. Aeschinus and Ctesipho congratulate one another on the state of affairs. Sannio is pacified by the assurance of receiving the stipulated sum.

156. Otiose, sc. *jam incedamus.* Aeschinus addresses the slave-girl. **Nunciam** = an emphatic *now.* **158. Ego,** sc. *tangam.* **161. At ita, etc.,** *But yet I am as true to my word as any one ever was.* He at first attempts to gain his property by threats and intimidation. Py. **162. Quod, etc.,** *As for your trying to, etc.* M. 398, b, Obs. 2; Z. 627. The subjunct. here, bec. the clause is 'a future possibility.' Key, 1454, *e.* **163. Huius.** M. 294, Obs. 1; Z. 444, note. **166. Indignis Quom, etc.,** i. e. when the *only* thing that is *unworthy* is *the way in which, etc.* Mt. **167.** Addressed to his slave, Parmeno. **Nili,** genitive of value; i. e. *your doing so is of no use.* **169. Nimium abisti,** *You've gone too far.* **Istoc,** *that way;* lit. to that place where you now stand. **171. Mala,** *cheek.* **172. Istuc — experiri,** sc. *whether you dare strike me.* **Serua.** See Lex. *s. v.* II., A. 1. **173.** A blow from Parmeno causes the exclamation **O — facinus,** and another, **Ei — mihi.** For the cases, M. 236, and Obs. 2. **174. In istam partem,** *on that side,* sc. on which *you* are now *erring.* On the use of the pronouns, see *Andr.,* l. 32, note. **Tamen,** made emphatic by its position. When it modifies a particular notion only or especially, it follows that notion. Arn. **175. Regnumne, etc.,** i. e. Do you think you can commit any outrage with impunity. Mt. Cf. Sall. *Jugurth.* 31: *Impune quaelibet facere, id est, regem esse.* **177. Desidero,** sc. *noscere.* **180. Non erit melius** implies a threat. **185. Autem** is used not only in corrective questions, but also in other impassioned questions of appeal, especially in the comic writers. Arn. **187. Aequi aliquid,** *something that's fair,* sc. *dicas.* **190. Nam — restat.** *No; for that is yet to come,* i. e. If you *had* injured me, you would not have got off as cheaply as you have. Py. **191. Loqueris,** an emendation of Krauss from *loquae res,* the reading of the Bemb. MS. So Wr. and Fn. The common reading is *quae res,* and the whole line is put into the mouth of Aeschinus. **192. Dabitur,** sc. *a me.* **194.**

Liberali, etc. See Lex. s. v. I. The allusion is to the practice of the courts in which a person maintained before the praetor that another was a free person, not a slave. See Dict. Antiqq., s. *Assertor*. 195. **Causam meditari,** sc. for trial in court. Cf. *Andr.*, l. 406, note. 197. **Qui.** M. 321. 198. **Domo — eripuit,** Wr. thinks is hardly a correct expression for Sannio, as Aeschinus would willingly have left him at home if only he would have stayed there; and he reads *Domi — arripuit*. 199. **Colophos.** M. 306. 200. **Tantidem emptam,** *bought at the same price,* sc. *quanti a me empta fuerit,* i. e. *at cost price.* Py. 201. **Bene promeruit,** said ironically. 202. **Hariolor.** See Lex. II. 203. **Dare,** i. e. *offer to sell* her. **Testis faciet,** *he will call witnesses.* 204. **Mox — redi.** The excuses of Aeschinus as foreseen by Sannio. 206. **Res,** *a fact.* **Eum quaestum,** sc. *lenocinium.* Cf. *Andr.*, l. 79, and note. 208. **Dabit,** sc. *argentum.* **Has — puto,** *make all these calculations.* Mt. 209. **Tace — actum,** said to Aeschinus as he leaves the house. 212. **Comparatam,** *matched,* often used of gladiatorial contests. 213. **Usque,** connected with what precedes by Wr. and W. & R.; with what follows, by Fn. 214. **Culpa,** ablat. **Gestum.** M. 407, Obs. 1; and see *Andr.*, l. 239, 641, notes. 216. **In loco,** *on a fitting occasion.* 218. **Morigerasses.** So Fn.; *esses morigeratus,* the MSS. Uh. and Wr. 219. **Faeneraret,** *would not have paid, have brought in interest,* a use of the word peculiar to this place. Py. **Ego — emo,** i. e. a bird in the hand is worth two in the bush. 220. **Rem,** your *fortune.* 222. **Potius** belongs to quin. Wr. See M. 308, Obs. 2. **Auferre.** See Lex. s. v. 4: with **in praesentia,** *to make a present gain.* 223. **Usquam,** *of any account.* So Don., Wr., Py.; a meaning found nowhere else, but accounted for by the influence of *a Greek original.* Cf. τοῦτον δυάμου λέγω. It is, of course, ironical. 224. **Dum.** See Lex. s. v. I., B. 2. 226. **Pendet,** sc. whether to go to Cyprus or remain here. **Tamen,** i. e. notwithstanding the delay. 227. **Pedem,** sc. *profero, I'll not stir a foot.* 229. **Articulo,** sc. *temporis; how he has caught me in the very nick of time.* Py. Cf. Cic. *Pro. Quinct.* 5. 232. **Ac tum.** So Bentley. Uh., Fn., and Wr.: *actum,* the MS. reading, which Wr. thinks destroys alike the sense and the metre. 234. **Passu's,** sc. *rem refrigescere.* 235. **Tum,** sc. on my return. **Persequi.** Cf. l. 163. 236. **Quod — putes,** *which you reckon will be your profit* from this voyage. 237-8. This also is said aside by Sannio. And his change of purpose is shown by his entirely deserting the ground of legal right, and declaiming against the unworthy behavior of Aeschinus; a sign of weakness of which Syrus immediately takes advantage. Py. 239. **Unum hoc,** *this one thing,* sc. to offer. 241. **Diuiduom face,** *split the difference.* 243. **Sorte.** See

Lex. s. v. II., C. 2, and cf. Livy VI. 14. **Uenio — dubium**, *Am I now in danger of losing.* Cf. The Merchant of Venice, IV. 1 : "Shall I not barely have my principal!" **247. Numquid — abeam?** *Have you any commands to prevent my going?* usually expressed more briefly by *Numquid vis?* = *Good-by.* **248. Litis.** See *Andr.*, l. 811, note. **251. Sedulo.** See *Andr.*, l. 146, 679, notes. **259. Homini nemini**, a tautology which serves here for emphasis. Wr. Cf. *Eunuch.* 549, *Hecyra*, 281. **Artium**, *qualities.* **260. Ellum.** See *Andr.*, l. 855, note. **261. Sit.** Cf. l. 84, and note. **262. Qui ignominias.** So Ub., Fn., and Wr., an emendation of the Bemb. MS. reading, *quignominia.* **Post**, i. e. *secondary, of less moment.* **263. Laborem**, *troubles, difficulties.* So Ub. and Fn., from Nonius, instead of *amorem*, the MS. reading. **264. Potis.** So Fn. and Wr., and it is often used in the neuter gender. Cf. l. 521; *Eunuch.*, l. 113; *Lucret.* I. 451; Catull. LXXVI. 24. The Bemb. MS. here reads *potest ;* Ub., *pote.*, which is the more common neuter form. **Supra**, sc. *dici.* **Crepuit.** See *Andr.*, l. 682, note. **265. Numquid**, i. e. *any money* for me. See *Andr.*, l. 235, note. **266. Quid fit.** A familiar expression *among equals,* like the Eng. *How d' ye do?* Mt. **270. Adsentandi**, sc. *causa.* M. 417, Obs. 5; Z. 764. **Quo** = *eo quod.* **272.** The reading of Fn. and Wr. *Paene*, before **sero**, and *scisse*, instead of *rescisse*, are retained by Ub. **Rescisse**, sc. that the slave-girl was to be taken to Cyprus. **274. Pudebat**, sc. *fateri.* **275. E patria**, sc. *exsulare*, or *ejici.* Mt. **276. Nobis.** M. 248; Z. 408. It is here used ironically, as frequently. Key Lat. Gr., 978. **Iam — est**, *Oh he is pacified at last.* Py. **278. Insta**, sc. the matter which I entrusted to you just now. Cf. l. 247, *et seqq.* **Ne tam quidem**, lit. *not even so much — not at all; I'll not stir a step.* Mt. **285. Lectulos**, *eating-couches.* **286. Obsonio.** See *Andr.*, l. 360, note. **287. Hilare**, an emendation adopted by Fn. and Wr., instead of the MS. reading, *hilarem.* Terence nowhere uses *hilaris*, but always *hilarus.* Wr.

ACTVS III.

Geta bewails his mistress's misfortune in the supposed faithlessness of Aeschinus, relates what he has seen to Sostrata, and is sent by her to Hegio to ask his advice. Demea is alarmed at hearing unfavorable reports of Ctesipho. Syrus humors his self-conceit, confirms him in his delusion as to his son's merits, and assures him that Ctesipho has gone back to the farm. Demea, starting to return, stops to talk with Hegio. Hegio, having heard the story about Aeschinus, communicates the facts to Demea, and appeals to him to see that justice is done to Pamphila.

The latter promises in behalf of Micio, and determines to see him about the matter. Hegio consoles Sostrata.

304. Hocine saeclum! *Is this the character of this age!* **306. Illum,** pleonastic; an idiom not infrequent. Cf. Virg. *Aen.* V. 334, 457. **313. Meo modo.** So Fn. and Uh.; *modo, probe.* Wr. **314. Illud scelus,** sc. Aeschinus. **316. Sublimem.** See *Andr.,* l. 861, note. **320. Eram, malo.** II. 384, II. 1; Al. 51, 1, c; A. 249, Rem. 3; B. 859; G. 318. **321. Sine me,** *permit me,* sc. to hasten to my mistress. It was a common practical joke to detain slaves in the street, that they might be whipped when they came home for staying out so long. Dacier. **322. Expecto.** So Fn. and Uh.; *expeto,* Wr. **Oppido** occurs in several other places in Terence, and is a very common word in Plautus; generally used in an intensive sense. **324. Prorsus,** *Utterly.* **325. Actumst.** See *Andr.,* l. 465, note. **328. Occulte fert,** *conceal.* **330. Quoi.** See *Andr.,* l. 1, note. **331. Nostram omnium.** M. 297, a; Z. 424. **336. Sanun =** *sanusne.* **337. Hau,** regarded by Fn. and Wr. as the original reading instead of *non,* which Uh. retains. It occurs in early Latin before consonants instead of *haud.* **339. Infitias.** M. 232, Obs. 4. **340. Uita,** i. e. position in life. Ps. **Si maxume,** *if even.* **342. Tacito.** See *Andr.,* l. 490, note. **Gentium.** II. 396, III. 4); Al. 50, 2, d; A. 212, Rem. 4, Note 2; G. 371, 4. **345. Secunda dos,** i. e. what might have been considered her dowry, figuratively speaking. Wr. Cf. Hor. O. III. 24, 21; Plaut. *Amphit.* II. 2, 209 :

> *Non ego illam mihi dotem esse duco quae dos dicitur,*
> *Sed pudicitiam, et pudorem, et sedatum cupidinem,*
> *Deum metum et parentum amorem, et cognatum concordiam,*
> *Tibi morigera, atque ut munifica sim bonis, prosim probis.*

346. Nuptum. M. 411, Obs. 1. **347. Mecum,** *in my possession.* **349. Pretium,** sc. as a compromise for the wrong done to my daughter. **350. Experiar.** See Lex. *s. v.* II., B. **Quid istic.** Cf. l. 133, and *Andr.,* l. 572, note. **Cedo.** So Fn., Uh., and Wr., after Bentley, as necessitated by the metre; *accedo,* the MSS. The whole clause is difficult to explain satisfactorily, and the text is probably corrupt. *I concede to you that you speak better.* Wr. thinks Terence wrote *dicis,* i. e. *I yield, since you advise better.* **Quantum — potest.** See *Andr.,* l. 861, note. **352. Simulo,** sc. her late husband. **Summus,** sc. *amicus.* See Lex. *s. v.,* l. 2, b. **353. Respicit.** See *Andr.,* l. 642, note. **358. Aliquoi rei,** *fit for something.* II. 390, II. 2; Al. 51, 5; A. 227, Rem. 3; B. 853; G. 350. **Meum.** So Fn.; *eum,* Uh., Wr. **361. Scibo.** M. 115, c; Z. 162. **364. Seni,** sc. Micio. **365. Haberet,** sc. *sc.* **Enarramus,** considered a contracted form for *enarravimus* by Py. and others. It may, however, be an historical present. See II. 481, IV. 2; Al. 58, 10, e; A. 258, II.; B. 1167; G. 511, R. 1. Brix (Plaut. *Trinum.* 14) thinks it cannot be a contracted perfect. **369. Adnumerauit,** *counted out, paid.* W. & R. **370. In sumptum,** *to make an entertainment.* Colman. **371. Ex sententia,** sc. *mea.* Cf. l. 420. **373. Quid agitur,** *How goes it with you.* **375. Rationem,** *style of acting.* Cf. l. 812. **Ne — dolo,** *to speak the truth.* **382. Vtrum — ne — an.** See M. 452, Obs. 1; Z. 554. Wr. and Py. consider **Vtrum,** in such a case as this, as a pronoun with its verb understood, and that it states generally the alternative which is particularized by **ne** and **an** following. Cf. *Eunuch.*, l. 721: *Utrum praedicemne an taceam;* Plaut. *Capt.* 268. Some have considered **Vtrum** separated from **ne** by tmesis. But, according to Wr. (Plaut. *Aul.* 427), there is not a single instance of *utrumne an* in the comic writers. That usage belongs to the silver age. **Studio,** i. e. *purposely.* The alternative is that either Micio is making the ruin of his adopted son his direct aim and *study,* or that he merely permits its progress with the idea that it will redound to his praise as an indulgent father. Ps. **385. Aliquo militatum.** Oftentimes, as a last resort, those who had squandered their fortunes, or had been piqued in love, went and enlisted in the army of one of the Asiatic kings, between whom the empire of Alexander the Great had been divided, and who were constantly at war with one another. Wr. Cf. *Havt.*, l. 117: *In Asiam ad regem militatum abiit.* **386. Istuc,** i. e. such as *you* possess. **389. Ellam.** See *Andr.*, l. 855, note. **Habiturus,** sc. *Aeschinus psaltriam.* **394. Quantus quantus** = *quantuscumque,* i. e. *every inch of you.* Cf. *quisquis* = *quicumque; quoquo* = *quocumque; utut.* Z. 521. **395. Somnium,** i. e. *a dotard.* **398. Mihi,** sc. who know it so well. **Siet,** sc. Ctesipho. For the form, see *Andr.*, l. 234, note. **399.** On the sentiment, cf. Prov. XXII. 6. Mt., however, thinks this is said aside, and interprets **itast,** *so it is,* i. e. in his own eyes. 'Geese are swans to those that own them.' **401. Abigam — rus,** said aside to the spectators. **402. Qui.** So the Bemb. MS., Fn. and Uh.; *quem,* Bentley and Wr. **Produxi,** *conducted him on his way.* Cf. l. 561. **421. Ei.** So Fn.; *hi,* Uh. and older editions. Wr. omits. See l. 23, note. **Cautiost.** See *Andr.*, l. 400, note. **422. Tam** = *tantum.* Cf. l. 278, and note. **429. Quid.** See *Andr.*, l. 490, note. **Usus.** M. 266, *in fin.;* Z. 464, Note 2. 'This parody of Demea's serious advice to his son is one of the best hits in Terence. The whole scene goes some way to redeem his character from the charge of deficiency in comic vigor.' Py. **430. Nos,** *our people*, i. e. Micio, Aeschinus, and Micio's household. Ds. **431. Ut homost**, etc., probably a proverbial saying: 'You must take a man as you find him, and *humor him* accordingly.' The application of the words here is: 'Aeschinus' habits are confirmed, and we must only let him have his way.' Ps. **432. Numquid uis?** The ordinary form of taking leave. See l. 247, note. **Mentem**, etc., replies to uis in its literal meaning, when the appropriate answer would be *valeas*. Ps. Demea will not even use the ordinary formalities of society, but must say something bitter. Py. **441. Ne** = *vai.* (See *Andr.*, l. 17, note.) **442. Antiqua.** See Lex, *s. v.* 4, and *Andr.*, 817, note. **443. Publice,** *in a public point of view.* Ds. **444. Etiam.** See *Andr.*, l. 116, note. **448. Quid?** So the best MSS., Uh. and Wr.; *Quod*, Fn. **450. Haud — dedisti,** *this was not acting like your father.* Colman. **Dedisti** is in the sense of *fecisti*, according to Py. and Ds., in that of *put forth, exhibit*, according to Mt. **453. Adsit, audiat;** the MSS. Uh. and Wr., *adesset, audiret.* **454. Sic auferent,** sc. *inultum.* Cf. *Andr.*, l. 610. **458. Dixeris,** sc. *"deseris."* M. 375, a, Obs. 1; Z. 624. **464. Officium.** The accusative always follows *fungi* in the comic poets. Wr. Cf. *Haut.*, l. 66; 580; *Phorm.* 282; and according to Fn. and Wr. *Adelph.*, l. 603, though the MSS. have in that passage the ablat. Cf. also *Andr.*, l. 5, note. **466. Aequalem.** See *Andr.*, l. 453, note. **Quid ni,** sc. *noverim;* = *Of course I did.* **473. Ducturum.** See Lex. *s. v.* I., B. 2. **476. Si — placet,** said ironically. Wr., however, considers **si** = *sic;* i. e. 'We can't help it, it is nothing of our doing.' **479. In mediost,** lit. *is in the midst of us,* i. e. can be produced to prove it. Mt. **480. Ut captus,** etc., *considering what slaves are.* See Lex. *s. r.*, 2. **482. Quaere rem** implies torture, as the means of eliciting the truth. Ds. **484. Coram — cedo,** i. e. *Question me in his presence.* Mt. On **Cedo,** see l. 123, note. **490. Quod — uos.** Cf. M. 228, b; Z. 393; Virg. Aen. III. 56. **Ius.** So Fn. and Wr.; *vis*, Uh. and others. **491. Uobis.** See Z. 390, *in fin.*, Note; and cf. l. 928, and *Haut.*, l. 965. **Decet,** sc. *facere.* **497. Experiar.** See l. 350, note. After l. 499, the MSS. insert a line which is merely an interpolation from *Phorm.*, l. 461. Wr. **501. Quam ... Tam,** here, as elsewhere in the comic writers, used with superlatives where we use the comparative. Cf. *Haut.*, l. 9, 97; Sall. *Jugurth.* 31; Plaut. *Aul.*, l. 234; Z. 725. Wr. renders *in such proportion . . . in the same proportion.* **Facillume agitis,** *live in the greatest ease, are well off.* **503. Noscere,** i. e. *exercere.* **505. Redito.** Hegio has just spoken somewhat angrily, and is turning to leave, when Demea calls him back and promises further. **507. Indicente** occurs only here and in Livy XXII. 39, 2. **Sit defunctum,** here a passive impersonal.

Py. Cf. Livy II. 35. **Modo,** *only,* i. e. with no worse consequences than these. Mt. **511. Quod** = *quoad.* **514. Si est, is.** So Uh. and Fn.; *Si ita est, If the fact be that, etc.* Wr. and others. **515. Faciat** and **Respondeat** are Subjunct. of Desire.

ACTVS IV.

Ctesipho's questioning of Syrus about his father's movements, his perplexity as to the most plausible excuse for absence from home, and fear of discovery. Demea's soliloquy upon his family troubles, delight at Syrus' story of ill treatment from Ctesipho as evidence of the latter's virtue, and departure by a circuitous route, suggested by Syrus, in search of Micio. Interview of the latter with Hegio; his promise of full reparation to Pamphila, and of a satisfactory explanation of Aeschinus' conduct. Aeschinus' soliloquy upon Pamphila's suspicions about him and the danger of compromising his brother; his self-reproach for neglect to ask at the first his father's leave to marry, and resolve to make full explanations. His interview with his father, confession of his love-affair, and gentle reproof from Micio with assent to the marriage. Demea's return from his fruitless search; reproach of Micio for the more serious misconduct of Aeschinus, just made known to him, and greater indignation on learning of Micio's approval of the marriage. Interview of Syrus and Demea interrupted by a message from Ctesipho to Syrus, which leads Demea to search the house for his son. Again reproaching Micio for spoiling both his sons, he is with difficulty pacified by the explanations of his brother, and consents to remain to the wedding of Aeschinus.

517. Sodes. See *Andr.,* l. 85, note. **518. Quom maxume.** See *Andr.,* l. 823, note. **Vtinam quidem,** sc. *faciat.* **519. Fiat.** M. 364, Obs. 2; Z. 559. **520. Triduo.** So the MSS. Uh. and Fn. Wr. thinks the accusative necessary to correspond to similar phrases in *Hec.,* l. 87; Plaut. *Rudens,* 370, etc. **521. Istoc,** ablat. Syrus hints a wish for the old man's death. But Ctesipho seems to take it as a kind of addition to his own wish. Py. **Potis.** See l. 264, note. **527. Ego hoc te.** An emendation adopted by Uh., Wr., Fn.; *Quem ego hodie,* the MSS. **528. In mentem.** M. 230, b, Obs. 2; Z. 316, *in fin.* In this phrase the accusative seems to be the rule in archaic language; instances also occur in later writers, and especially in juridical language. Wr. **Nequior,** *the worse,* sc. *es.* **530. Hisc — sit,** depends upon **in mentem,** or a similar expression to be supplied from what precedes. **533. Quin.** See *Andr.,* l. 45, note. **534. Ouem.** Cf. M. 303, b; Z. 484. **535. Te—deum.** This expression is used in sober prose by Cicero, *De Orat.* II. 42, but with reference to *power* instead of, as here, to *goodness*. Mt. **537. En tibi.** *Mind yourself.* **Lupus in fabula.** Wr. states that the origin of this expression is a tale in which a nurse says to a crying child, 'Be quiet, else the wolf will come and eat you'—and lo, there is the wolf to speak for itself. Servius, however, connects it with the popular notion that the sight of a wolf deprived a person of speech, and so, he says, the proverb is applied to the appearance of one of whom we are talking, whose arrival cuts short our conversation. Py. **539. Tu,** sc. *vidisse—dicas.* **540. Gentium.** M. 284, Obs. 10; Z. 434. **543. Syre.** Ctesipho speaks from within. Cf. l. 538. **Verum.** See *Andr.*, l. 769, note. **544. Malum,** a common exclamation, frequently occurring in Plautus and Terence. Py. Cf. *Hart.*, l. 318, 716; *Eunuch.*, l. 780. **545. Nisi.** See *Andr.*, l. 664, note. **547. Obnuntio,** always used of *evil* tidings. **550. Etiam.** See *Andr.*, l. 849, note. **554. Syrus,** pretending not to see Demea, rushes in in great haste, as if he were just smarting from a severe whipping, and thought of running away. **561. Produxe.** See l. 402, note; M. 113, **b**, Obs. 3; II. 234, 3; Al. 30, 6, **b**; A. 162, 7, **c**; B. 320; G. 191, 5. **562. Puduisse.** See *Andr.*, l. 215, 870, notes. **564. Patrissas,** from πατρίζειν, which is, however, mentioned by Priscian alone, and is not found in any Greek writer. Wr. See II. 332, I. 2); Al. 44, 2, **b**; A. 187, 5; B. 587. **Abi.** See Lex. *s. v.* S. **566. Perquam,** stronger than *valde* or *magnopere*. Arn. **568. Caput.** See *Andr.*, l. 458, note. **575. Uorsum** is pleonastic. **576. Ad — manum,** explained by a gesture accompanying the words. **577. Illi,** *there.* See l. 116, note. **578. Angiportum,** here *a court* without an outlet; sometimes any narrow lane terminating at both ends in some public street, or leading to the less frequented parts of the city. Rich's Dict. Antiqq. **579. Censen — esse?** i. e. You see I am a poor fallible mortal. Py. See M. 6, Obs. 2; 451, a; Z. 352. Wr., however, renders: *Would you believe me to be in my senses?* **580. Erratio,** here, *danger of missing the way.* **582. Dianae,** sc. *aedem*. M. 280, Obs. 3; Z. 762. Cf. Hor. *Sat.* I. 9, 35; and in Eng., "St. Peter's," "St. Paul's." **583. Lacum.** With these directions of Syrus, cf. Shakesp. *Merchant of Venice*, II. 2. **585. Lectulos in sole,** *couches for sunning oneself,* i. e. for use in the *solarium*, *sunny chamber*, or *terrace* on the top of a house. **Faciundos dedit,** *has ordered to be made,* sc. Micio. **587. Silicernium,** i. e. old enough to die and furnish an occasion for a *funeral feast*. Wr. See Lex. *s. v.* **589. In — totus,** *entirely taken up with his love.* Cf. Hor. *Sat.* I. 9, 2. **593. A nobis,** *on our part,* identifying himself with his adopted son. **595. Ultro,** *moreover.* Cf. *Andr.*, l. 100, and note. **597. Atque.** See *Andr.*, l. 515, note. **In,** omitted and *esse* substituted by Wr. **600. Fn.** and Wr. assume a gap after this line, and to fill it suggest: *Ab Aeschino raptum esse fratrem quo adiuvaret clanculum*, on the ground that Sostrata was aware that the suspicions against Aeschinus arose on account of the *psaltria*, and that what ought now to be told her was the precise truth. **601. Facto.** See *Andr.*, l. 490, note. **605. Minus secundae**, a euphemism for *miserae*. **607. Ludier.** So Bentley, Fn., and Wr.; *claudier*, Bemb. MS.; *negligi*, other ed. **608. Ipsi,** *to her, i. e. in her eyes.* Mt. So Uh., Fn., and Wr.; others, *ipsis*. **Placabilius.** M. 185, b, Obs. 1; Z. 249, 3, *in fin.* **610. Animi.** M. 296, b, Obs. 3; Z. 437, Note 1. This usage was as old and original in Latin as it was in Greek. **611. De me.** M. 267, and Obs.; Z. 491. **614. Turba,** *trouble, scrape.* **615. Incidit,** sc. *illis.* **620. Abi,** here with a reproachful signification. Cf. l. 564, and note. **621. Dedisti uerba.** See *Andr.*, l. 211, note. **622. Ualeas.** See *Andr.*, l. 696, note. **625. Opus,** *expedient.* An instance of litotes. H. 705, VI.; A. 324, 9; G. 448, 2. **626. Mitto** = *Not to dwell on that, for,* etc. **627. Id,** sc. *fratris esse hanc.* **629. Adeo** strengthens **mea.** See *Andr.*, l. 579, note. **631. Nunc porro.** See *Andr.*, l. 22, note. **633. Pultare.** See *Andr.*, l. 682, note. **634. Aliquis** is here used distributively. Py. Cf. M. 217, Obs. 1; Z. 367. **638. Quid—negotist,** said aside. So also **Tacet**—**dicere,** and l. 643 to **est. 639. Ludo** = *illuda.* **641. Istas,** sc. *fores populi.* **643. Sodes.** See *Andr.*, l. 85, note. **646. Aduocatum,** technically denoted a person who gave his advice and aid to another in the management of a cause, but did not signify the orator or *patronus* who made the speech. See Dict. Antiqq. **648. Vt,** etc. On the punctuation of this and the preceding line, Uh., Fn., and Wr. agree. There is a mixture of two constructions: Regularly either *Vt opinor . . . noristi* or *Opinor . . . nosse* would be expected. **652. Huic leges,** etc. See *Andr.*, l. 71, note. In *Phorm.*, l. 125, a recital of the law is given:

    Lex est ut orbae, qui sunt genere proxumi,
    Eis nubant, et illos ducere eadem haec lex iubet.

655. Animo malest, *I feel as if I should faint.* Py.; said aside. Cf. Plant. *Amphit.* 1058; *Rudens,* 510. **656. Nil enim,** *Nothing of course worth thinking of.* Mt. See *Andr.*, l. 503, note. **659. Priorem esse,** i. e. has a prior claim. **660. Poscere.** An emendation adopted by Uh. and Wr. *Postea,* the MS. reading = *after what you had heard.* Py. **664. Inliberaliter,** here in its literal meaning. **666. Animi** limits **quid. Qui cum ea.** So Bentley and Wr. **Ea** has then a monosyllabic pronunciation. The MS. reading, *cum illa,* is against the metre. Fn.

has *qui illa*, but according to Wr. no passage can be quoted where *consuescere* takes an ablat. of the person. To another reading, *quicum illa*, there are also objections on account of the metre. **671. Auctor.** See Lex. s. v. 9, c. **672. Alienam.** As an orphan, she belonged to her next of kin, and was thus virtually *betrothed to another*. **673. Grandem,** *grown up.* **674. Haec** refers to the words used, *id* to the matter of the argument. Py. **678. Nostra,** sc. *e re sunt*. **683. Tui,** *because of my respect for you.* The gen., with **pudet,** sometimes denotes the person *before whom the shame is felt*. M. 292; Z. 443. **684. Indiligens,** *reckless*. We must suppose Aeschinus to show great remorse, and Micio, who has had some difficulty in being angry enough with him, now takes up the question as one of expediency. Py. **687. Humanum.** Cf. l. 471, and see l. 107, 579, and notes. **693. Dormienti,** *without any exertion of yours.* **695. Rerum.** M. 289, b. **700. Eam, Eam.** So Fn., Wr.; *iam, iam,* the Bemb. MS., and Ub. **Quantum potest.** See *Andr.,* l. 861, note. **702. Perbenigne,** sc. *dicis, you are very kind,* a common form of polite refusal. So here Micio expresses his incredulity by the same form. Cf. *Phorm.* 1051. **707. Quid negoti?** *What a marvel is this?* expresses surprise and commendation. Don. **708. Qui,** *how*. **Morem gereret.** See l. 431, note. **709. Gestandus in sinust.** Cf. Shakespeare, *Hamlet,* III. 2: 'I will wear him in my heart's core; ay, in my heart of hearts.' **711. Sciens** — *prudens.* **716. Illic fabrica.** The MSS. add *ulla*. Ub. reads *fabrica illi ulla . . . nec*; Wr., *illi ulla fabrica . . . nec.* **719. Illis,** sc. Sostrata and her daughter. **722. Ecce — noua.** *See, now, new officers!* So Fn. and Wr.; *Ecce autem.* De *Noua,* Ub. and older ed. **723. Capitalia,** lit. *deserving capital punishment.* **727. Clamas,** *cry out against, complain of.* **Malim quidem.** Here he is interrupted by Demea. **728. Uortant,** *cause to turn out, prosper.* See Lex. s. v. l., B. 1. **730. Res - fert,** *the situation suggests.* **732. Isto pacto,** sc. without a dowry. **Oportet,** *nuptias fieri.* **Amplius.** Micio pretends to misunderstand his brother, as though he were complaining that the preparations for the wedding were not on a sufficient scale. Mt. **733. Ipsa re,** *really.* **734. Hominis,** here a man of *proper* feeling, in l. 736, a man of *kind* feeling; a play upon the meaning of the word. Py. **735. Fiunt,** i. e. *are about to take place.* **741. Id.** M. 489, a. **Ut corrigas.** sc *ɩuc.* **742. Corrector,** *Fine mender, indeed!* ironical. Py. **743. Quantum,** sc. *celerrime.* **744. Abiciendast,** sc. by selling under the real value. Wr. But see Lex. s. v. l. **754. Haec.** See l. 85, note. **756. Hilarum.** M. 59, Obs. 3; Z. 101, Note. **761. Salus.** The personification of health, prosperity, and the public welfare among the Romans. A temple to this deity on the

Quirinal was dedicated B. C. 203. **763. Syrisce,** a term of endearment, as such diminutives often are. **765. Postquam.** See l. 1, note. **766. Sis** = *si vis.* **769. Sapientia,** *old wiseacre,* the abstract for the concrete. **770. Dis** = *Dives.* **775. Exitum,** sc. *esse;* said aside. **780. Nostin?** *Don't you know him?* **Iam scibo,** *I'll soon know who he is.* **788. A me,** i. e. *at my house.* M. 253, Obs.; Z. 304, *b;* and cf. *Andr.,* l. 156, and note. **792. Lites,** sc. between Demea and Ctesipho. **Succurrendumst,** sc. *Ctesiphoni.* **796. Rem — putemus.** *Let us take account of the facts as they really are.* Mt. **797. Adeo** strengthens *ex te: The suggestion arose from yourself.* Ds. **799. Recipis,** often used of giving shelter to a thief or runaway. Ps. **800. Numqui — aequomst,** *Is it anywise unfair?* **801. Mihi,** sc. *tecum,* **ius,** *my right as regards you.* **804.** The Greek proverb κοινὰ τὰ τῶν φίλων occurs three times in Aristotle, and is quoted by Cicero, *De Off.* I. 16; *De Leg.* I. 12, and called *illa Pythagorea vox.* **805. Demum,** i. e. *for the first time;* with **istaec — oratiost,** *this is a novel sentiment in your mouth,* i. e. is opposed to your own practice. Mt. Cf. l. 113, 129, *et seqq.* **807. Sumptum.** See *Andr.,* l. 3, note. **809. Pro re tua,** *according to your means.* **812. Illam,** i. e. that which was yours, but which you abandoned. Py. **Rationem,** *plan.* **Antiquam.** Cf. *Andr.,* l. 817, and note. **813. Parce.** *Be thrifty.* Py. **814.** This is the reading of Uh. and Fu.; *gloriamque istaec tibi,* sc. *relinquas.* Wr., from the MSS. **815. Mea.** See *Andr.,* l. 5, *operam,* note. **816. Summa,** sc. *rei tuae, your estate* or *principal.* **Hinc,** *from me.* **817. De lucro,** *clear gain.* Cf. *Hecyra,* 287, and *Phorm.* 246, *In lucro;* Hor. O. I., 9, 14: *Lucro appone.* **820. Mitto,** etc., *I do not mind the money; their character* is what I care about. Py. On the construction of **consuetudinem,** cf. *Andr.,* l. 624, note. **Ipsorum.** So Fn. and Uh.; *amborum,* Bemb. MS., Wr. **821. Istuc ibam,** *I was coming to that.* **In homine,** *in man's nature.* **824. Hoc — facere,** i. e. Some men will not be spoilt by a little indulgence in early life; others will. **Impune,** *without bad consequences to himself,* refers simply to the effect on the person's own character, not to any external consequences of indulgence or folly. Py. **825. Is,** sc. *dissimilis est.* Wr. **826. Quae,** sc. *signa.* **827. In loco,** *when occasion requires.* **828. Vereri,** = *verecundos et modestos esse.* Delph. **Liberum,** *worthy of a man, noble.* **830. Redducas,** sc. *ad officium.* **Ab re,** *as regard interests.* **835. Quod,** accusative of specification, refers to the preceding sentence. **Ne,** sc. *timeo* or *carendum est.* **836. Boationes,** *fine arguments.* **841. Luci.** So Fn., Uh., and Wr. This frequently occurs in the older latinity. Cf. Plaut. *Aul.* 741; *Cist.* I 48. *Veteres masculino genere dicebant lucem.* Don. Z. 78, note.

nocte, lit. *after nightfall; to-night.* **843. Pugnaueris,** *you will have won the day,* i. e. will have fought and conquered. Py. **844. Prorsum,** *certainly.* **Illi,** = *illic,* locative. **847. Sit.** See *Andr.,* l. 854, note, and M. 372, b. Obs. 4. **853. Sentio,** *I feel,* sc. while you are insensible. **854. Est,** sc. *dies dicatus.* **Ei rei,** sc. the nuptials.

ACTVS V.

Demea's soliloquy upon the contrast between his own course of life and that of his brother, and the greater happiness of the latter. He resolves to imitate Micio. His courteous demeanor towards Syrus, Geta, and Aeschinus, in succession, and congratulation of himself upon the success of the experiment. Aeschinus' amazement at the change in his father's disposition, and delight at his suggestions. Appearance of Micio to satisfy himself of the reality of this unexpected and complete alteration in his brother's behavior; his astonishment at Demea's proposal that he shall marry Sostrata and present Hegio with a farm, to which, however, he finally assents. Emancipation of Syrus and his wife through the solicitation of Demea; his explanation of his sudden fit of liberality, and offer to be henceforth a friendly adviser of his sons; their acceptance of it.

855. Subducta — **fuit,** *made his calculations.* See Lex. s. *Subduco,* II., B., and cf. l. 208, and note. **856. Res,** *circumstances.* **Usus,** *experience.* **858. Prima,** sc. in importance, *most desirable.* **860. Prope** — **spatio,** *when at last my course is well-nigh run.* The metaphor is from the race-course. Cf. Cic. *De Senect.* 23. **Mitto,** *abandon.* **861. Clementia.** Cf. l. 42. **864. Nulli** — **os,** *he would offend no one to his face.* Cf. l. 269. On the construction, cf. *Andr.,* l. 62, note. **866. Agrestis,** *churlish.* Cf. Hor. *Epist.* I. 18, 6. **867. Ibi,** *thereby.* Ds. **Uidi,** *experienced.* Cf. Virg. Aen. II. 5: *Quaeque ipse miserrima vidi;* Psalm XXXIV. 12, *that he may see good.* **870. Fructi.** See *Andr.,* l. 365, note. **871. Commoda.** See *Andr.,* l. 5, note. **874. Illum.** M. 439, Obs. 1. This kind of attraction is very frequent in Plautus and Terence, but rarer in later writers, occurring often, however, in the dialogues letters of Cicero. The verbs with which it is generally found are *udi et declarandi,* and sometimes *efficiendi.* **Expectant.** See l. *.* **878. Hoc** = *huc.* **879. Me amari.** M. 389, Obs. 4; II. 558, l. 70, 2, 3; A. 271, Rem. 4; B. 1140; G. 424. **Magni.** See . 293, note. **880. Posteriores,** sc. *partes.* See Lex. *s. v.* II., B. .eerit, sc. *si pecunia.* M. 442, a, Obs. 2; Z. 780. **884. Iam** *,* etc., said aside, as also l. 896, *Meditor,* etc., and l. 898. **886.** **aaud inliberalem,** *well behaved.* Cf. *Andr.,* l. 38. **889. Ad hos,** *to*
13 — Ter. R

our neighbors, sc. Micio and Aeschinus. **891. Qui uocare?** i. e. *What is your name?* **893. Spectatus,** *of well-proved character.* See *Andr.,* l. 91, note. **895. Usus.** See Lex. s. v. II., C. 2 and l. 429, note. Py. considers **usus uenerit** as a single verb, with **quid** as its subject. **897. Existumas.** M. 358, Obs. 2. **898. Plebem — meam,** sc. as if he were a candidate for office, securing the votes of the plebs before he went to the higher classes. Py. **899. Nimis sanctas,** *so very formal, with overmuch ceremony,* explained by l. 905 and 907. **905. Tibicina,** etc. See *Andr.,* l. 365, note, and Becker's Gallus, p. 161. **906. Huic seni** = *mihi.* **908. Maceriam,** a rare word; not found elsewhere in Terence or in Plautus. Py. See D. s. *Murus.* **909. Hac,** sc. *via.* **913. Quid mea?** sc. *refert.* **915. Dinumeret.** M. 390, Obs. 2; Z. 617. Bentley and others regard **Iube** = *Age.* **Ille Babylo,** i. e. *that prodigal brother of mine:* he shall see the ruinous consequences of his liberality. So Don., Bentley, Ruhnken, Wr., and Ds. **Babylo,** because the Medes and Persians were reputed luxurious and extravagant beyond other nations. Cf. Hor. O. I. 38, 1; Juv. 3, 221. Colman and Py. read *illi* = *Aeschino,* and understand **Babylo** to be the name of one of Demea's slaves; while others interpret it *banker.* **917. Illas,** the object of **traduce.** **919. Factum uelle,** i. e. *that you wish us well,* an idiomatic expression. Cf. *Phorm.* 787; Plaut. *Bacch.* 495; *Asin.* 685. *Factum volo* = *Cupio tibi fieri quod uis et quantum in me est, ut fiat, operam dabo.* Gronov. ad *Gell.* VII. 3. **921. Per uiam,** *through the street.* **923. Sic soleo,** *Such is my wont.* **932. Solast.** See *Andr.,* l. 381, note. **Quam — agit?** *What is he driving at?* **933. Et te,** etc., addressed to Aeschinus, as is also **934. Si — homo.** Cf. l. 107, and note. **935. Agis.** See Lex. s. v. III. 1. d. **937. Aufer,** sc. *nugas.* **Da — filio,** *indulge your son's wish.* **939. Id.** M. 229, b, Obs. 2, and see *Andr.,* l. 157, note. **940. De te** = *de tuo, of what's your own.* **943. Age prolixe,** *Act liberally.* **950. Qui.** See *Andr.,* l. 6, note. **Fruatur,** used technically. Hegio was to have the *usufructus* of the farm, but not the ownership. It would still belong to Micio. See Lex. s. v. II. **952. Non.** So the MSS., Uh., and Fn.; *nunc,* Bentley, Wr., and Ds. **Non — facio,** *these words I'm using are not mine,* Ds.; *I will not arrogate to myself,* etc. **953. Uitium,** etc. Cf. l. 833 et seq. **956. Quid istic?** See *Andr.,* l. 572, note. **958. Suo sibi.** Z. 746. Cf. Plaut. *Capt.,* l. 50. **Quod iussisti.** Cf. l. 908, 916. **965. De die,** lit. *immediately after mid-day.* Py. See Lex. s. *De,* B. 2. The usual time for the *coena* was the ninth hour. To begin a feast earlier in the day was a mark of dissipation. **968. Prodesse,** i. e. that he should be rewarded. **Alii — erunt,** *Other slaves will be the better for it.* Ironical. **969. Hic,** sc. Aeschinus. **970. Accede,** etc. See Dict.

Antiqq., s. *Manumissio.* **971. Seorsum,** lit. *separately,* then *especially.* **972. Perpetuom,** *complete.* **973. Uxorem,** a nobler word than *contubernalis,* the common term for the wife of a slave. Wr. **977. Quantist,** *which she is worth.* **980. Prae manu,** i. e. *in ready money.* **981. Unde utatur** = *quo victum habeat,* i. e. he was to make this loan his capital, and by and by pay it back. Py. **Istoc,** e. g. a snap of the finger. **Uilius,** sc. *quicquam non dabo.* Don. **985. Prolubium,** this *whim* of yours. Py. **986. Quod.** See l. 162, note. **987. Uera uita,** *well-regulated mode of life.* **Aequo et bono,** technically used in the sense of 'equity,' as opposed to 'law!' Py. **990. Iusta,** etc., are accusat. of specification. **Obsequor,** sc. *vobis.* **991. Missa facio,** *I abandon all things to you;* i. e. you may henceforth do as you please. **994. Obsecundare — loco,** *humor in due season.* **996. Quid — facto.** See *Andr.,* l. 490, note. **De fratre.** Cf. *Andr.,* l. 614. M. 267, Obs.; Z. 491. **997. In — faciat,** i. e. Let him not engage in an intrigue with any other. **Istuc recte,** i. e. *you are indulging your son in a most fitting manner.* Ironical. It is a sort of humorous retort on Demea, who has now carried his newly-acquired indulgence beyond all bounds. Py. **Cantor. Plaudite.** See *Andr.,* l. 981, note.

This last act is not necessary to the plot, and is a sort of after-piece. Still, Terence may have purposely introduced these supplementary scenes as a sort of set-off to the strong contrasts of character in the former part of the play, to show that indulgence may easily be assumed, and that a man is not to value himself too much upon popularity obtained by mere easiness of manner. This act may thus be said to be the application and moral of the preceding. Py. Wr., however, thinks that great injustice is done in it to Micio as well as to Aeschinus, who maintain too high a character in the first four acts to warrant their sudden change in the fifth, as it seems hardly consistent that Aeschinus should lend himself to the jokes Demea plays upon his brother, or that Micio should oppose so tame and spiritless a resistance.

APPENDIX.

A. ON THE PROSODY OF TERENCE.

(ABRIDGED FROM WAGNER'S INTRODUCTION.)

I. The Latin language, in its most remote period, was possessed of an abundance of suffixes with long vowels. It was the subsequent tendency of the language to shorten many of these, in which it was assisted by the general inclination of many, if not all, languages to obscure final syllables when not accented. This tendency became at last so powerful that all final vowels of original long quantity became indifferent when preceded by a short syllable under the accent; i. e. in archaic Latin, and consequently in the prosody of the comic poets, $\acute{\smile} - = \acute{\smile} \smile$.

1. The number of instances where original *long vowels retain their old quantity* is in proportion far smaller in Terence than in Plautus. Instances are as follows: (1) a in the neutr. plur. in *omniā*, Havt. 575, *debiliā*, Ad. 612. (2) us in the nom. sing. of the second decl. in *filiūs*, Havt. 217, *Aeschinūs*, Ad. 260, 588, 634, and in the neuter of the comparative, e. g. *faciliūs*, Havt. 803. (3) e in the ablat. sing. of the third decl., e. g. *temporē*, Hec. 531, *lubidinē*, Havt. 216, *virginē*, Ad. 346, *fratrē*, Ad. 40. (4) it in the third pers. sing., pres. indic. act. of the third conj. in *accipīt*, Eun. 1082 (analogously āt in the subj. *augeāt*, Ad. 25), and in the third pers. sing., perf. act. in *profuīt*, Hec. 463, *stetīt*, Phorm. 9. (5) **erē** in the pres. inf. act. in *dicerē*, Andr. 23, *ducerē*, 613.

2. Instances of originally long final vowels shortened: (1) a in the nom. sing. of the first decl. *always* in Terence, though still appearing long in Plautus. (2) o in the ablat. (and dat.) sing. of the second decl., e. g. *novŏ*, Phorm. 972. (3) i in the ablat. *levĭ*, Hec. 312, in *herĭ*, 416. (4) a, e, i frequently in dissyllabic imperatives of originally iambic measure, e. g. *rogă*, Hec. 558, *iubĕ*, Phorm. 922, *cavĕ*, Andr. 300, *redĭ*, Ad. 190.

II. By a further extension of the influence of accent, originally long vowels could be shortened when standing before an accented long and after a short syllable, i. e. $\smile - \acute{-} = \smile \smile \acute{-}$.

Instances are: *cavĕ te esse*, Andr. 403, *cavĕ quoquam*, 760, *manĕ non dum*, Ad. 467, *iubĕ dirui*, 908, *darĭ mi obviam*, 311; even **is** in the dat. plur. in Hec. 202; **as** in the acc. plur. first decl. in Havt. 388; *tacĕs*, Hec. 527, *verĕbamini*, Phorm. 902.

III. This tendency of shortening long unaccented vowels after short accented or before long accented syllables was greatly assisted by another, which manifests itself in the metres of the comic poets and in the ancient inscriptions, viz., a tendency *to drop the final consonants of many words*. This will help to explain the seeming violation of the ordinary laws of '*positio*' in numerous passages of the comic writers.

1. Final **m** should not be pronounced in *paru̅m mi*, Hec. 742, *eni̅m lassam*, 238, *eni̅m scio*, Andr. 503, *eni̅m vero*, 91, Ad. 255, *eni̅m ducet*, Phorm. 694; in *quide̅m* in many instances; and in the case of many other words.

2. Final **s** is dropped in many instances: *auctus sit*, Hec. 334, *nullus sum*, 653, etc. In *foris sapere*, Havt. 923, and *bonis Latinas*, Eun. 8, the long ending *also* appears shortened. That this did not fall into disuse until the age of Cicero is proved by his testimony, *Orat.* 48, 161, and the Inscriptions of the Republican period. In the case of **s** and **m**, the prosody of the comic writers went beyond the limits explained in I. and II.

3. Final **r** in several instances: *amor misericordia*, Andr. 261, *pater venit*, Phorm. 601, *miser quod*, Eun. 237, etc.

4. Final **t** and **d**: *dabit nemo*, Andr. 396, *ipse erit*, *vos*, Ad. 4, *studet par*, 73, *erat missa*, 618, etc.; **nt** either entirely or in part: Ad. 900, Havt. 993, Eun. 384; **d** in *ad:* Phorm. 150, 648.

5. **l** in *semol* or *simul*, Havt. 803, Eun. 241; **n** in *tamen*, Ad. 145, Hec. 874, Eun. 889; **x** in *senex* in some lines, in others pronounced as **c** or **s**.

6. The final consonant in all monosyllabic prepositions *may be dropped*.

IV. The tendency of shortening long unaccented syllables was also assisted by the great indifference of the language of that period in regard to double and simple consonants. In fact, double consonants were entirely unknown in Latin before Ennius.

1. **ll** does not affect the quantity of the preceding vowel in *supĕllectile*, Phorm. 666; *ille*, with its derivatives, is frequently used as a pyrrhic, Terence himself writing *ile;* **mm** does not lengthen the first syllable of *immo;* nor do **nn** or **mn** (without much doubt sounded like **nn**) or **pp** the preceding syllable, as in *omnis*, Andr. 694, and other passages, *opportune*, Ad. 81, *oppressionem*, 238. This law holds good of *all* double consonants.

2. **n** before **s**, and in general before dentals and gutturals in this period, was attenuated, and in many cases entirely disappeared: e. g. *quod intellexi*, Eun. 737, *sed interim*, Haut. 882, *sine invidia*, Andr. 66, *bonum ingenium*, 466, etc.; the first syllable of *unde* and *inde*, when a short syllable precedes, is short in various passages: also that of *ignave*, Eun. 777; and the vowel preceding **x** in *uxorem*, Andr. 781, Hec. 514, and in *exemplum*, Hec. 163, **x** seeming there to have the soft pronunciation of **s**, and in *excludor*, Eun. 159, to disappear entirely.

V. Many other deviations of comic prosody from that of the Augustan period can only be properly understood by extending the general laws given in I. and II. to all metrical combinations of words or syllables instead of confining them to single dissyllabic words.

VI. SYNIZESIS. In the comic writers,

1. *Deo dei deae deis deos deus*, and *meo mei meae meos meas meis* are frequently treated as monosyllables; and *deorum dearum, meorum mearum* as dissyllables. It is the same with *eo ei eodem eidem eas easdem eos eosdem eae eaedem ea eadem* (abl.) *eorum earum*.

2. *Eius* and *huius* admit of a threefold pronunciation: *éius* (trochee), *ĕius* (pyrrhic, after a preceding short syllable), and *eis* (monosyllabic), with the extrusion of *u*. *Cuius* or *quoius* also is either a trochee or a monosyllable (*quois*).

3. *Dies die diu, scio nescio, ais ain ait aibam, trium*, are among the rest of those words which admit of synizesis; while *gratiis* and *ingratiis* are always fully pronounced.

4. Compounds, in which two vowels come together, are always pronounced with synizesis.

[See also M. 6, Obs. 1; Z. 11; H. 669, II.; A? 306, 1; B. 1519, 3; G. 721.]

VII. HIATUS is of very rare occurrence in Terence. In general, it is justified only (1) where the line is divided among two or more speakers, or (2) in the legitimate caesurae of all metres.

Quite different from this are those instances in which monosyllables ending in a long vowel or **m** do not coalesce with a following short vowel, e. g. in Andr. 191, 825, Eun. 119, 193, 563, 1080, Hec. 343, Phorm. 27. Cf. Virg. *Ecl.* VIII. 108; Lucr. II. 404.

[See M. 502, **b**; Z. 8; H. 669, I. 2; Al. 80, 3, and 83, 5, **h**; A. 305, 1, (2); G. 714, Rem.]

See also Brix's Introduction to the *Trinummus* and Wagner's to the *Aulularia* of Plautus; Parry's Introduction to Terence; M. 502, **a**, Obs. 2; Al. 83.

B. THE METRES OF TERENCE.

I. TROCHAIC.

1. TROCHAIC TETRAMETER CATALECTIC or *Trochaic Septenarius*. M. 506; Z. 833; H. 680, 3; Al. 82, 3; A. 315, I.; B. 1512, 3; G. 749. This metre is very frequent in Terence.
2. TROCHAIC TETRAMETER ACATALECTIC or *Trochaic Octonarius*. H. 680, 4; A. 315, I., Rem. 2; G. 748.
3. TROCHAIC DIMETER CATALECTIC. H. 681; A. 315, IV.; G. 747, 3. This occurs only in connection with other metres, and is never continued for any great number of lines.
4. Two *trochaicae tripodiae catalecticae*. *Andr.*, l. 635.

II. IAMBIC.

1. IAMBIC TETRAMETER CATALECTIC or *Iambic Septenarius*. M. 507, a, Obs.; Z. 839; H. 686; Al. 82, 2, b; A. 314, IV.; B. 1511, 5; G. 757.
2. IAMBIC TETRAMETER ACATALECTIC or *Iambic Octonarius*.
3. IAMBIC TRIMETER or *Iambic Senarius*. M. 507, a; Z. 837; H. 683, 3; Al. 82, 2, a; A. 314, I.; G. 754. The easiest and most frequent of all the metres employed by Terence. All the prologues are written in it, and also the first scenes of each play. Wr.
4. IAMBIC DIMETER or *Iambic Quaternarius*. H. 685; Al. 82, 2, c; A. 314, VI.; G. 752. This occurs in a considerable number of passages.
5. IAMBIC DIMETER CATALECTIC occurs in a few places, e. g. *Andr.*, l. 485.

III. OTHER METRES.

The more intricate metres are seldom used by Terence, and he has no anapaestic lines at all.

1. CRETIC TETRAMETER. M. 499, c; Z. 850; H. 656, I.; Al. 82, 6; A. 302, I., 2; B. 1502; G. 771; *Andr.*, l. 626–634.
2. BACCHIAC TETRAMETER. M. 499, d, Obs. 1, *foot-note;* Z. 851; Al. 82, 5; *Andr.*, l. 481–484, 637, 638.
3. CHORIAMBIC VERSES. Z. 856; H. 688; Al. 82, 7, k; A. 316; B. 1515, 2; G. 770; *Adelph.*, l. 612, 613.

See also Parry's Introduction to Terence.

C. METRICAL KEY TO THE ANDRIA AND ADELPHOE.

ANDRIA.

METRA HVIVS FABVLAE HAEC SVNT.

V.
1 ad 174 iambici senarii.
175 et 177 iambici octonarii.
176 iambicus quaternarius.
178 et 179 trochaici septenarii.
180 ad 195 iambici octonarii.
196 ad 198 iambici senarii.
199 ad 214 iambici octonarii.
215 ad 226 iambici senarii.
227 iambicus octonarius.
228 ad 233 trochaici septenarii.
234 ad 239 iambici octonarii.
240 et 244 iambici quaternarii.
241 et 242 trochaici septenarii.
243 iambicus octonarius.
245 et 247 trochaici octonarii.
246 trochaicus dimeter catalecticus.
248 ad 251 trochaici septenarii.
252 iambicus quaternarius.
253 ad 255 iambici octonarii.
256 ad 260 trochaici septenarii.
261 ad 269 iambici octonarii.
270 ad 298 iambici senarii.
299 et 300 iambici septenarii.
301 et 305 et 307 trochaici octonarii.
302 et 306 et 308 trochaici septenarii.
303 et 304 309 ad 316 iambici octonarii.
317 trochaicus septenarius.
318 iambicus senarius.
319 ad 383 trochaici septenarii.
384 ad 393 iambici senarii.
394 ad 403 iambici octonarii.
404 ad 480 iambici senarii.
481 ad 484 bacchiaci tetrametri acatalecti.
485 iambicus dimeter catalecticus.
486 iambicus senarius.
487 ad 496 iambici octonarii.

V.

497 et 498 iambici senarii.
499 ad 505 iambici octonarii.
506 iambicus septenarius.
507 ad 509 iambici octonarii.
510 ad 515 trochaici septenarii.
517 trochaicus dimeter catalecticus.
518 ad 523 trochaici septenarii.
524 ad 532 iambici senarii.
533 ad 536 iambici octonarii.
537 iambicus quaternarius.
538 ad 574 iambici senarii.
575 ad 581 iambici septenarii.
582 ad 604 et 606 iambici octonarii.
605 iambicus quaternarius.
607 et 608 trochaici octonarii.
609 trochaicus septenarius.
610 ad 620 iambici octonarii.
621 ad 624 trochaici septenarii.
625 dactylicus tetrameter acatalectus.
626 ad 634 cretici tetrametri acatalecti.
635 compositus ex duabus trochaicis tripodiis catalecticis.
636 iambicus quaternarius.
637 et 638 bacchiaci tetrametri acatalecti.
639 et 640 trochaici septenarii.
641 et 642 iambici octonarii.
643 ad 649 trochaici septenarii.
650 ad 654 iambici octonarii.
655 ad 681 iambici senarii.
682 et 683 iambici octonarii.
684 ad 715 iambici septenarii.
716 ad 819 iambici senarii.
820 ad 856 trochaici septenarii.
857 iambicus octonarius.
858 et 859 trochaici septenarii.
860 ad 863 iambici octonarii.
864 trochaicus septenarius.
865 iambicus octonarius.
866 ad 895 iambici senarii.
896 ad 928 trochaici septenarii.
929 ad 958 iambici octonarii.
959 ad 981 trochaici septenarii.

ADELPHOE.

METRA HVIVS FABVLAE HAEC SVNT.

V.
1 ad 154 iambici senarii.
155 ad 157 trochaici octonarii.
158 trochaicus dimeter catalecticus.
159 iambicus octonarius.
160 et 162 trochaici octonarii.
161 163 164 trochaici septenarii.
165 trochaicus octonarius.
166 ad 169 trochaici septenarii.
170 ad 196 iambici octonarii.
197 ad 208 trochaici septenarii.
209 iambicus septenarius.
210 ad 227 iambici octonarii.
228 ad 253 iambici senarii.
254 ad 287 iambici octonarii.
288 trochaicus septenarius.
289 ad 291 iambici octonarii.
292 et 293 trochaici septenarii.
294 iambicus octonarius.
295 ad 298 trochaici septenarii.
299 ad 302 iambici octonarii.
303 et 304 trochaici septenarii.
305 ad 316 iambici octonarii.
317 iambicus quaternarius.
318 et 319 trochaici septenarii.
320 iambicus octonarius.
321 ad 329 trochaici septenarii.
330 et 331 iambici octonarii.
332 et 333 trochaici septenarii.
334 ad 354 iambici octonarii.
355 ad 516 iambici senarii.
517 trochaicus octonarius.
518 trochaicus septenarius.
519 ad 523 iambici octonarii.
524 iambicus quaternarius.
525 trochaicus octonarius.
526 trochaicus septenarius.
527 ad 539 iambici octonarii.
540 ad 591 trochaici septenarii.

APPENDIX.

V.

592 ad 609 iambici octonarii.
610 et 611 trochaici septenarii.
612 et 613 versus choriambici.
614 iambicus senarius.
615 iambicus quaternarius.
616 trochaicus dimeter catalecticus.
617 trochaicus octonarius.
618 trochaicus septenarius.
619 ad 624 iambici octonarii.
625 ad 637 trochaici septenarii.
638 ad 678 iambici senarii.
679 ad 706 trochaici septenarii.
707 ad 711 iambici septenarii.
712 iambicus octonarius.
713 ad 854 iambici senarii.
855 ad 881 trochaici septenarii.
882 ad 933 iambici senarii.
934 ad 955 iambici octonarii.
956 et 957 iambici senarii.
958 iambicus octonarius.
959 ad 997 trochaici septenarii.

THE END.

Model Text-Books

FOR

Schools, Academies, and Colleges.

CHASE & STUART'S CLASSICAL SERIES,

COMPRISING EDITIONS OF

Cæsar's Commentaries
First Six Books of Æneid
Virgil's Æneid
Virgil's Eclogues and Georgics
Cicero's Select Orations
Horace's Odes, Satires and Epistles
Sallust's Catiline et Jugurtha
Livy
Cicero De Senectute, et De Amicitia
Cornelius Nepos
Cicero De Officiis
Cicero's Tusculan Disputations
Terence
Tacitus
Juvenal
Cicero De Oratore.

A SERIES OF TEXT-BOOKS
ON THE
ENGLISH LANGUAGE.

By JOHN S. HART, LL.D.,
Late Professor of Rhetoric and of the English Language in the College of New Jersey.

The Series comprises the following volumes, viz.:

Language Lessons for Beginners.
Elementary English Grammar.
English Grammar and Analysis.
First Lessons in Composition.
Composition and Rhetoric.
A Short Course in Literature.
A Class-Book of Poetry.
A Manual of American Literature.
A Manual of English Literature.

THE
MODEL SERIES OF ARITHMETICS.
By EDGAR A. SINGER, A. M.,
Principal of the Henry W. Halliwell Grammar School, Philada.

COMPRISING

The Model Primary Arithmetic
The Model Elementary Arithmetic
The Model Mental Arithmetic
The Model Practical Arithmetic

ELEMENTS OF PHYSICAL GEOGRAPHY. By EDWIN J. HOUSTON, A.M., Professor of Physics and Physical Geography in the Central High School of Philadelphia.

HOUSTON'S PHYSICAL GEOGRAPHY is just such a work on the subject as has long been needed, and its publication supplies a long felt want in schools of all grades. Especial pains have been taken, and no expense spared, to bring up every feature to the highest possible standard of excellence. With the design of rendering the book peculiarly adapted for the class-room, new features have been introduced, the importance and utility of which will be appreciated by teachers. The syllabus at the end of each chapter is a feature which teachers will appreciate. The work has grown out of the wants of the author in the school-room, and presents the labor of years in this branch of study. With this book the subject can be mastered in less time than with any other text-book heretofore published.

CHRISTIAN ETHICS; or, THE SCIENCE OF THE LIFE OF HUMAN DUTY. A New Text-book on Moral Science, by Rev. D. S. GREGORY, D.D., Professor of the Mental Sciences and English Literature in the University of Wooster, Ohio.

GROESBECK'S PRACTICAL BOOK-KEEPING SERIES. By Prof. JNO. GROESBECK, Prin. of the Crittenden Commercial College. In Two Volumes, viz.

    COLLEGE EDITION, for Commercial Schools, Colleges, &c.

    SCHOOL EDITION, for Schools and Academies.

THE CONSTITUTION OF THE UNITED STATES. For Schools, with Questions under each Clause. By Prof. JOHN S. HART, LL.D. Should be taught in every school.

AN ELEMENTARY ALGEBRA. A Text-Book for Schools and Academies. By JOSEPH W. WILSON, A.M., Professor of Mathematics in the Philadelphia Central High School.

KEY TO WILSON'S ELEMENTARY ALGEBRA. For the use of Teachers only.

THE MODEL MONTHLY REPORT. Similar to the Model School Diary, excepting that it is intended for a *Monthly* instead of a *Weekly* report of the Attendance, Recitations, etc., of the pupil.

Circulars, giving full descriptive notices of our publications, will be sent to any address on application.

Please address

   ELDREDGE & BROTHER,
    No. 17 North Seventh Street,
     PHILADELPHIA, PA.

www.ingramcontent.com/pod-product-compliance
Lightning Source LLC
Chambersburg PA
CBHW020905230426
43666CB00008B/1314